AF825320

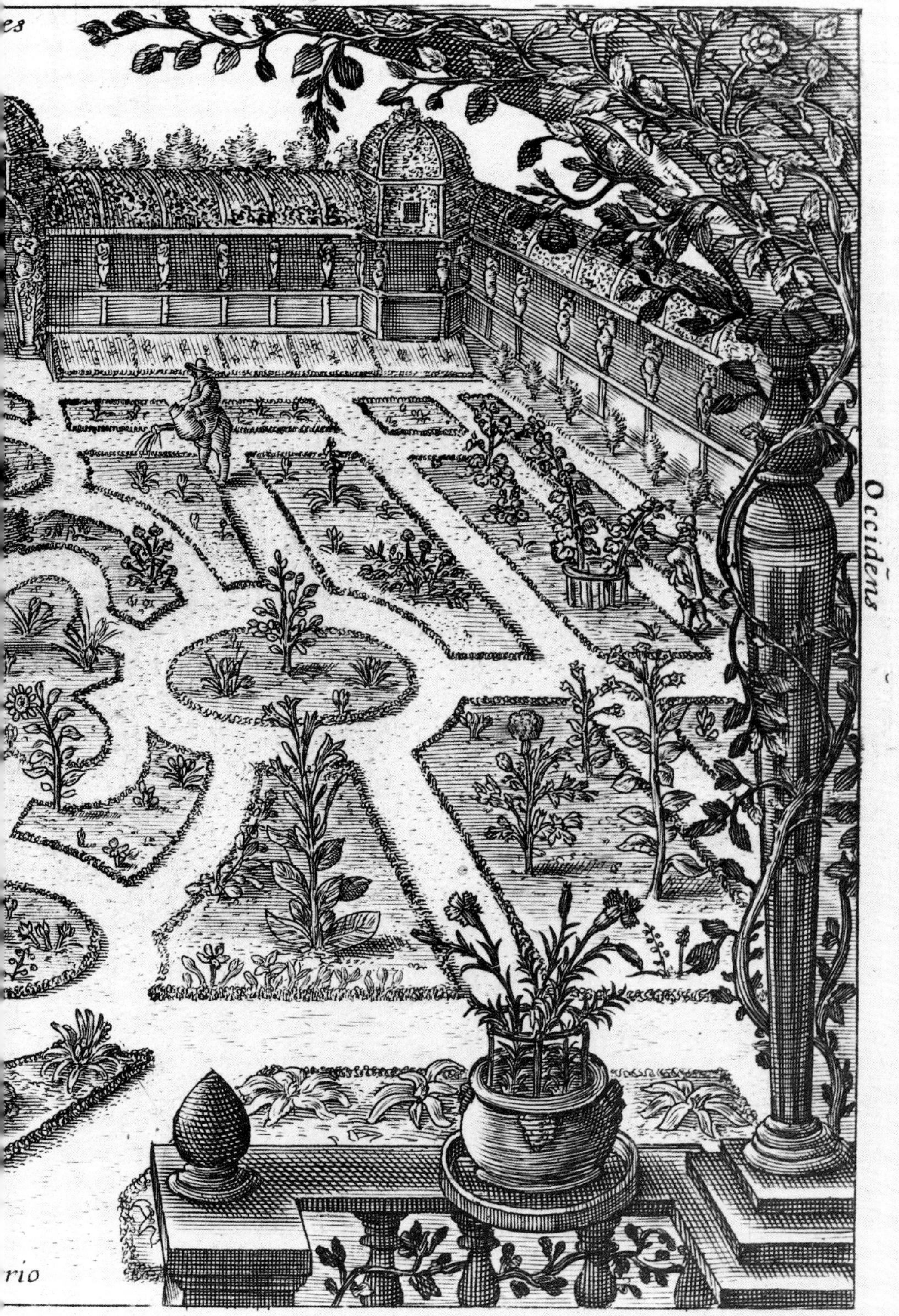

NATURE ILLUSTRATED

■

FLOWERS, PLANTS, AND TREES 1550-1900

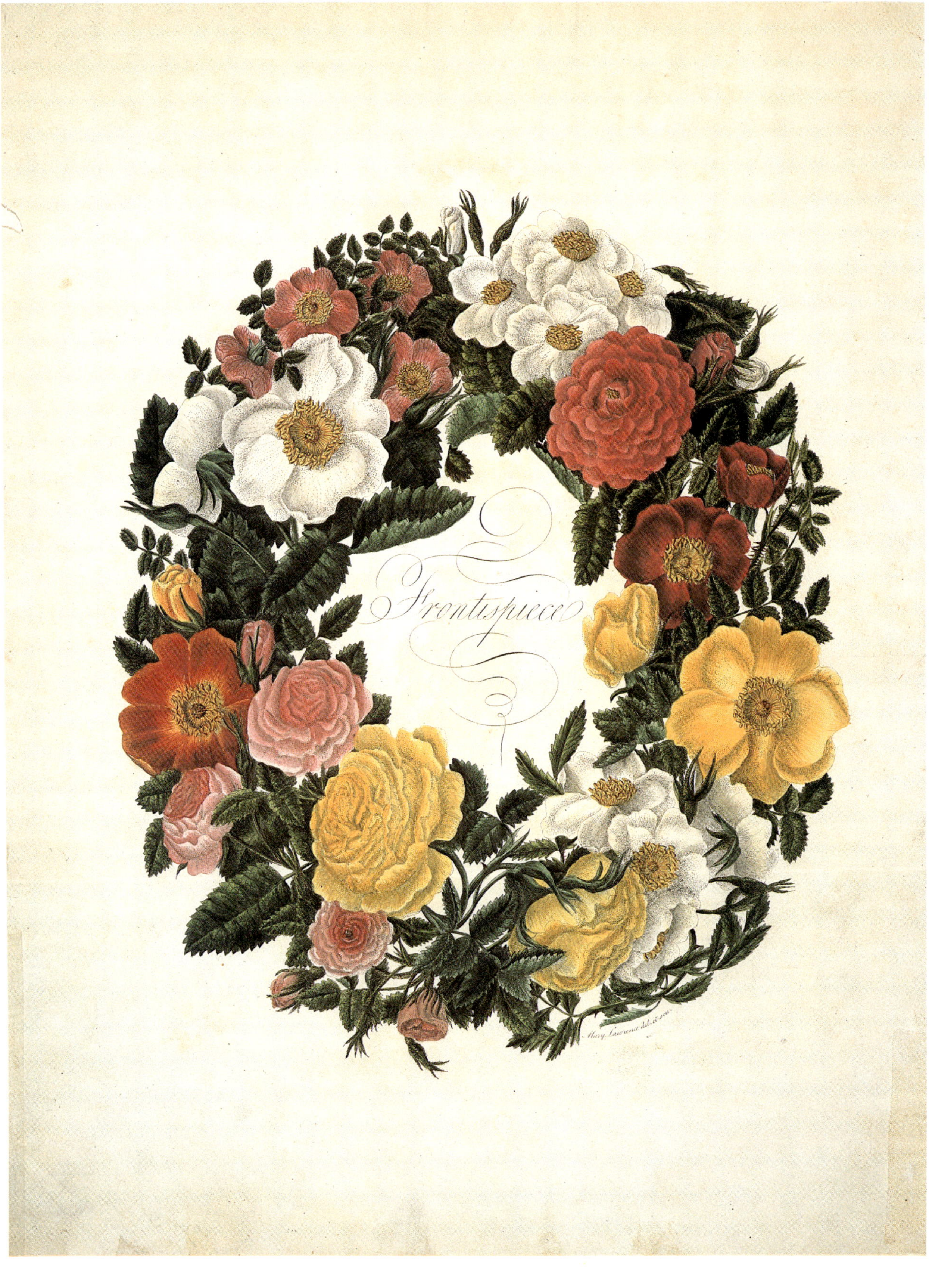
Frontispiece
Mary Lawrance del. et sculp.

NATURE ILLUSTRATED

■

FLOWERS, PLANTS, AND TREES 1550-1900

From the Collections of
The New York Public Library

■

FOREWORD BY ELEANOR PERÉNYI
TEXT BY BERNARD McTIGUE,
CURATOR OF THE ARENTS COLLECTIONS
AND KEEPER OF RARE BOOKS

■

Harry N. Abrams, Inc., Publishers, New York

Editor: Ruth A. Peltason
Designer: Elissa Ichiyasu

Photographs by Philip Pocock

Endpapers:
Septentria. Engraving. In HORTUS FLORIDUS *by Crispijn van de Passe (1614–16).*

Page 2:
Floral Wreath. Hand-colored engraving. In A COLLECTION OF ROSES . . . *by Mary Lawrance (1799).*

Page 7:
Title Page. Color-printed engraving. In LES FLEURS ANIMÉES *by J. J. Grandville (1847).*

Page 8:
Title Page. Engraving. In LA BOTANIQUE . . . *by Nicolas François Regnault (1774–80).*

Page 117:
Floral Wreath. Color-printed and hand-finished stipple engraving. In LES ROSES *by Pierre-Joseph Redouté and Claude Antoine Thory (1817–24).*

This book has been published to coincide with the exhibition of botanical illustrations presented at The New York Public Library in the Summer of 1989. This exhibition was made possible by a generous gift from Enid A. Haupt.

Library of Congress Cataloging-in-Publication Data
New York Public Library.
Nature illustrated: flowers, plants, and trees:
illustrations 1550–1900:
from the collections of the New York Public Library /
by Bernard McTigue: foreword by Eleanor Perényi.
p. cm.
Bibliography: p.
ISBN 0–8109–1176–0
1. Botanical illustration—Catalogs.
2. New York Public Library—Catalogs.
I. McTigue, Bernard. II. Title.
QK98.3N49 1989
581'.022'2—dc19 88–7582

Foreword copyright © 1989 Eleanor Perényi
Text copyright © 1989 Bernard McTigue
Illustrations copyright © 1989 The New York Public Library

Published in 1989 by Harry N. Abrams, Incorporated, New York
All rights reserved.
No part of the contents of this book may be reproduced
without the written permission of the publisher
A Times Mirror Company
Printed and bound in Japan

CONTENTS

FOREWORD BY ELEANOR PERÉNYI

All great institutions have their hidden treasures. Still, one wonders how so many gardeners and other interested parties could for so long have been ignorant of the remarkable collections of botanical books that The New York Public Library has been harboring (and adding to) since the end of the last century. The specialists, I assume, have been aware of them all along but too many amateurs like myself have not, and my first feeling on learning of their existence has been one of regret for the hours of pleasure missed. No matter. Here at last are examples culled from the finest of them—and if by the exigencies of the format a single page must inevitably stand for a whole book, the sensation of holding it in one's hand is nevertheless there, the next best thing. ▪ Why are they so fascinating? There is, of course, no valid comparison between, to choose at random, a Van Gogh sunflower and a botanical study of the same subject. The first is a work of art whose purpose is to convey the artist's vision of sunflowers, not an exact representation of them. But from its rough beginnings in the woodcuts of fifteenth-century herbals to its high point of achievement in the exquisite color plates of the eighteenth and nineteenth, accuracy has been the first requisite of botanical illustration—and this is true even of the masterpieces of the genre like Besler's *Hortus Eystettensis* (1613) and Redouté's *Les Roses* (1817–24). Today we would think of them as art books to be displayed on library (or cocktail) tables; and in fact many of them were so treated even then, especially those devoted to flowering plants. But that was never their true purpose. Strictly speaking, they belonged to science, and to a lesser degree to commerce; and if we value them for aesthetic reasons only we miss the historical point. To the entrepreneurial societies of the West, books like these brought, in addition to botanical knowledge, potentially profitable news of exploitable crops: tobacco, cotton, sugarcane, unfamiliar fruits and vegetables, medicinal herbs like quinine, being discovered on other continents. There were fortunes to be made from the new flora, and botanists weren't the only ones who wanted to know what they looked like, what they were "good for." The botanical books made that information available to anyone who could read. ▪ But this is also why, though it often paralleled the development of the still life in painting, and indeed borrowed from it, the botanical illustration belongs in another category. Even Redouté's roses, always the crown jewels of any collection, are artifacts produced by the industrial revolution, not pure works of art. Their primary purpose is to identify the members of the species—which is also why, as is never true of the pure work of art, the reproduction serves as well as the original painting and perhaps, when the engraving is particularly fine, even better. In that sense the botanical illustration isn't a copy of the real thing: it *is* the real thing. That is at once its strength and its limitation. ▪ None of which is to say that these books aren't authentic treasures. They are, if only because we won't see their like again. The great botanical adventure is over. No longer do artists plunge, as many of these did, into jungle and high sierra in search of the unknown orchid, the just-discovered rhododendron. Worse, familiarity has dulled the curiosity once aroused by exotic flora. Schoolchildren may still be amused by the sprouting of mung beans on a windowsill, but though many of our medicines are still manufactured from plants in the vanishing rain forest, taking them in the form of pills has killed our interest in the source. Cooks know all about Chinese ginger and Spanish saffron, and are unimpressed to find papaya, mangoes, and kiwi fruit in the supermarket. And if we are still curious, there are always photographs and a few, a very few, artists trying to emulate the glories of the past in gardening and cookbooks. ▪ In theory these should perhaps do as well. In practice, neither begins to satisfy as the old illustrations did. Photographs especially, shying from the banality of the representational, too often veer into abstraction after the manner of paintings by Georgia O'Keeffe: eerie close-ups of plants that could be mistaken for sexual parts. But O'Keeffe did that better. And when the photographer does opt for realism, the banality of the catalogue is indeed the usual result. Modern illustrators haven't solved the problem either. The truth is that no fresh or original way to portray plants that unites scientific accuracy with aesthetic pleasure has been invented since the eighteenth century. At best, what we get are pale copies of the earlier models. Inspiration is lacking, and there is simply no substitute for these books that descend to us from a time when craftsmanship could be combined with a sense of wonder at the marvels of the natural world.

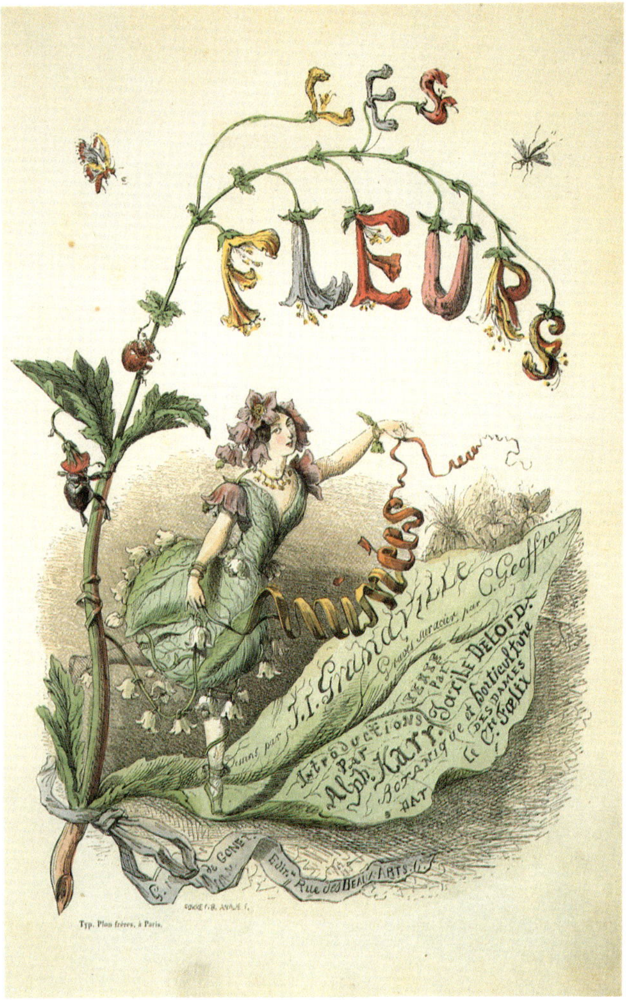

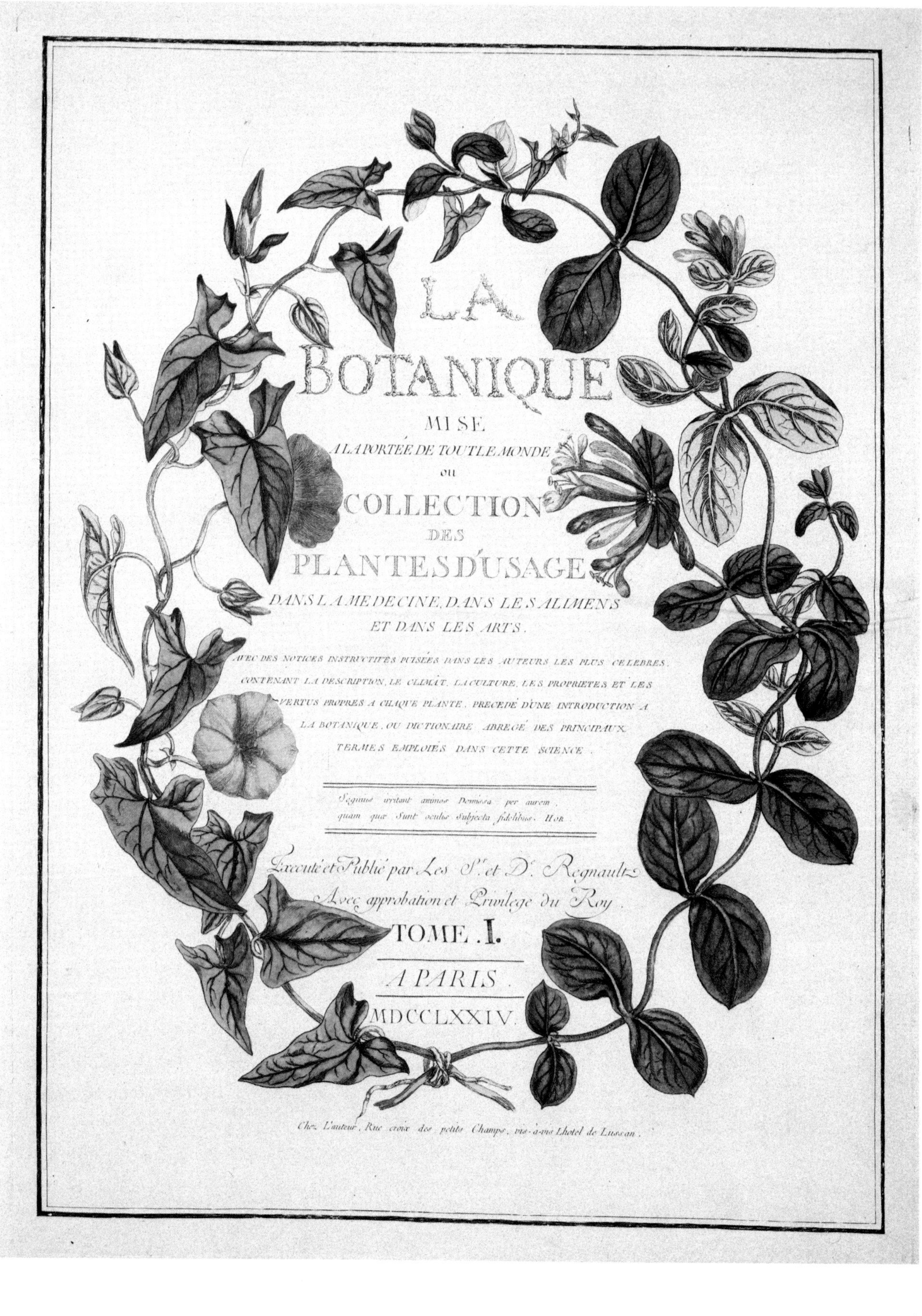
LA BOTANIQUE
MISE
A LA PORTÉE DE TOUT LE MONDE
ou
COLLECTION
DES
PLANTES D'USAGE
DANS LA MEDECINE, DANS LES ALIMENS
ET DANS LES ARTS.
AVEC DES NOTICES INSTRUCTIVES PUISÉES DANS LES AUTEURS LES PLUS CELEBRES.
CONTENANT LA DESCRIPTION, LE CLIMÂT, LA CULTURE, LES PROPRIETES ET LES
VERTUS PROPRES A CHAQUE PLANTE, PRECEDÉ D'UNE INTRODUCTION A
LA BOTANIQUE, OU DICTIONAIRE ABREGÉ DES PRINCIPAUX
TERMES EMPLOIÉS DANS CETTE SCIENCE.

Segnius irritant animos Demissa per aurem,
quam quæ Sunt oculis Subjecta fidelibus. Hor.

Executé et Publié par Les S.r et D.e Regnault
Avec approbation et Privilege du Roy.
TOME. I.
A PARIS.
MDCCLXXIV.
Chez L'auteur, Rue croix des petits Champs, vis-à-vis Lhotel de Lussan.

INTRODUCTION

One of the pleasant surprises that midtown New York can offer the stroller is the sight of roses in bloom in late spring in front of the Fifth Avenue entrance to The New York Public Library. Here in the middle, perhaps the very heart, of the "asphalt jungle" bright red flowers call out a reminder of nature's beauty and kindness. Just as surprising as this vision are the plants and flowers that lay hidden up the steps and behind the walls of The Library. These are between the covers of some of the most beautiful books ever printed, books which lie quietly in the shade of The Library's stacks. Surprising because, although it is known for many things to many people, The Library is not generally known for its botanical collections, and yet it possesses copies of most of the great illustrated botanical books printed between 1550 and 1900. ▪ Like The Library itself, this collection exists not due to the generosity of a single individual but rather as a result of the largesse of a number of collectors and philanthropists. The first of these was John Jacob Astor, whose benefaction enabled the Astor Library to acquire, in the second half of the nineteenth century, the core collection of English and French botanical and horticultural works. The second collector was James Lenox, whose interest in Americana brought into his private library works relevant to the plants of the Americas. These collections came together in 1895 with the Tilden Trust to form The New York Public Library. ▪ In the twentieth century the Astor and Lenox collections have been joined by the gifts of a number of private donors that contain important botanical works. Among these is the Spencer Collection of Illustrated Books and the Arents Collections. The latter is devoted to the history of tobacco; its coverage of the subject includes that plant's documentation in botanical literature from the sixteenth through the nineteenth centuries. ▪ These botanical collections form one of the many hidden treasures of The Library. They have been rarely displayed and seldom studied. Thus we have adopted a rather archaic approach to the organization of this book, one that harks back, in a way, to the herbals of the sixteenth century. We have divided the plant world into four parts: Useful Plants, Edible Plants, Ornamental Flowers and Ferns, and Trees and Shrubs. For each section we have chosen illustrations from among the most beautiful and important works ever produced on the subject. Many of these plants will be quite familiar, even to the reader who can barely tell a rose from a rhododendron, others will be unfamiliar to all but the aficionado. In this way we hope to provide the opportunity for the reader to encounter the familiar perhaps in a new light and the unfamiliar through eyes of scientific and artistic genius. ▪ That genius will be most apparent in the spectacular colorplate books of the eighteenth and nineteenth centuries, produced primarily in England and France. But these works rest on a more subtle gathering of genius, a cumulative brilliance which had been gathering force since the sixteenth century. ▪ The sixteenth century was the era of the herbal, one in which the plant lore of the Old and New worlds was documented, usually by physicians, with a viewpoint that emphasized the curative powers of both common and uncommon plants. William Turner's discussion of mint in his *A New Herball* (1551), for example, suggests that it is good for the memory, but does not mention mint's marvelous taste and smell. This is also the era of woodcut illustration, common to most books published with pictures in the sixteenth century. These woodcuts are often modest in their artistic ambitions, usually appearing uncolored, creating the impression more of line drawings than of finished works. But some of the works published in this period suggest the power and the éclat possible when the technique was handed by a master. The illustrations in Pier Andrea Matthioli's *Commentarii in Sex Libros Dioscoridis* (1565) are strong and impressive, filling the printed page with confidence and vigor. They have a vividness and graphic appeal impressive even by today's standards, and at a distance of some four hundred years. This forcefulness of imagery is carried through into the next century in books such as Basil Besler's *Hortus Eystettensis* (1613), the pictorial record of the famous garden owned by Johann Conrad von Gemmingen, prince bishop of Eichstadt in Bavaria. The book's visual impact is due in part to the large folio size of the book and also to the use of engraving as an illustrative technique. With this process the image put down on paper made greater use of contrasting shading and finer details than woodcuts were capable of. ▪ Two other engraved botanical works of the seventeenth century suggest that something greater than a change in the technique of illustration has taken place. There has also been a change in attitude. Crispijn van de Passe, in his *Hortus Floridus* (1614), and Nicolas Robert, in his *Diverses Fleurs* (1660), were not merely offering the viewer documentary evidence of certain flowers; they were expressing and communicating sheer delight in the visual and painterly qualities of their subjects. Where art begins and nature departs is not easy to discern in these engravings. This is not, of course, to suggest that all engraved work in the seventeenth century was of a pronounced aesthetic character. In John Jonston's *Dendographias* (1662), a book on fruit and fruit trees, we find a page illustrating the variety of pears that is more reminiscent of a nineteenth-century nurseryman's catalogue than of Dutch still-life painting. ▪ The interplay in botanical illustration between art and documentation, between visual delight and scientific discovery, is most pronounced in works produced in the eighteenth century. It is in this period, too, that the contribution of women to the corpus of botanical literature begins to be evident. In two books, in particular, we may note these trends. There is Maria Sibylla Merian's *Dissertation sur la Génération et les Transformations des Insectes de Surinam* (1726) which, from its title, would seem to have nothing at all to do with plants. In fact, the native caterpillars and butterflies that were this indomitable woman's primary interest are portrayed against backgrounds of the trees, flowers, and fruits in the South American Dutch colony of Surinam. Elizabeth Blackwell's *A Curious Herbal* (1737–39) is, visually, a less complex book than Merian's. Its straightforward hand-colored engravings of flowers, trees, and herbs are portrayed with a simple grace. The accompanying text, in the tradition of herbals, relates the herbs' curative powers. Mrs. Blackwell had created her herbal in order to raise money to spring her husband from jail, wherein he had been ensconced for bankruptcy. It seems she should have left him there, if only for his own good; he was later beheaded in Sweden for political intrigue. ▪ Less melodramatic in background but highly dramatic in visual impact are the floral illustrations that Georg Dionysius Ehret provided for a number of works published in the mid-eighteenth century. The calla lily that he created for Christoph Jacob Trew's *Hortus Nitidissimus* (1750–86) transcends the idea of documentary illustration. Yes, it is an accurate image of a readily identifiable flower, but it is also a marvel of composition, with an almost rococo sense of energy and movement. ▪ Then there is the majestic art of Pierre-Joseph Redouté. Although his output was prodigious, his work always seems meticulous, precise, balanced, an evocation of the calm and quiet grandeur that is sometimes associated with the classical spirit in art. This is actually not too surprising given the fact that Redouté developed as an artist when the neoclassical spirit in the arts in France was in the ascendant. Indeed, the first book to which he contributed illustrations, the *Stirpes Novae* (1784), by Charles Louis L'Héritier de Brutelle, appeared at the time of the full flowering of the Louis XVI style. His reputation grew during the Empire with its pronounced classical character. Just as Napoleon emphasized the grandeur of France in world politics, so too Redouté in his *Les Liliacées* (1802–16), with its 488 plates, suggests the grandeur of French botanical illustration. ▪ In pronounced counterpoint to this French taste are the fruits that peer out at us from the pages of George Brookshaw's *Pomona Britannica* (1804–12), a work compiled, its author tells us, for "Nurserymen, Gardeners and even Gentlemen." It seems almost to be an embodiment of that national characteristic of the British whom Napoleon scorned as "a nation of shopkeepers." The fruits do appear to be on display; like elaborate advertisements for an exemplary greenmarket, they are shown in all their enticing succulence. They do not speak to us of majesty; rather, they are about basic human needs and activities, however refined, gastronomic as well as economic. There was another side, of course, to the British character that found its expression in the Romantic movement in English poetry and painting. Nature and beauty were among its gods, so it is not surprising to find evidence of a romantic sensibility in the illustrations of flowers and trees. In Dr. Robert John Thornton's *The Temple of Flora* (1798–1807) flowers are portrayed against landscapes of an evocative and poetic character. Poetry accompanies many of the images. We are asked to worship in this temple, not merely to contemplate works of art that adorn it. In H. W. Burgess's *Eidodendron* (1827), we find images of trees that mingle the idea of the picturesque, with its atmospheric haziness, with the particular nobility and character of individual trees. Some of this romantic spirit spills over into mid- to late-nineteenth century English works such as Joseph Dalton Hooker's *The Rhododendrons of Sikkim-Himalaya* (1849), the result of Hooker's trek through that region. This is the work of a botanist and an adventurer, one in which the hidden treasures of far-off lands are recorded with results that are both intellectually and aesthetically satisfying. ▪ As with Hooker's work, *Nature Illustrated: Flowers, Plants, and Trees 1550–1900* will have served its purpose if readers come away from it with the sense of having visited lands in which science and art grew together in harmony.

USEFUL PLANTS

When Pierre Pena and Matthias de L'Obel illustrated papyrus in their *Stirpium Adversaria Nova* (1571) they were showing their readers a plant that was quite unfamiliar. To Europeans of that time, Egypt, the native habitat of papyrus, was an exotic place, part of a Moslem empire with which they were still, if intermittently, at war, as they had been for some seven hundred years. Besides being attributable to religious and political history, this unfamiliarity also had a cultural aspect. For several thousand years in the Mediterranean world papyrus had been commonplace as a writing surface. The ancient Egyptians, Greeks, and the Romans recorded their literature, philosophy, theology, and legal contracts on papyrus. Then, around the fourth century A.D., parchment, made from young animal skins, began to replace papyrus as the stuff from which books were made. By the time of Pena and L'Obel's publication, paper had been introduced into Europe from the East only about two hundred years previously. The simple woodcut of this rather unprepossessing plant belies its historic significance and its cultural impact at the dawn of literacy. ▪ Cotton as a fabric is as familiar to us as papyrus was to ancient Egyptians. And yet, this was not always so. The plant may have been around for thousands of years but its general use in the West in clothing and furnishings dates back only about three hundred years. Looking at the spare and unadorned illustration of the plant in Joseph Pitton de Tournefort's *Institutiones Rei Herbariae* (1719), one would be hard pressed to gauge its social and economic impact. This is the plant that made Manchester and other cities in the English midlands rich in Victorian times. And it is the plant that was once termed "King Cotton" in the southern United States. Cotton remains an important part of the international economy and is popular in today's fashions, yet one cannot help but wonder whether, in the not so distant future, like papyrus it will become a plant familiar more in books than in everyday life. ▪ This passing into and out of a useful phase on the part of plants is something we can observe firsthand in our own time in the case of the tobacco plant. Tobacco was unknown outside of the Americas until the European conquest and exploration of the New World. In the sixteenth century, as botanists began to document the natural life in the Americas, tobacco was included among those plants that were thought to have medicinal value. This usage is alluded to in Elizabeth Blackwell's *A Curious Herbal* (1737–39), where the oil of the leaves of the tobacco plant is suggested as a cure for ulcers, piles, and the King's Evil. In Blackwell's time tobacco was taken in the form of snuff and smoked in clay pipes. It also formed an increasingly important part of the trade between Europe and the Americas. This trade grew over the next century with the advent of the cigar and, then, in the latter part of the nineteenth century, with the arrival of the cigarette. ▪ Tobacco use was not without its opponents. As early as 1604 King James I of England railed against the "stinking weed." In the centuries since, the opponents of tobacco use have grown more vociferous. The tobacco plant appears to be headed the way of papyrus.

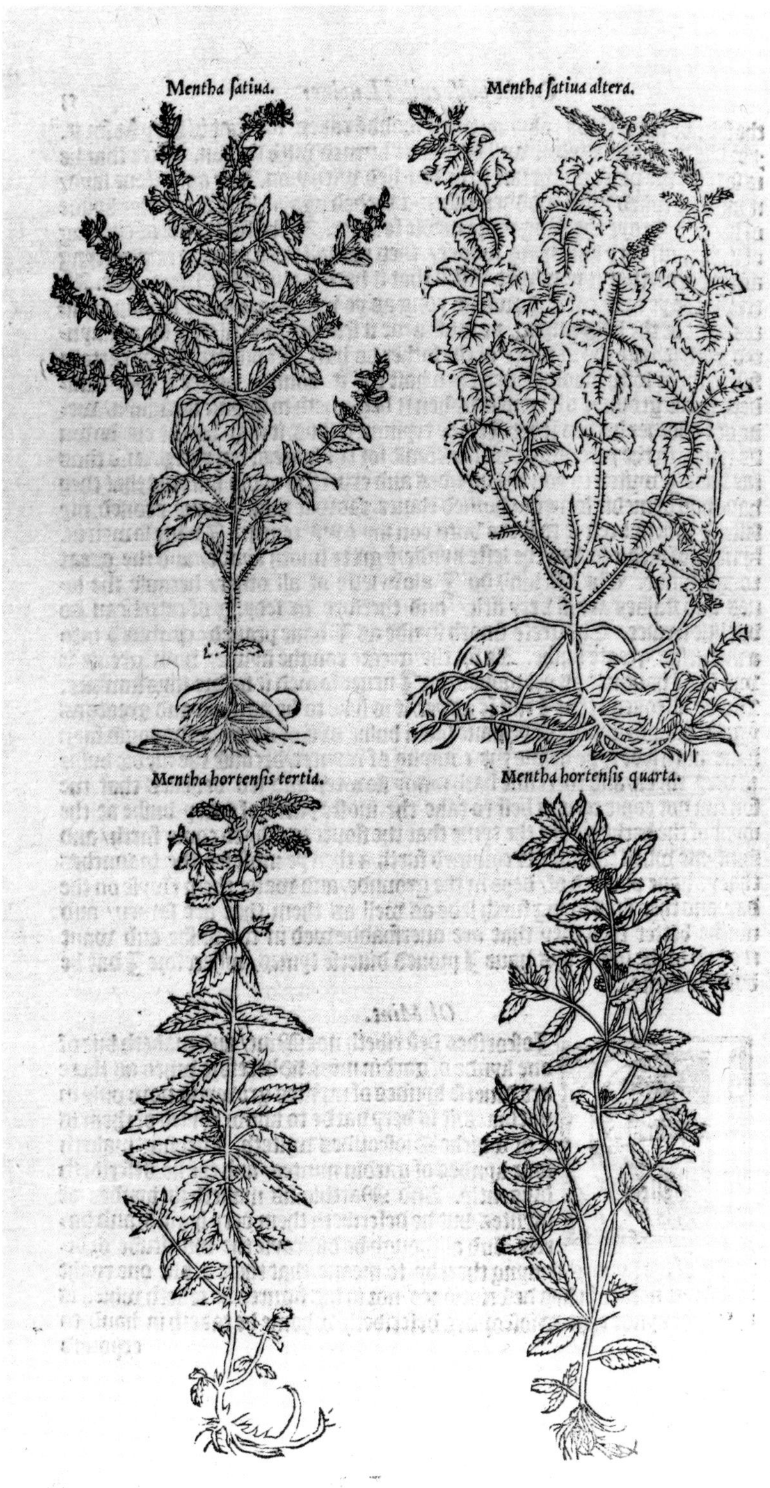

1 ▪ MINT *Mentha spp.*

Woodcut. In *A New Herball* by William Turner (1551). ▪ Among the virtues ascribed to the four kinds of mint shown in Turner's work are that it kills roundworms, encourages virility in men, heals dog bites, and is good for the memory.

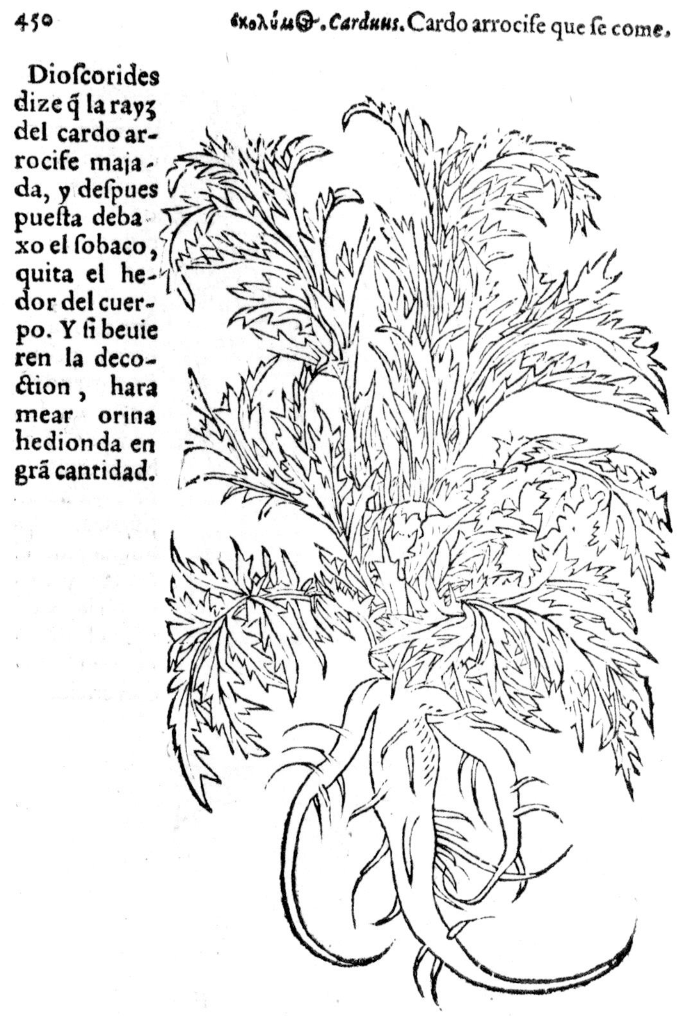
450 σκόλυμος. *Carduus.* Cardo arrocife que ſe come.

Dioſcorides dize q̃ la rayz del cardo arrocife majada, y deſpues pueſta debaxo el ſobaco, quita el hedor del cuerpo. Y ſi beuieren la decoction, hara mear orina hedionda en grã cantidad.

2 ▪ THISTLE *Carduus sp.*

Woodcut. In *Historia de Las Yeruas, y Plantas . . . .* by Leonhart Fuchs (1557). ▪ First published in Latin in 1542, this is one of the most important contributions to botanical knowledge of the sixteenth century. But its greatness may seem elusive considering Fuchs's commentary on the thistle. Drinking a liquid made from thistles, he reports, will result in a great quantity of stinking urine.

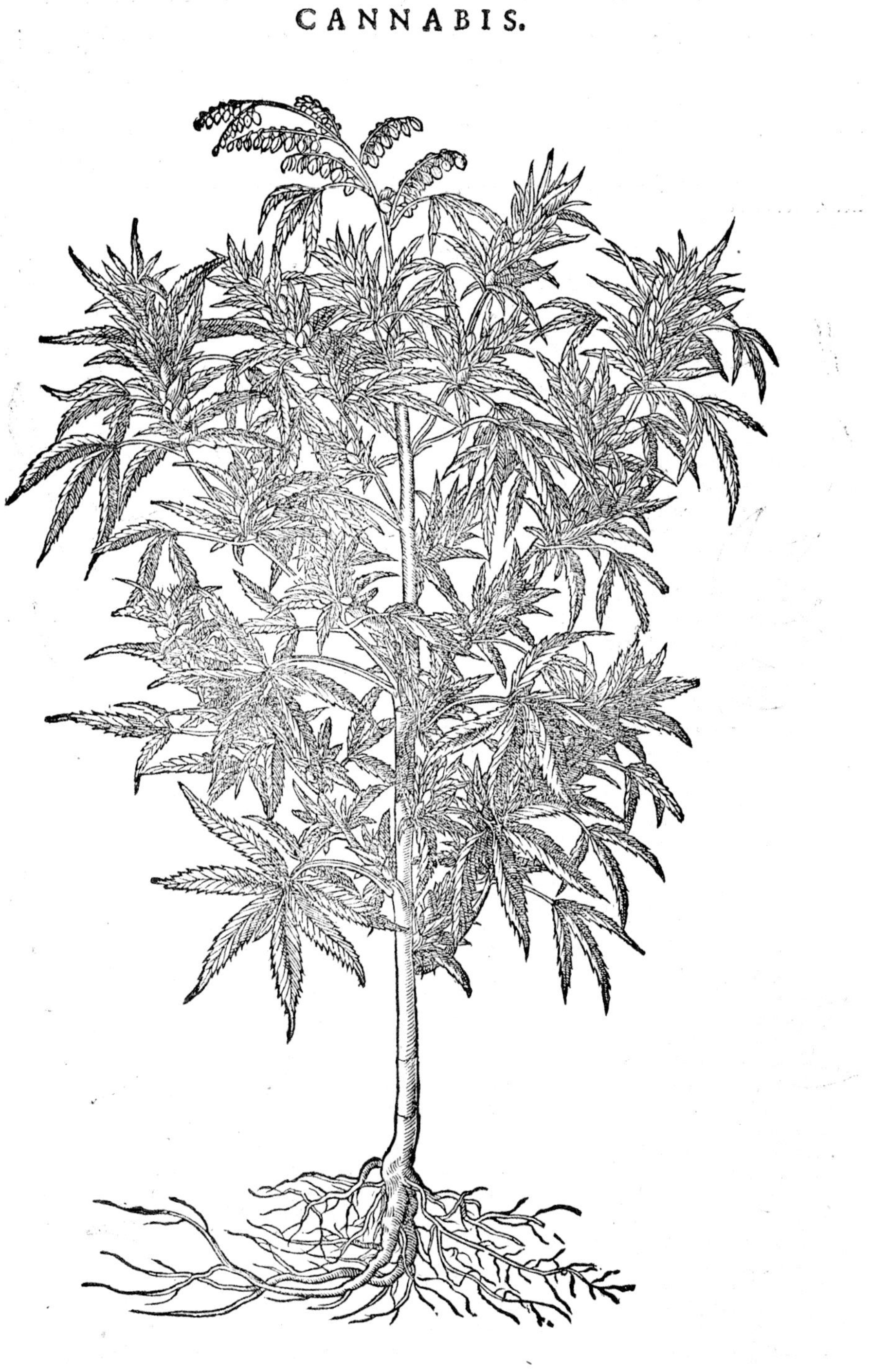

3 ▪ HEMP *Cannabis sativa*

"Cannabis." Woodcut, by Giorgio Liberale or Wolfgang Meyerpeck. In *Commentarii in Sex Libros Dioscoridis* by Pier Andrea Matthioli (1565). ▪ While cannabis is associated largely with its use as a narcotic stimulant, the principal use of hemp was for rope and sailcloth in support of the shipping industry.

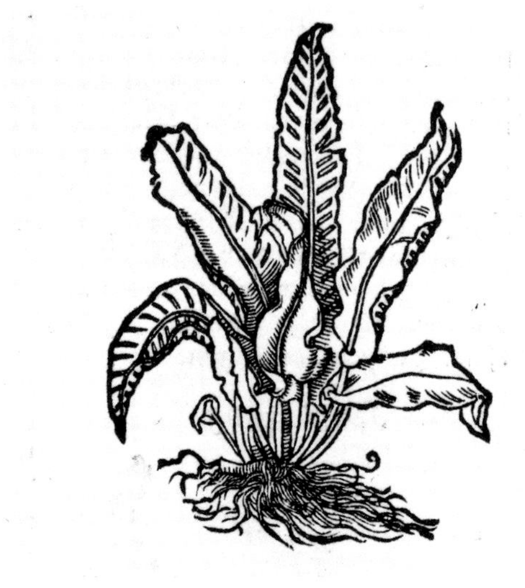

4 ▪ HART'S TONGUE FERN *Phyllitis scolopendrium*

Woodcut. In *Kleines Distillierbuch* by Hieronymus Brunschwig (c. 1565). ▪ This work by a fifteenth-century physician recommends a distillate of this fern, taken twice a day, as a good remedy for ailments of the heart. It was perhaps more commonly used in treating dysentery and diarrhea.

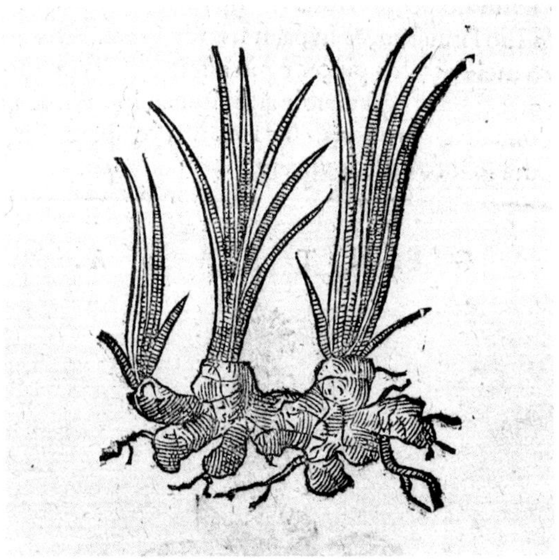

5 ▪ GINGER *Zingiber officinale*

"Gengevo." Woodcut. In *Herbario Novo* by Castore Durante (1602). ▪ Physician to Pope Sixtus the Fifth, Durante compiled his herbal out of the generally accepted body of medical knowledge of the day. Here ginger is prescribed as good for stomach ailments. As a spice imported from the East, it was highly coveted in Europe. Partly due to the costliness of the trade and potential profits to be made, voyagers were encouraged to find a new route to the Orient after the fall of Constantinople to the Turks in 1453.

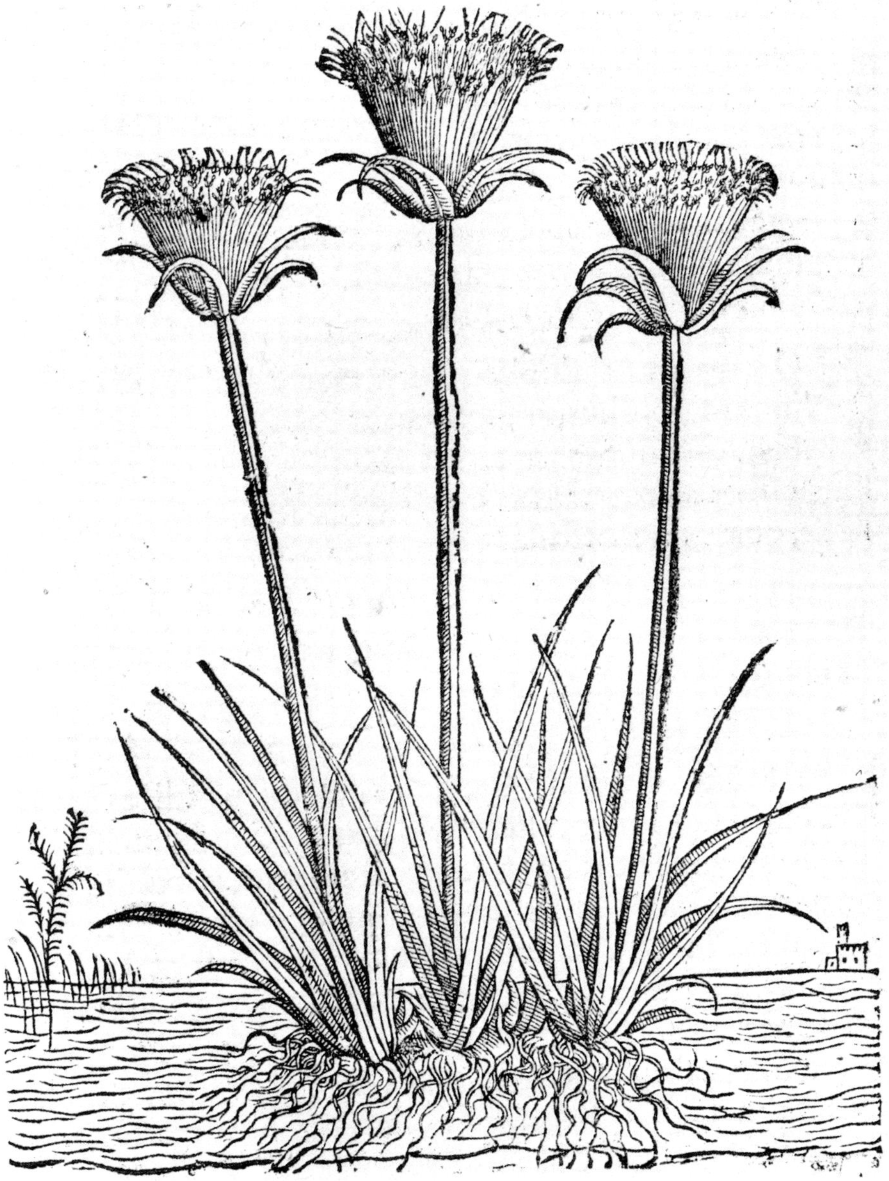

6 ▪ PAPYRUS *Cyperus papyrus*

"Papyrus Nilotica." Woodcut. In *Stirpium Adversaria Nova* by Pierre Pena and Matthias de L'Obel (1571). ▪ This Egyptian plant had been used for thousands of years in the Mediterranean world as a writing surface. By the sixteenth century in Europe it was a mere curiosity, an evocation, perhaps, of a far-off country.

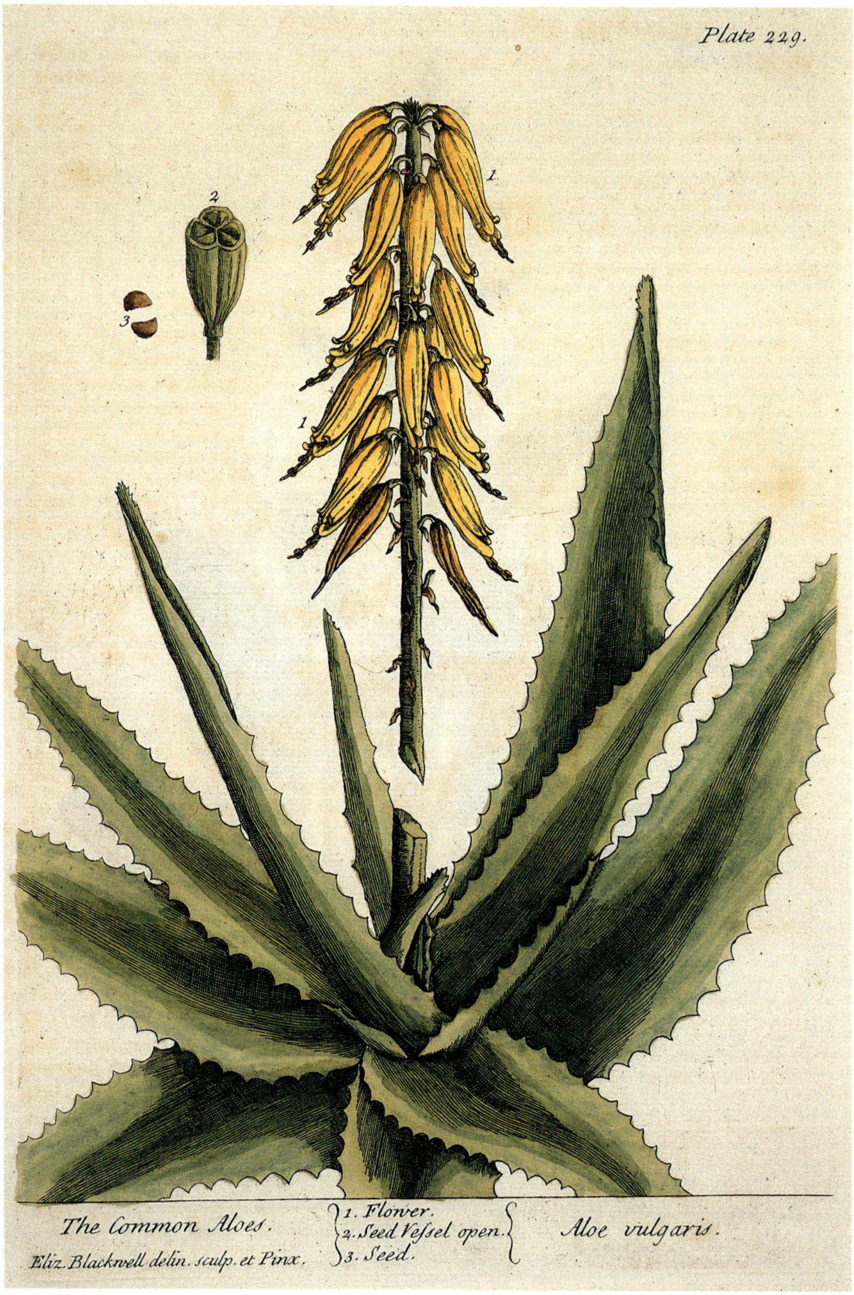

7 ▪ COMMON ALOE *Aloe vulgaris*

"The Common Aloe. 1. Flower; 2. Seed vessel open; 3. Seed." Hand-colored engraving, by Elizabeth Blackwell from her own drawing. In *A Curious Herbal, Containing 500 Cuts, of The Most Useful Plants Which Are Now Used in The Practice of Physick* by Elizabeth Blackwell (1737–39). ▪ Blackwell produced this work in order to free her husband from debtor's prison, where he had been committed after some financial difficulties in his printing business caused him to go bankrupt. In her comment on the uses to which the aloe may be put, Mrs. Blackwell makes no mention of it as a healing agent for the skin, a use to which we put it today. She does, however, note that when taken internally, it helps cure worms in children.

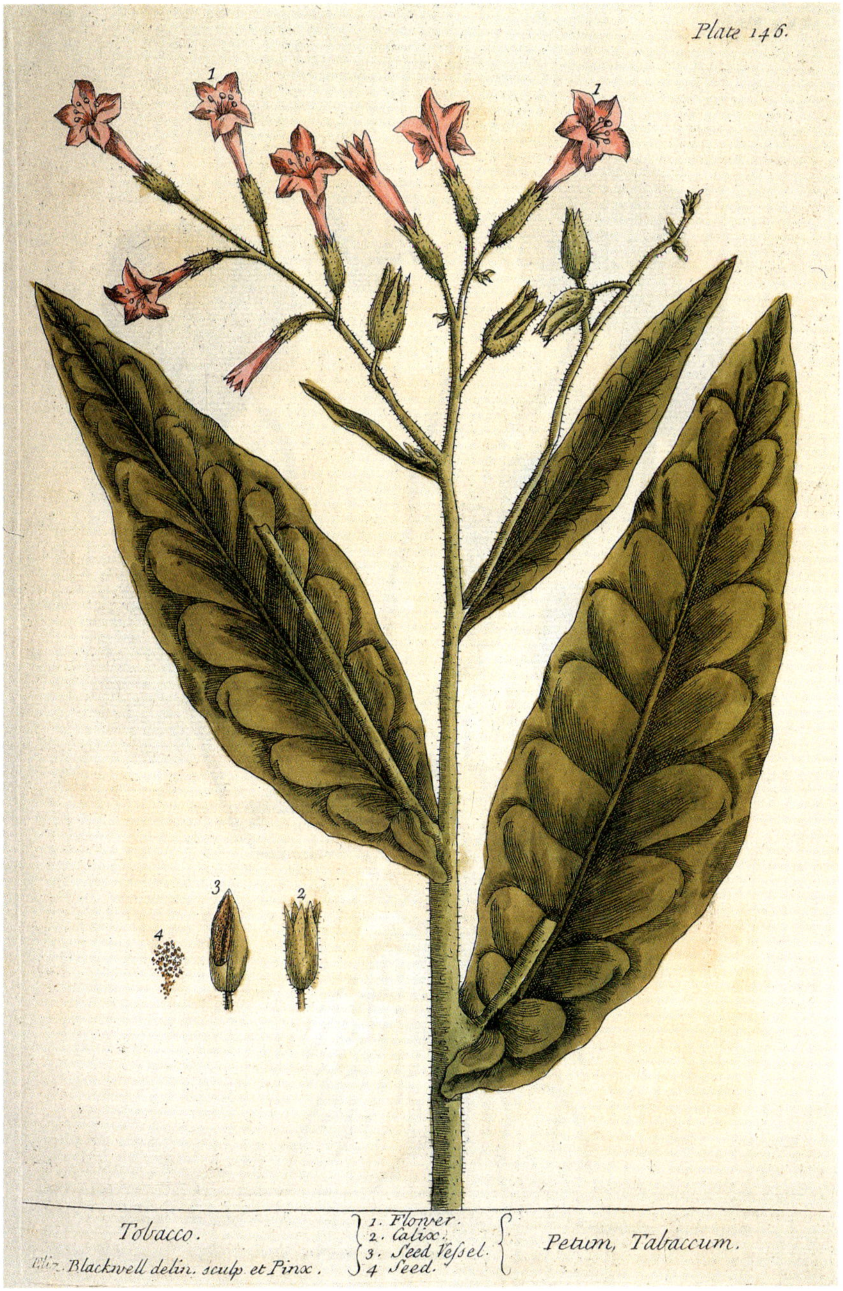

8 ▪ TOBACCO *Nicotiana tabacum*

"Tobacco. 1. Flower; 2. Calix; 3. Seed vessel; 4. Seed." Hand-colored engraving, by Elizabeth Blackwell from her own drawing. In *A Curious Herbal, Containing 500 Cuts, of The Most Useful Plants Which Are Now Used in The Practice of Physick* by Elizabeth Blackwell (1737–39). ▪ Among the illnesses that the oil of the tobacco leaf can cure, the author notes ulcers, piles (hemorrhoids), and the King's Evil (scrofula). At the time Mrs. Blackwell was preparing her herbal, tobacco had already come into general use in England in the form of snuff and pipe tobacco and it was an important factor in the trade between Britain and the North American colonies.

718 Liure XVIII. de l'Hiſtoire des Plantes,

enſemble, ou de l'vn d'iceux ſeparément. Ceſte ſeconde ſorte ſemble eſtre celle que Pena appelle *Palma ſancta*, ou *Palum ſanctum*, de l'Indie Occidentale, & dit que c'eſt vne eſpece d'arbre differente d'auec le *Guaiac*, combien qu'aucuns diſent que c'eſt vne meſme eſpece. Car il n'eſt pas grand comme vn Freſne, mais plus petit, combien qu'il ait l'eſcorce de meſme couleur. Ses fueilles ſont ſemblables à celles du Plantain, ſinon qu'elles ſont plus eſpaiſſes & plus graſſes, & ſi ſont moindres & plus courtes. Son fruict eſt de la groſſeur d'vne Noix, propre pour laſcher le ventre. Le meſme Pena dit qu'il a recouuert par le moyen des mattelots Anglois qui auoient fait le voyage d'Indie, des branches d'vn arbre ſemblable à la *Palme ſaincte*, deſquelles il met le pourtrait & la deſcription comme s'enſuit : Ce ſont, dit-il, les branches d'vn grand arbre, qui ſont droites, couuertes d'vne eſcorce ſemblable à celles du Guainier. Leurs fueilles retirent à celles des Citronniers, & ſont poulpues & nues, plus larges que celles du Laurier, & plus courtes, & nerueuſes. Au bout des brãches il y a des gouſſes blaffardes, qui ſemblent eſtre de cuir, rondes, & fort plattes, quaſi de la grandeur d'vn eſcu d'or de France, dans leſquelles il y a de la graine, de la figure & couleur d'vne Lentille; toutefois elle eſt plus platte & vn peu amere. Voila ce qu'en dit Pena. Au reſte voici comme lon dit que l'vſage du *Guaiac* vint à notice : C'eſt qu'vn certain Eſpagnol eſtant extremement tourmenté par les douleurs qu'il enduroit procedãtes de la verolle, qu'il auoit prinſe auec vne femme Indienne, ſon ſeruiteur, qui eſtoit Medecin en ce pays-là, luy fit boire la decoction du *Guaiac*, par le moyen de laquelle il ſe ſentit non ſeulement deliuré de ces grandes douleurs qu'il enduroit, mais auſſi du tout gueri, à l'imitation duquel tous les Eſpagnols qui ſe trouuerent entachez de ladite maladie, furent auſſi gueris. Ainſi ceux qui retournerent de ceſte Iſle-là, publierent incontinent la maniere de guerir ceſte maladie à Seuille, puis par toute l'Eſpagne, & en fin par tout le monde, comme ceſte maladie y euſt eſté ſemee peu à peu. Et de fait il n'y a point de plus ſouuerain remede contre icelle, Dieu ayant permis que le remede ſoit venu du lieu meſme d'où le mal eſtoit procedé : car ceſte maladie vint premierement de l'Indie Occidentale, & principalement de l'iſle S. Dominique, qui fut la premiere dont les Eſpagnols ſe ſaiſirent au nouueau monde, en laquelle ceſte maladie eſt auſſi commune, comme la petite verolle eſt en nos quartiers. Or elle fut ſemee par tout le monde en ceſte maniere : En la guerre que le Roy Charles huictieſme Roy de France mena au Royaume de Naples, Chriſtophle Colomb eſtant de retour de ſon premier voyage qu'il auoit entreprins pour cercher vn nouueau monde, auquel il auoit deſcouuert l'Iſle S. Dominique, & autres Iſles, & ayant amené auec ſoy des hommes & femmes à Naples (où eſtoit le Roy d'Eſpagne pour lors, & auoit fait paix auec le Roy de France) comme les ſoldats des deux armees frequentaſſent les vns auec les autres, les Eſpagnols commencerent à ſe meſler auec les femmes Indiennes qui eſtoient entachees de ceſte maladie, & les Indiens auec les Eſpagnolles, puis apres les Italiens & Allemans en voulurent auoir leur part, tant qu'à la fin les François en furent auſſi poiurez; ſi bien que par ce moyen la maladie fut ſemee par tout le mõde. Or pour la guerir entierement il n'y a point de plus ſouuerain remede que la decoction du *Guaiac*, quand elle eſt ordonnee à propos par vn bon Medecin, qui ait eſgard aux forces du malade, & à ſon temperamẽt: car c'eſt le vray contrepoiſon de ceſte maladie, entant qu'il ne la guerit pas par ſes qualitez manifeſtes, dautant que ſon gouſt, ſuiuant la doctrine de Galien en ſon liure des facultez des Simples, monſtre qu'il eſt fort ſec & chaud, pource que ſa decoction eſt amere & acre, tellement qu'il ſemble eſtre chaud iuſqu'au troiſieſme degré, & auoir des parties ſubtiles, deſquelles procede l'acrimonie; & des terreſtres aduſtes, qui luy cauſent l'amertume. Parquoy il ſouſtient d'eſtre longuement cuit, ſi bien que ſi on le cuiſoit dix fois, la derniere decoctiõ ſeroit quaſi auſſi amere, acre & eſpaiſſe que la premiere : tellement qu'on ne peut quaſi eſpuiſer ſa vertu. Ayant donc les qualitez ſuſdites, tant s'en faut qu'il deuſt guerir ladite maladie qui procede d'vne intemperie du foye chaude & ſeche, qu'il l'empireroit pluſtoſt. Ainſi il appert qu'il fait ceſte operation par vne qualité occulte, & par vne forme ſpecifique, comme il en prend à pluſieurs autres medicamens. Ceſte decoction eſt ſemblablement propre pour ceux qui commencẽt à eſtre hydropiques, aux aſthmatiques, contre le haut mal, aux maladies de la veſſie & des reins, aux gouttes, & à toutes ſortes de maladies qui procedent d'humeurs froides & de ventoſitez, & aux maladies inueterees, auſquelles on a eſſayé

Arbre retirant à la Palme ſaincte.

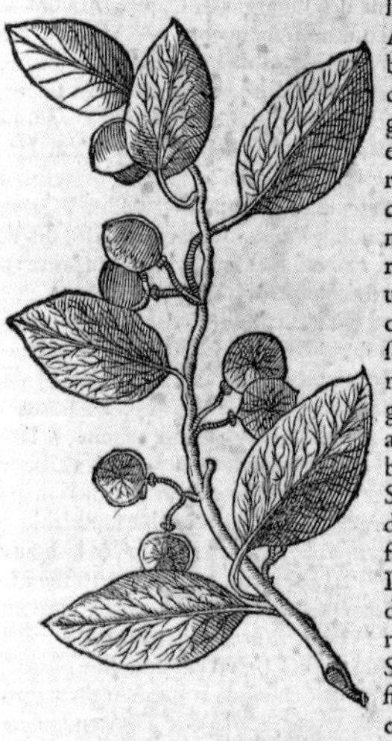

Le temperament & les vertus.

9 ▪ GUAIAC *Guaiacum sanctum*

Woodcut. In *L'Histoire Générale des Plantes* by Jacques D'Aléchamps (1615). ▪ Native to the New World, this tree received its Latin appellation "sanctum" or "holy" because of the cures ascribed to its sap, among them a cure of venereal disease. D'Aléchamps, a sixteenth-century French physician, ascribes the rise of venereal disease in Europe to the discovery of the New World. He suggests that the Indian women brought back to Europe by Columbus first infected the Spanish who, in the usual manner, spread the disease to the rest of the world. No "French disease" this, he seems to say.

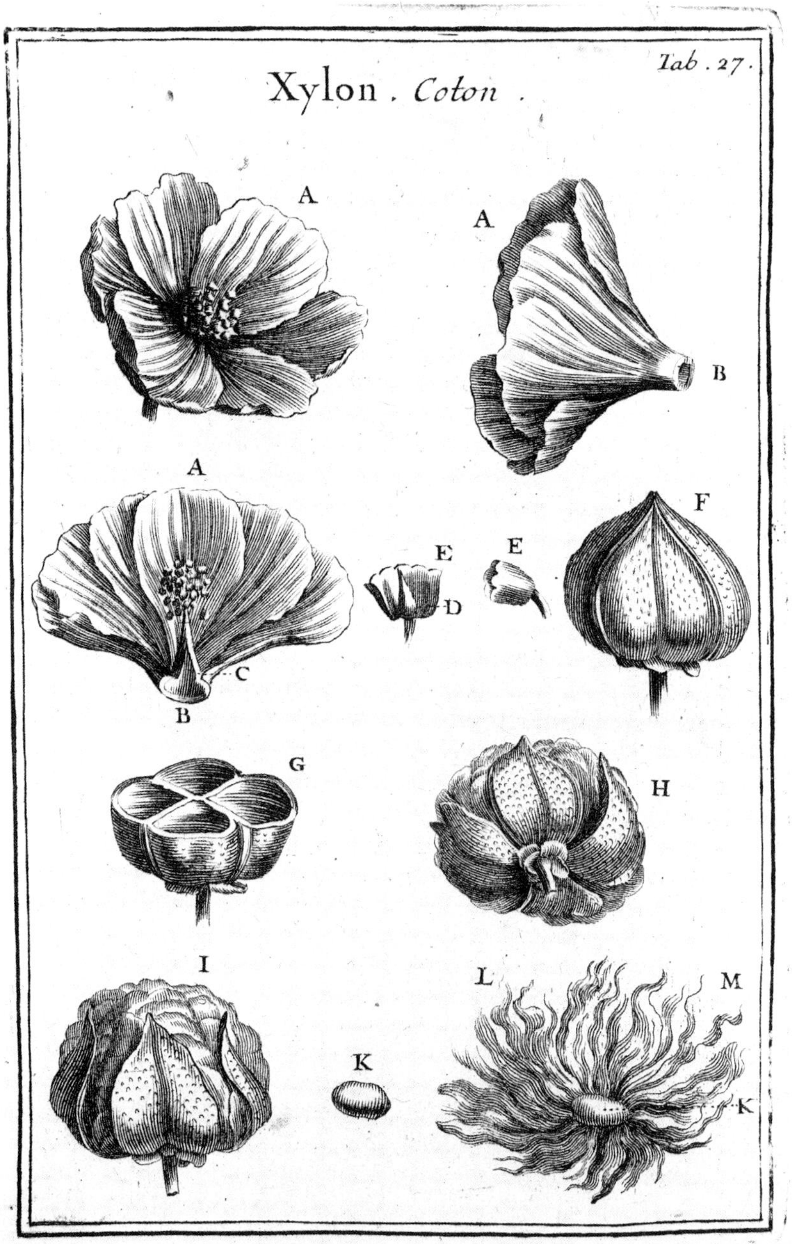

10 ▪ COTTON *Gossypium herbaceum*

"Xylon. Coton." Engraving. In *Institutiones Rei Herbariae* by Joseph Pitton de Tournefort (1719). ▪ Tales related by travelers in the sixteenth century, often the only source of information (or misinformation, as the case sometimes happened to be) incorporated in the herbals, included mention of the barometz, or vegetable lamb as it was known prior to the Linnaean system of classification. It was thought that as the plant produced a "wooly" pod, lambs were literally the resulting progeny. This was clearly the cotton plant imperfectly observed.

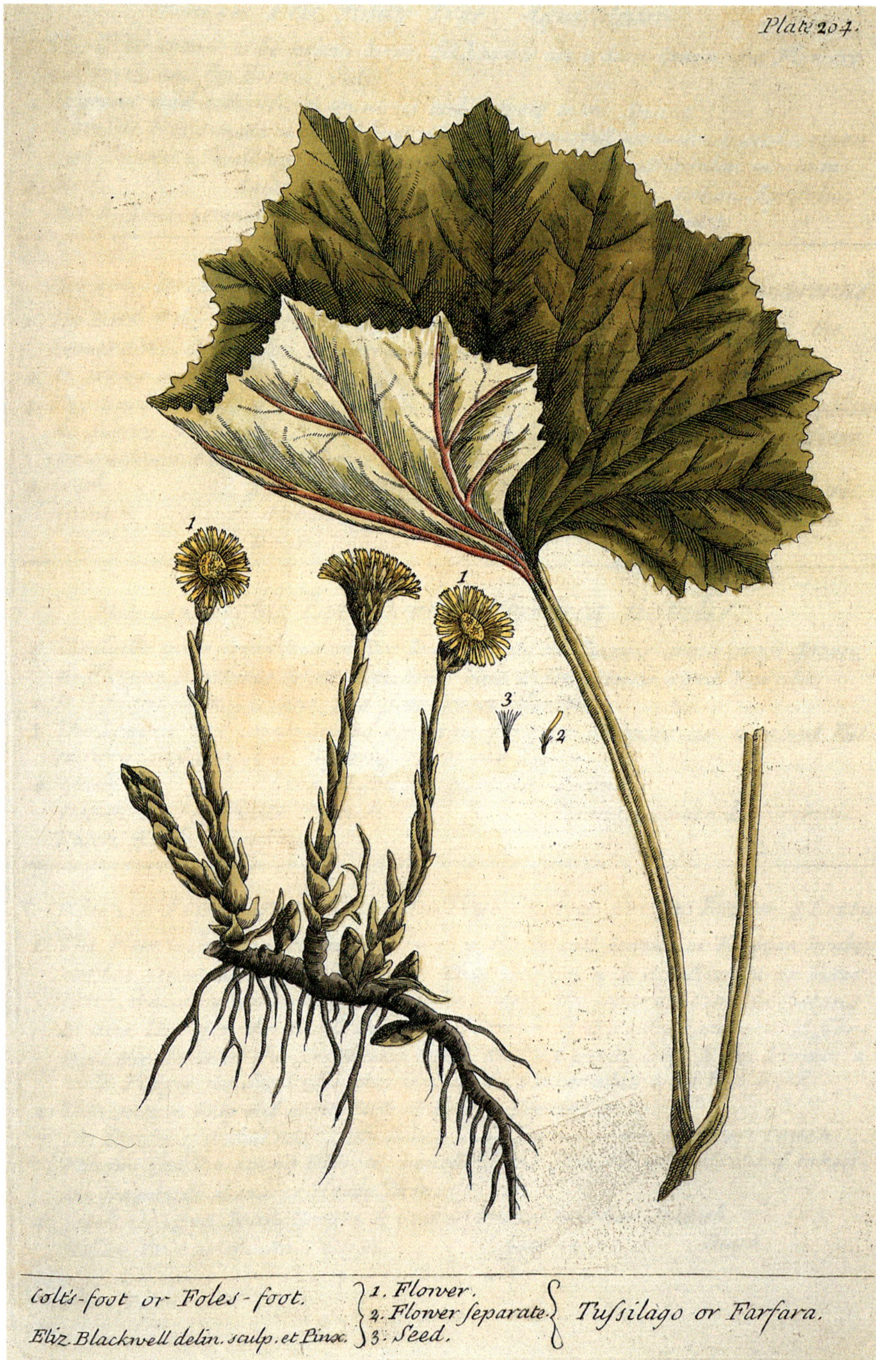

11 ▪ COLTSFOOT *Tussilago farfara*

"Colt's-foot or Foles-foot. 1. Flower; 2. Flower separate; 3. Seed." Hand-colored engraving, by Elizabeth Blackwell from her own drawing. In *A Curious Herbal, Containing 500 Cuts, of The Most Useful Plants Which Are Now Used in The Practice of Physick* by Elizabeth Blackwell (1737–39). ▪ The author reports that "some smoke the dryed leaves [of this plant] among tobacco for coughs and affections of the lungs."

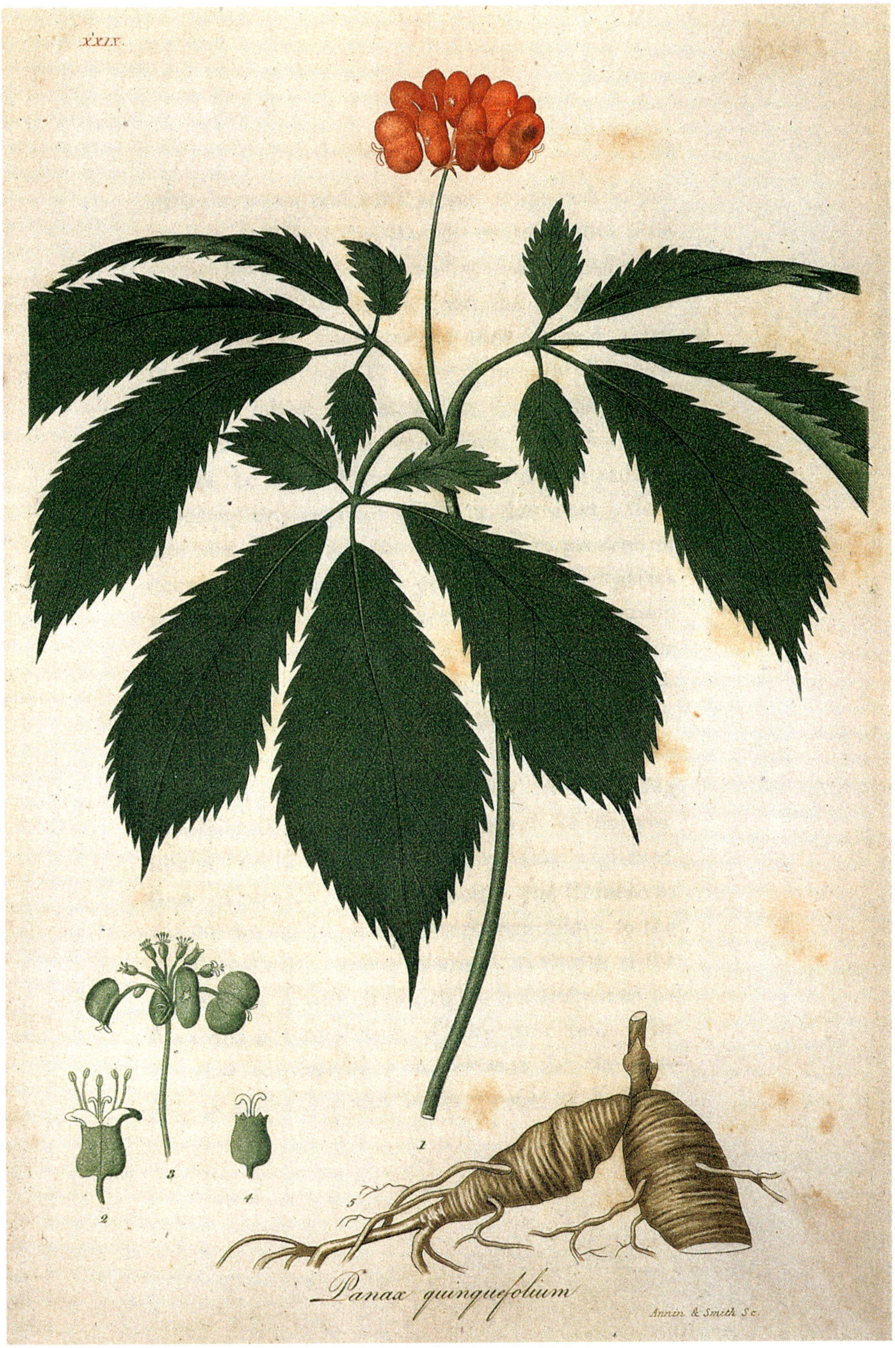

12 ▪ GINSENG *Panax quinquefolium*

"Panax quinquefolium." Hand-colored engraving, by Annin and Smith. In *American Medical Botany* by Jacob Bigelow (1817–20). ▪ In Chinese herbal medicine great curative powers were ascribed to the root of this plant, among them the ability to ease fatigue and to extend the life span. Professor of Materia Medica at the Massachusetts Medical College, Bigelow was of the opinion that "its virtues do not appear, by any means, to justify the high estimation of it by the Chinese." Bigelow's *Botany* was the first American book to be published with the plates printed in color.

EDIBLE PLANTS

If, after Eden, fruit required a good public relations person, it could not have found a better spokesman than George Brookshaw. In his *Pomona Britannica* we find "the most esteemed fruits . . . in Great Britain" (none of them from the "tree of the knowledge of good and evil," however) pictured at the height of their most tempting ripeness. Brookshaw published his work in two versions, first in 1812 and later in 1817. The earlier version was produced in a larger format than the latter, each plate being 24 × 19 inches in the 1804–12 book and 15 × 11 inches in the 1816–17 edition. The earlier version is also distinguished by the striking, dark brown aquatint backgrounds which throw the fruit illustrated into bold, dramatic relief. Brookshaw had written his work for "Nurserymen, Gardeners and even Gentlemen," and selected his specimens from the royal gardens at Hampton Court and other London gardens. His intent was a practical one, even though the luxurious quality of the books might suggest otherwise. He labored for ten years to produce a book that would help people improve their harvests and enhance the variety of their crops. ▪ Brookshaw's *Pomona Britannica* was the first major work devoted exclusively to fruit. Prior to his efforts, fruit and vegetables had been dealt with in the general context of agricultural and botanical literature. The sixteenth-century botanists, for example, dealt with vegetables as one element of the plant kingdom in their surveys. Pier Andrea Matthioli, an Italian physician and botanist, included them in his *Commentarii* on the works of Dioscorides (Venice, 1565) with its finely designed woodcuts by Giorgio Liberale and Wolfgang Meyerpeck, woodcuts which suggest that the influence of Italian art in the sixteenth century included botanical illustration. The practice of including vegetables in studies of plants persisted into the eighteenth century. In Joseph Pitton de Tournefort's *Institutiones Rei Herbariae* (Paris, 1719) we move through flowers and trees and ferns as well as fruit and vegetables. Finally, after the turn of the nineteenth century, we find books like Brookshaw's devoted exclusively to edible plants. Joseph Antoine Risso and Pierre Antoine Poiteau's *Histoire Naturelle des Orangers* (1818–22) presents us with the citrus world in a series of engravings, which like Brookshaw's, seem almost edible in themselves. Mathieu Bonafous's *Histoire Naturelle, Agricole et Économique du Maïs* (1836) deals exclusively with the subject of corn in all its varieties. Among its plates we find one painted by P.-J. Redouté, which was a change of subject matter for this master of flower paintings and also, as it turned out, one of his last works. ▪ Giorgio Gallesio's *Pomona Italiana* (1817–39) is the Italian counterpart to Brookshaw's book. Here grapes glisten, and a sheet of deeply colored figs suggests a meaty and juicy flavor unique to Gallesio's artistry. Like its English relation, it, too, has a practical purpose. Brookshaw's book was intended to assist growers and gardeners in their labors. The richly colored, engraved plates remind us of the purpose and fate of fruit and vegetables (with the possible exception of brussels sprouts), which are to be eaten.

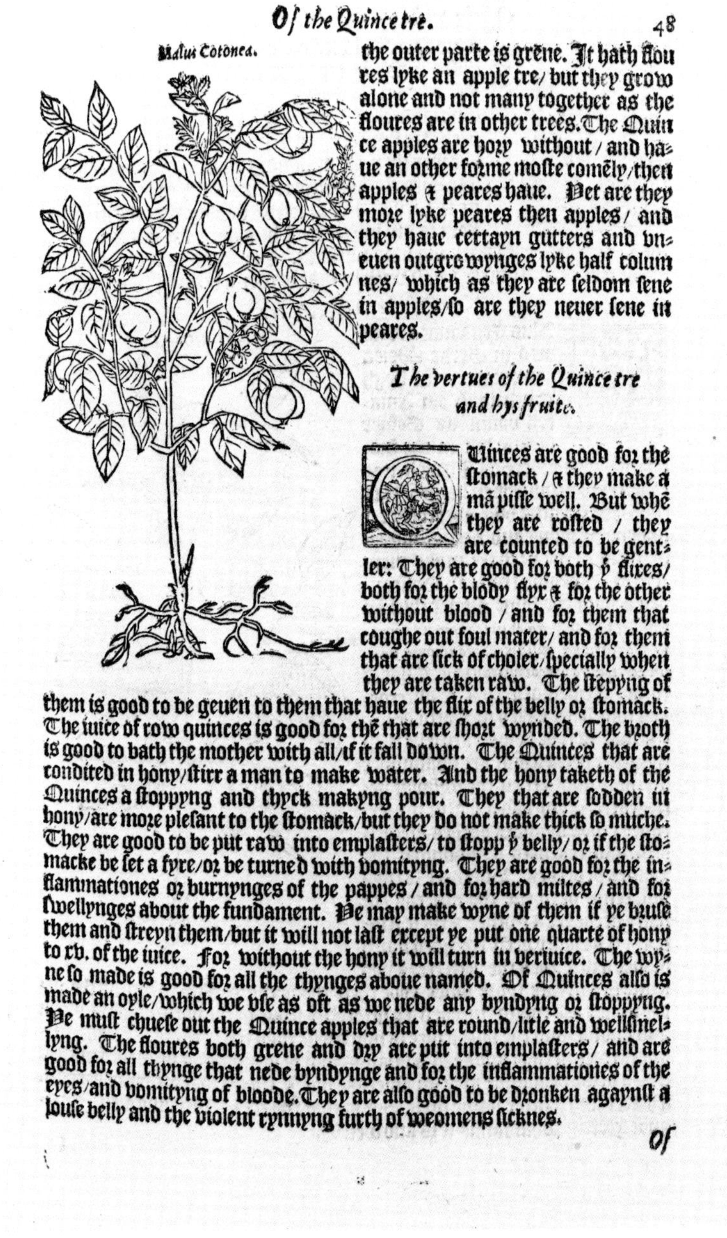

Of the Quince tre. 48

Malus Cotonea.

the outer parte is grene. It hath floures lyke an apple tre/ but they grow alone and not many together as the floures are in other trees. The Quince apples are hory without / and haue an other forme moste comely/ then apples & peares haue. Yet are they more lyke peares then apples/ and they haue certayn gutters and vneuen outgrowynges lyke half columnes/ which as they are seldom sene in apples/so are they neuer sene in peares.

The vertues of the Quince tre and hys fruite.

Quinces are good for the stomack / & they make a mã pisse well. But whẽ they are rosted / they are counted to be gentler: They are good for both ẏ flixes/ both for the blody flyx & for the other without blood / and for them that coughe out foul mater/ and for them that are sick of choler/specially when they are taken raw. The steppyng of them is good to be geuen to them that haue the flix of the belly or stomack. The iuice of row quinces is good for thẽ that are short wynded. The broth is good to bath the mother with all/if it fall down. The Quinces that are condited in hony/stirr a man to make water. And the hony taketh of the Quinces a stoppyng and thyck makyng pour. They that are sodden in hony/are more plesant to the stomack/but they do not make thick so muche. They are good to be put raw into emplasters/ to stopp ẏ belly/ or if the stomacke be set a fyre/or be turned with vomityng. They are good for the inflammationes or burnynges of the pappes / and for hard miltes / and for swellynges about the fundament. Ye may make wyne of them if ye bruse them and streyn them/but it will not last except ye put one quarte of hony to xv. of the iuice. For without the hony it will turn in veriuice. The wyne so made is good for all the thynges aboue named. Of Quinces also is made an oyle/which we vse as oft as we nede any byndyng or stoppyng. Ye must chuese out the Quince apples that are round/litle and wellsmellyng. The floures both grene and dry are put into emplasters/ and are good for all thynge that nede byndynge and for the inflammationes of the eyes/and vomityng of bloode. They are also good to be dronken agaynst a louse belly and the violent rynnyng furth of weomens sicknes.

Of

13 ▪ QUINCE *Cydonia oblonga*

"Malus Cotonea." Woodcut. In *A New Herball* by William Turner (1551). ▪ Physician and theologian, Turner is the father of English botany. In the period when Fuchs and Matthioli were active on the Continent, Turner provided the English with a great herbal based on contemporary scientific practice and his own rather hard-edged skepticism about the supposed magical properties assigned to some plants. As with all sixteenth-century herbals, his work provides medical as well as botanical information about the plants he describes. In writing of the quince—perhaps the "golden apple" of classical literature—he notes that they "are good for the stomack for they make a man pisse well." That said, it was more readily applied for its styptic and astringent qualities.

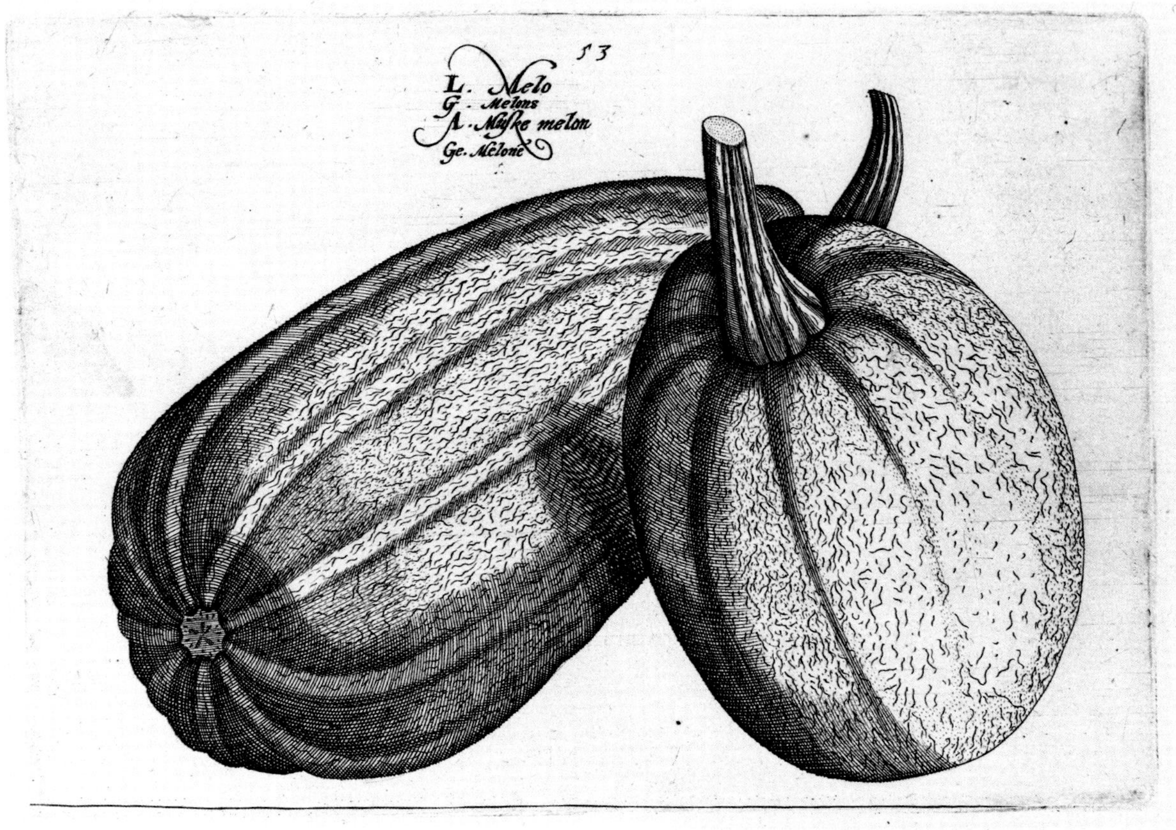

14 ▪ MUSK MELON *Cucumis melo*

"Melo." Engraving. In *Hortus Floridus* by Crispijn van de Passe (1614–16). ▪ The images in this work, whether of flowers or fruit, are reminiscent of contemporary Dutch still-life paintings. Van de Passe's melons are shown not merely to inform the gardener of what they look like, but also to delight the viewer with their appearance. Van de Passe imbued these melons with a heavy sensuousness that perhaps surpasses Nature's intentions.

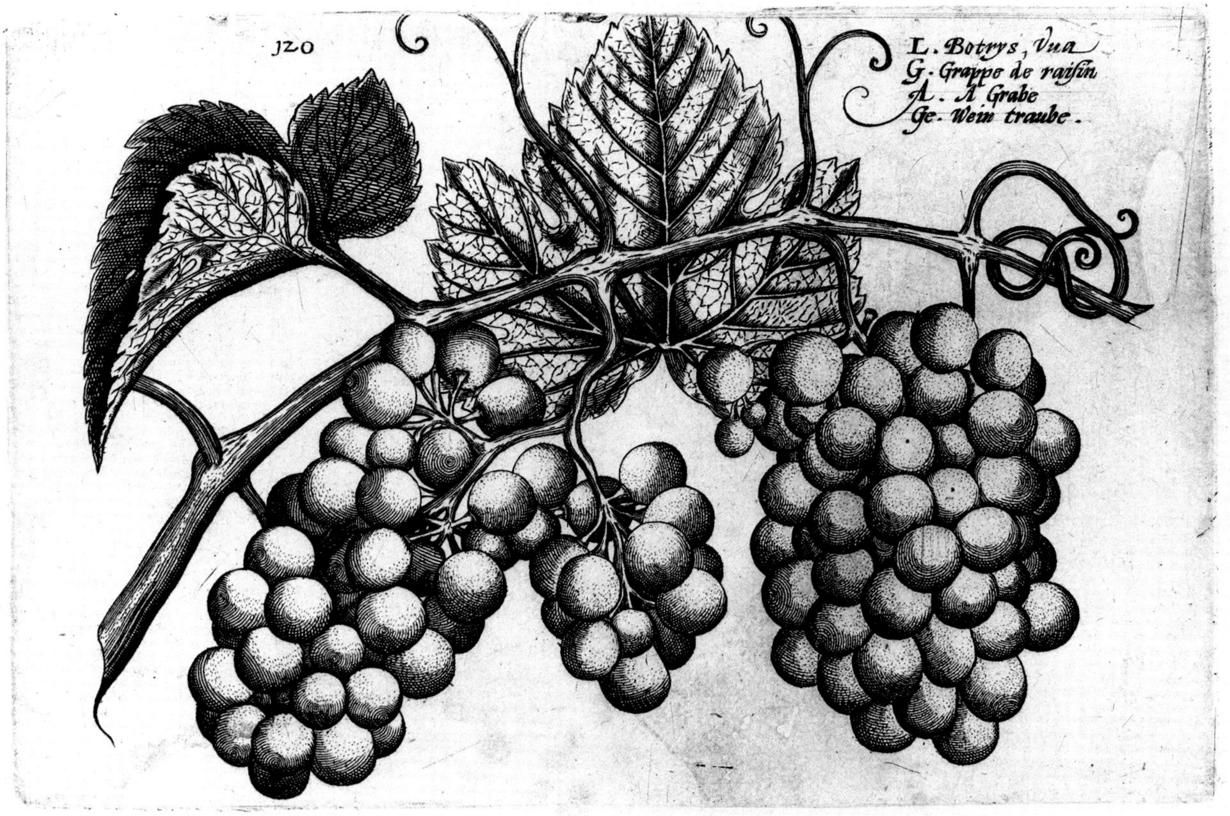

15 ▪ GRAPES *Vitis vinifera*

"Botrys Vua." Engraving. In *Hortus Floridus* by Crispijn van de Passe (1614–16). ▪ This work is best known for its illustrations of garden flowers, but edible plants were also included as part of the well-rounded garden. Except for the name of the fruit, Van de Passe provided no additional text for the plates, suggesting that the plates were to be seen as an ideal image against which garden realities were to be measured.

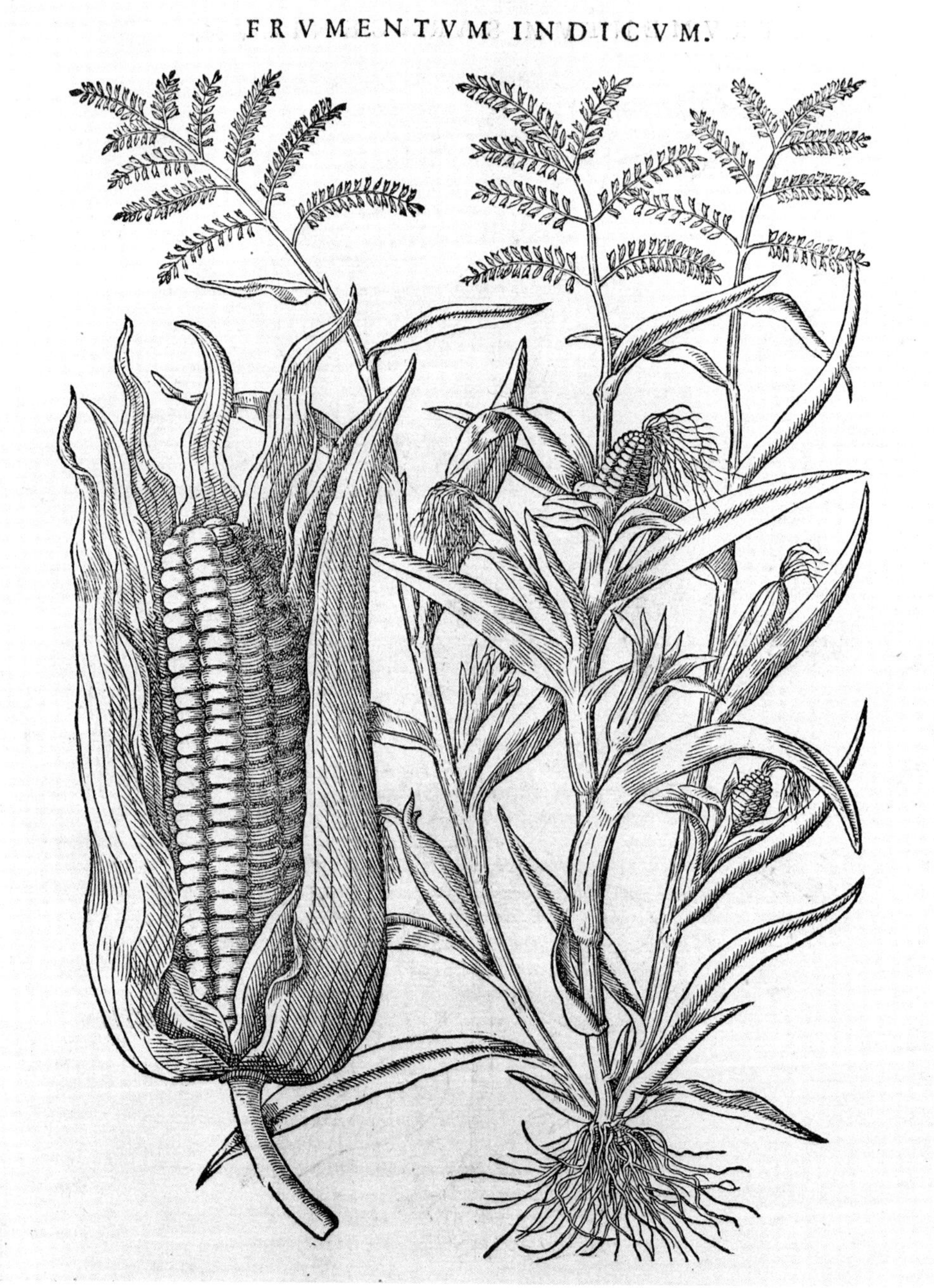

16 ▪ CORN *Zea mays*

"Frumentum Indicum." Woodcut, by Giorgio Liberale or Wolfgang Meyerpeck. In *Commentarii in Sex Libros Dioscoridis* by Pier Andrea Matthioli (1565). ▪ In the century after the discovery of the Americas, herbalists, of whom Matthioli was among the most distinguished, incorporated New World plants such as corn into the body of accumulated botanical knowledge. Along with the potato, the tomato, and tobacco, these plants, heretofore unknown to Europeans, were to become an important, and sometimes crucial, factor in the economics and agriculture of the Old World.

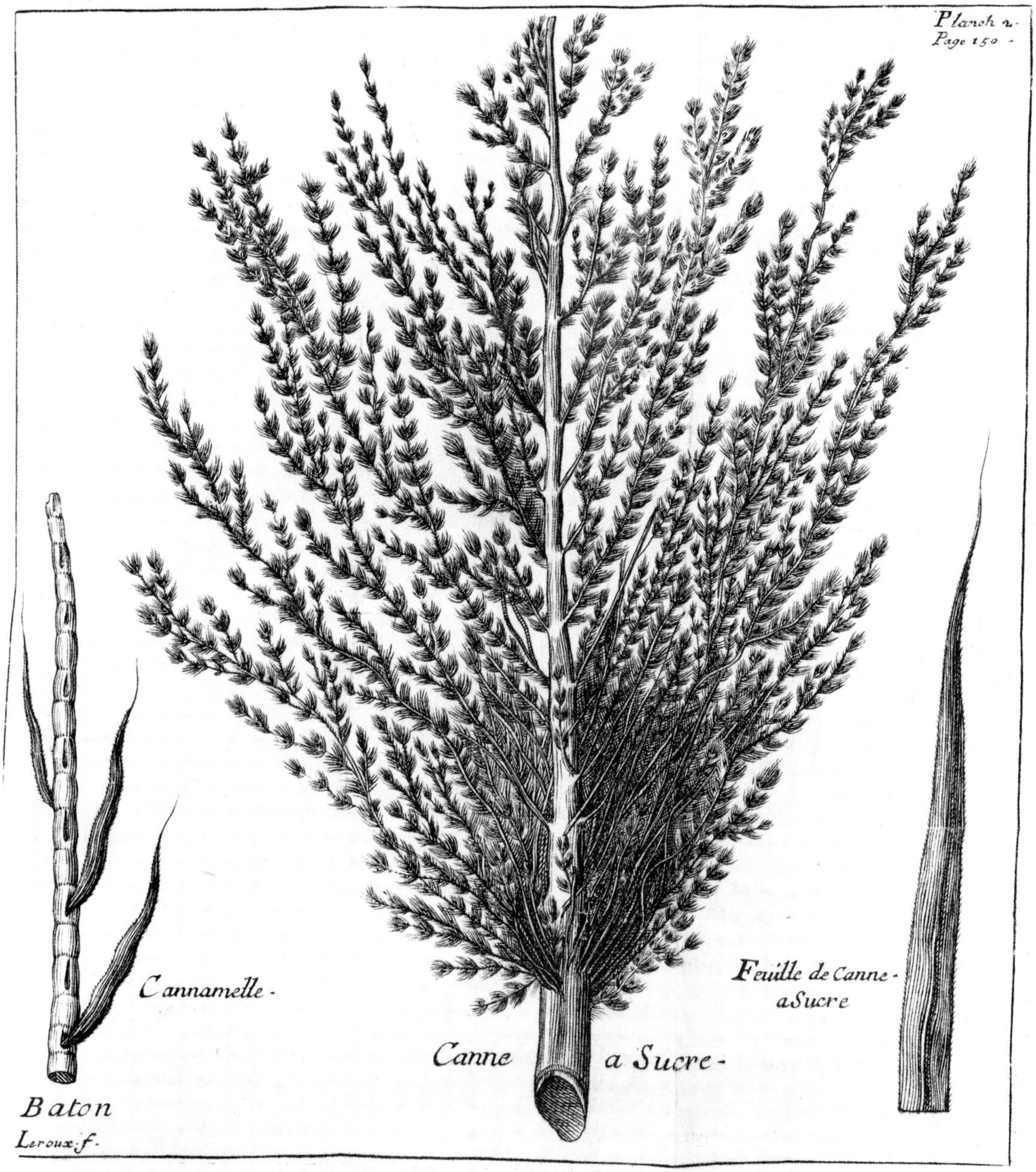

17 ▪ SUGARCANE *Saccharum officinarum*

"Canne a Sucre; Cannamette; Feuille de Canne a Sucre." Engraving, from the drawing by Leroux. In *Histoire Naturelle du Cacao et du Sucre* by D. de Quélus (1719). ▪ Introduced into the Americas by the Spanish, sugarcane rapidly became an important crop, particularly in the Caribbean islands, among them Santo Domingo and Cuba. Along with the sugar beet, sugarcane is a primary source of refined sugar. But at the time Quélus's work was written, sugar was very much a luxury item.

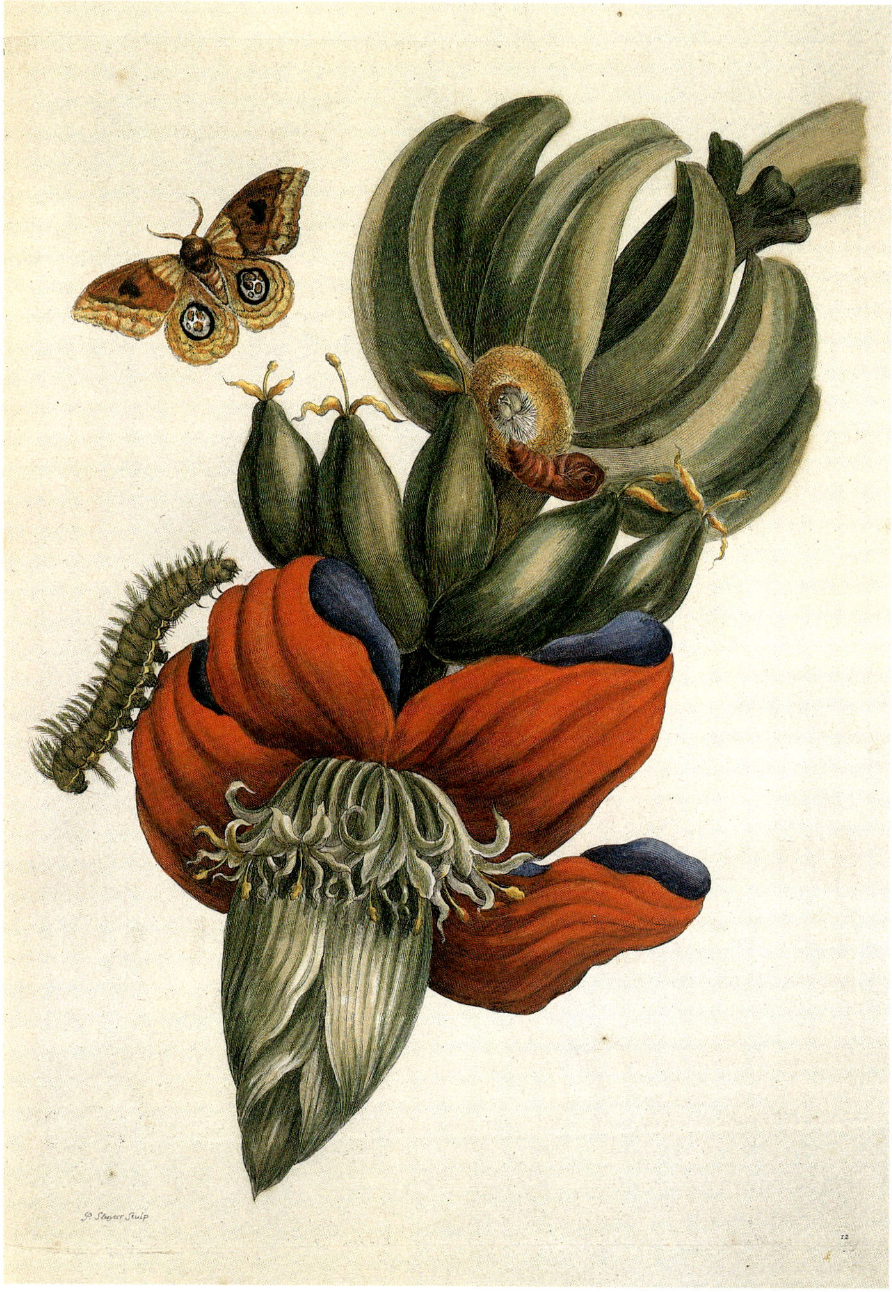

18 ▪ BANANAS *Musa paradisiaca*

Hand-colored engraving, by Jan Pieter Sluyter from the drawing by Maria Sibylla Merian. In *Dissertation sur la Génération et les Transformations des Insectes de Surinam* by Maria Sibylla Merian (1726). ▪ The daughter of the German engraver and publisher Matthias Merian, Maria Sibylla traveled to the Dutch colony of Surinam to study and paint the then undocumented insect life there. Although the first bananas to have appeared in England were immortalized on the engraved title page of Gerard's *Herball* (1633) revised by Thomas Johnson—and in whose apothecary shop they were displayed—still one hundred years later they were little known. Thus, given its rendering here, this particular tropical fruit must have seemed bizarre to European readers of Merian's work.

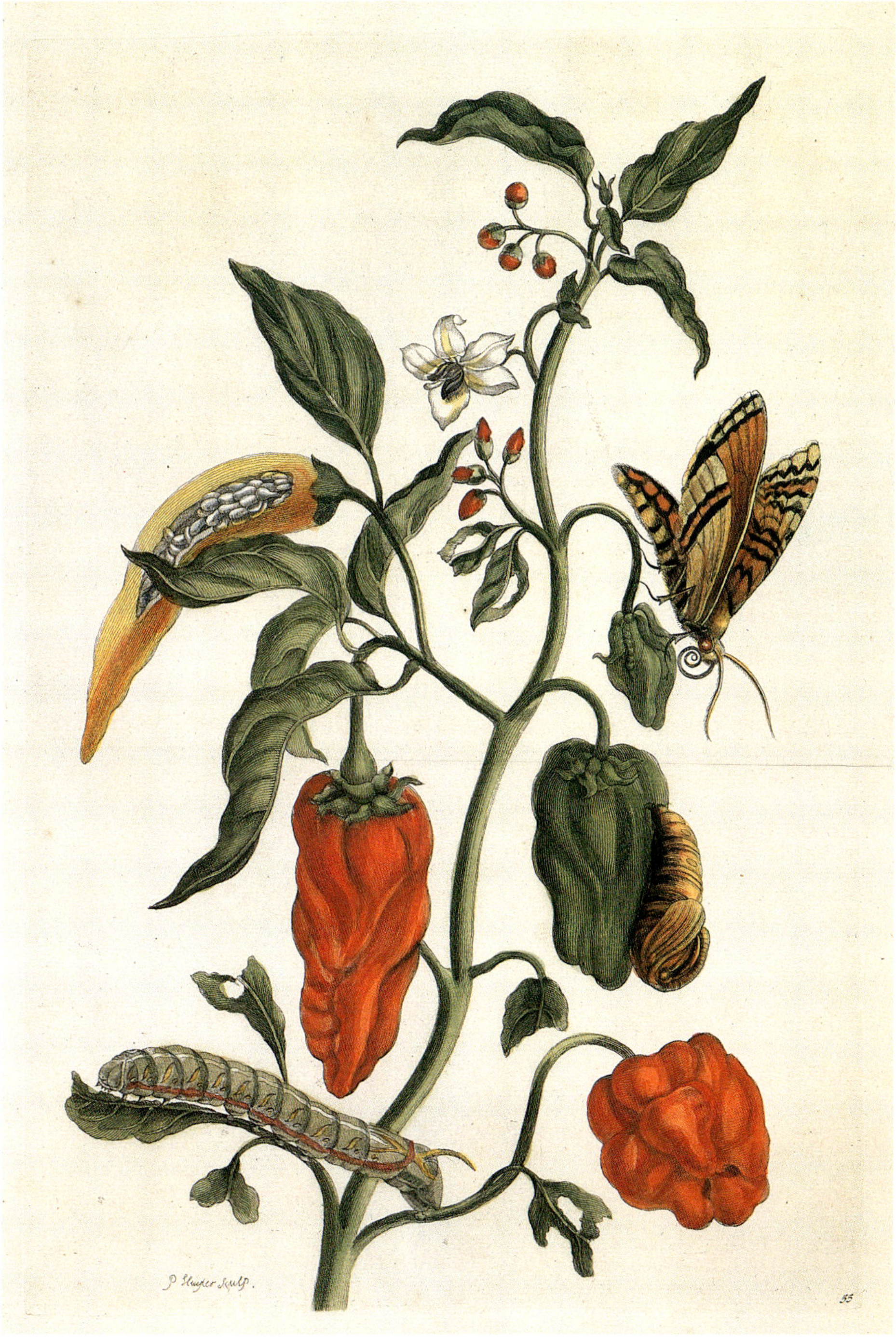

19 ▪ PEPPER *Capsicum annuum*

Hand-colored engraving, by Jan Pieter Sluyter, from the drawing by Maria Sibylla Merian. In *Dissertation Sur La Génération et Les Transformations des Insectes de Surinam* by Maria Sibylla Merian (1726). ▪ In this work the caterpillars and butterflies which were the object of Merian's study are portrayed against plants native to Surinam.

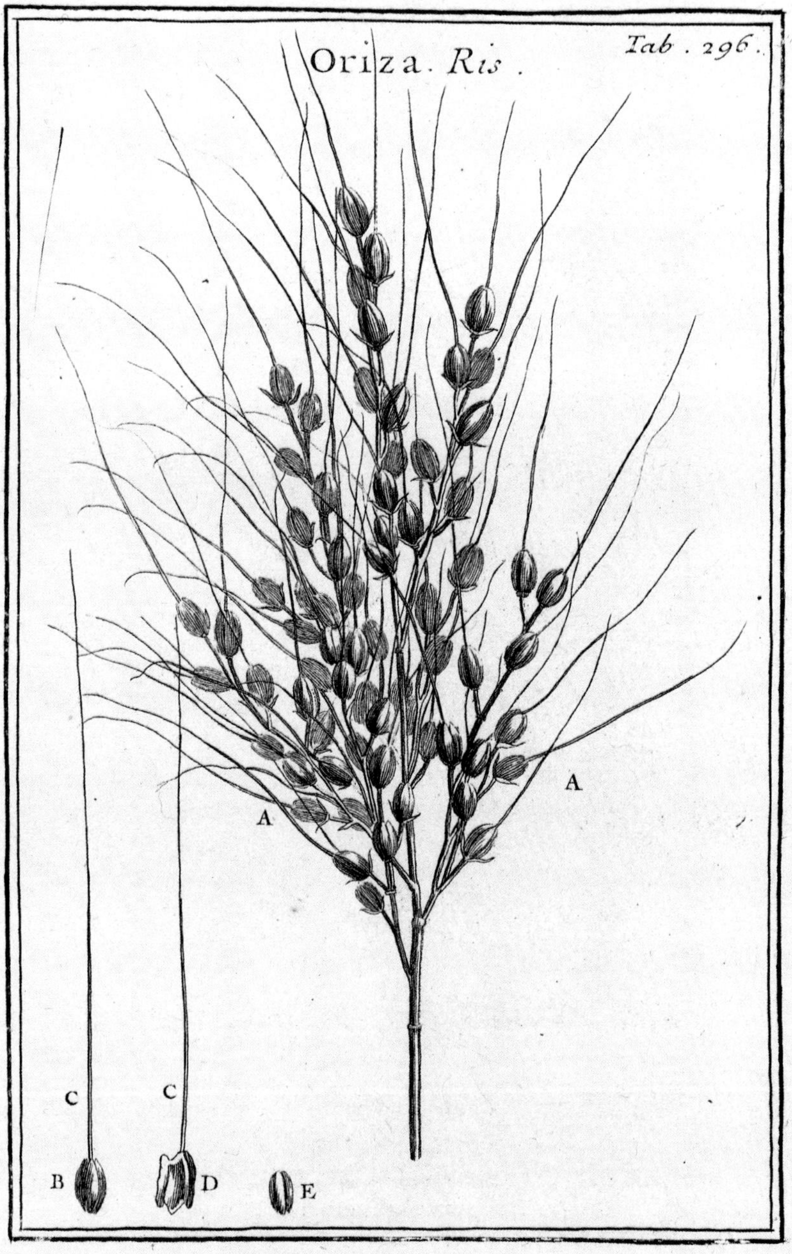

20 ▪ RICE *Oryza sativa*

"Oriza. Ris." Engraving. In *Institutiones Rei Herbariae* by Joseph Pitton de Tournefort (1719). ▪ As the head of the royal gardens of the King of France, to whom this work is dedicated, Tournefort traveled widely in Europe and the Near East in search of plants. Rice, although a food staple in the Far East, comparable to wheat in the West, did not achieve similar such status in Europe until the nineteenth century, when contacts with China and India became more frequent than they had been heretofore.

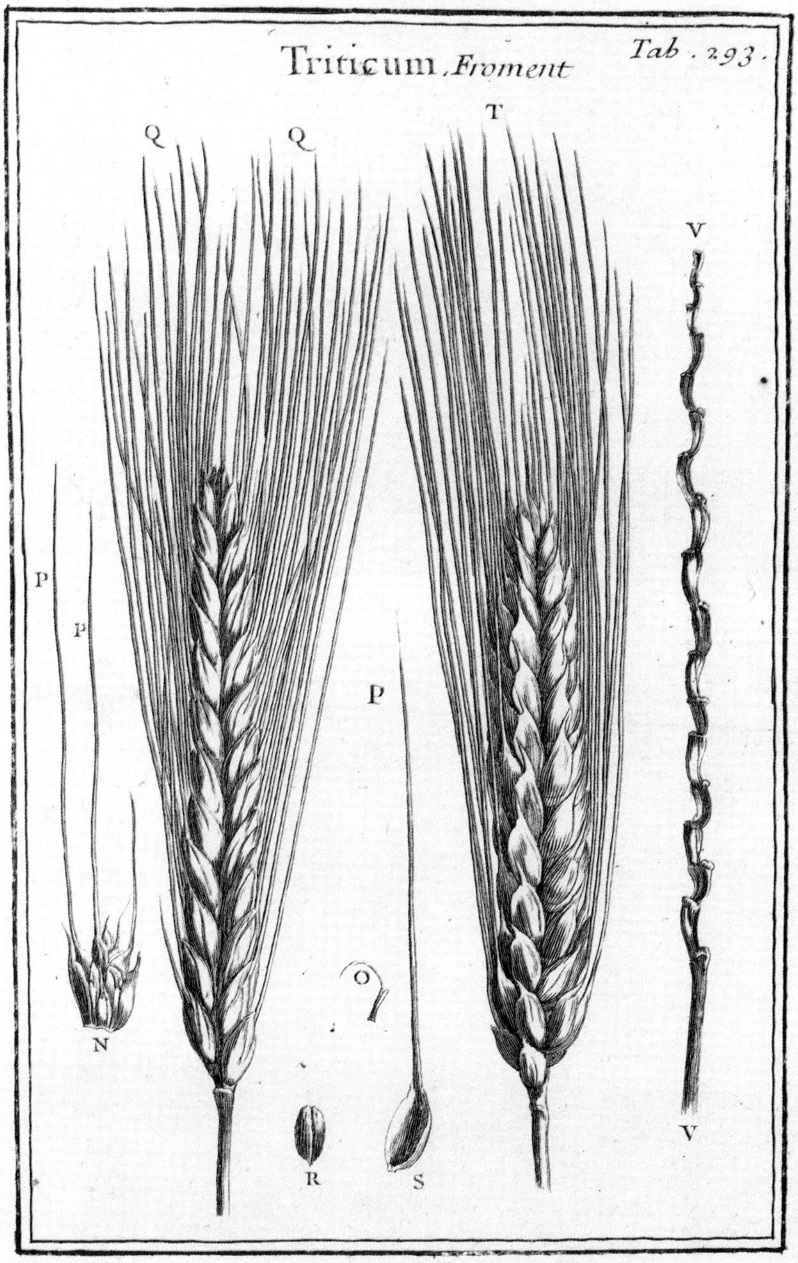

21 ▪ WHEAT *Triticum aestivum*

"Triticum. Froment." Engraving, after the drawing by Claude Aubriet. In *Institutiones Rei Herbariae* by Joseph Pitton de Tournefort (1719). ▪ The engravings that illustrate this three-volume work on the classification of plants are remarkable for their clarity; the inclusion of the dissections was particularly noteworthy for this time. Wheat, an important agricultural crop since ancient times, is elegantly presented in Tournefort's impressive taxonomic work.

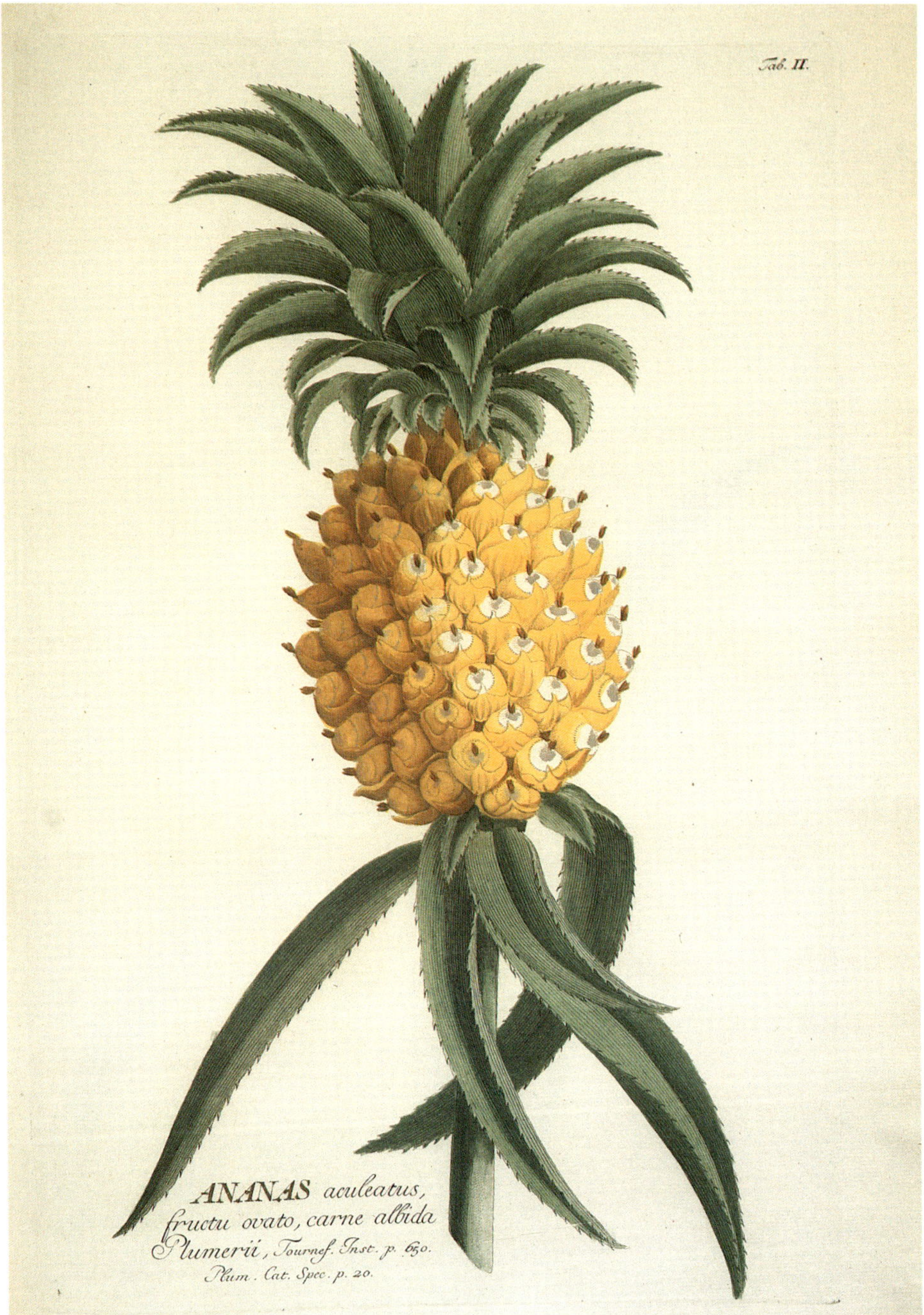

22 ▪ PINEAPPLE *Ananas comosus*

"Ananas." Hand-colored engraving, by Johann Jacob Haid from the drawing by Georg Dionysius Ehret. In *Uitgezochte Planten* by Christoph Jacob Trew (1771–73). ▪ Originally native to South America, the pineapple was planted in other tropical areas, most notably Hawaii, after the European discovery of the New World. Due to its rarity, it was offered as a special treat to guests, thereby making it a symbol of hospitality. In more recent periods in history, its elegant form made it attractive to designers in the fields of architecture and the decorative arts.

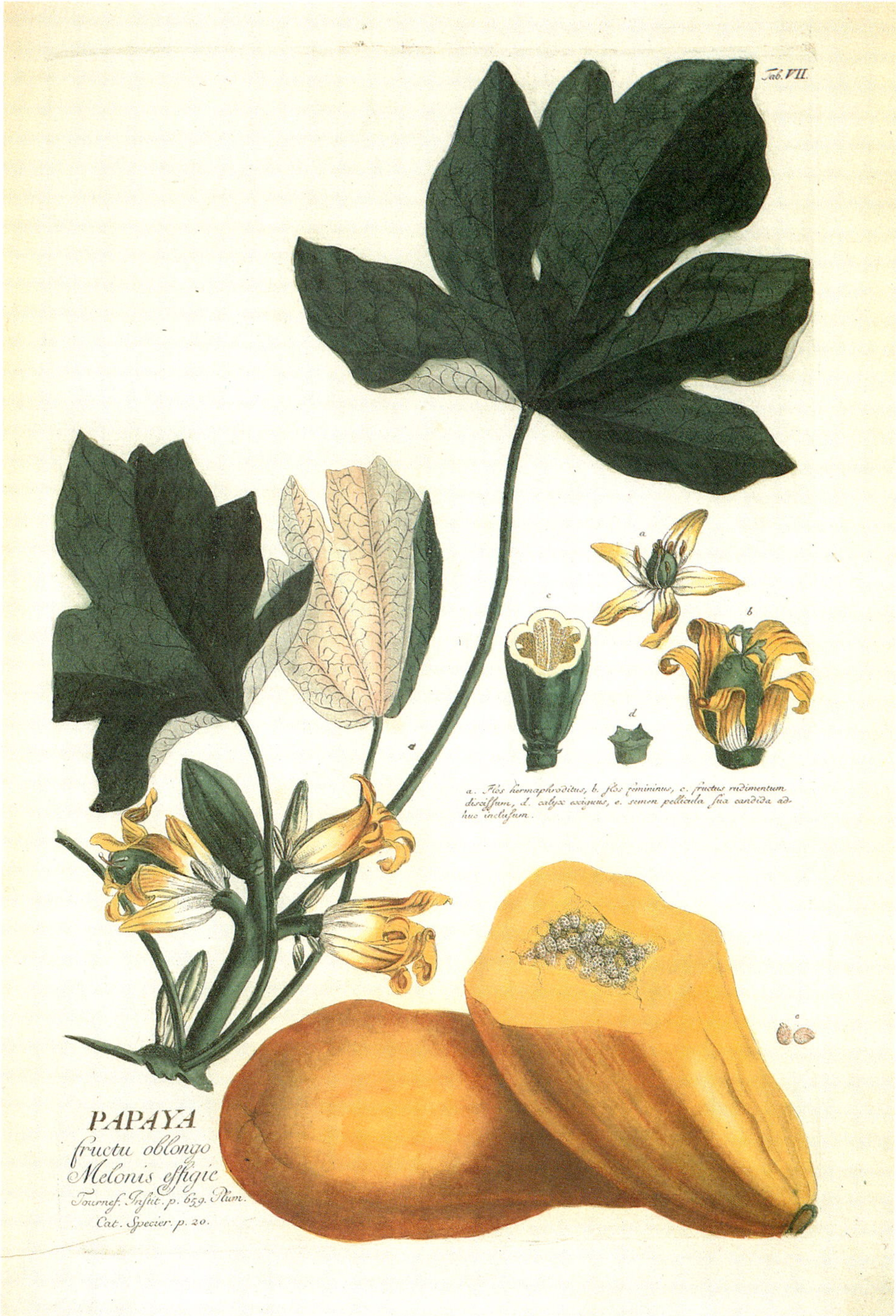

23 ▪ PAPAYA *Carica papaya*

"Papaya." Hand-colored engraving, by Johann Jacob Haid from the drawing by Georg Dionysius Ehret. In *Uitgezochte Planten* by Christoph Jacob Trew (1771–73). ▪ In this luxuriously produced Dutch translation of the author's *Plantae Selectae*, the artist and the engraver are both given credit on the title page. The papaya remains a somewhat exotic fruit in northern countries, even today.

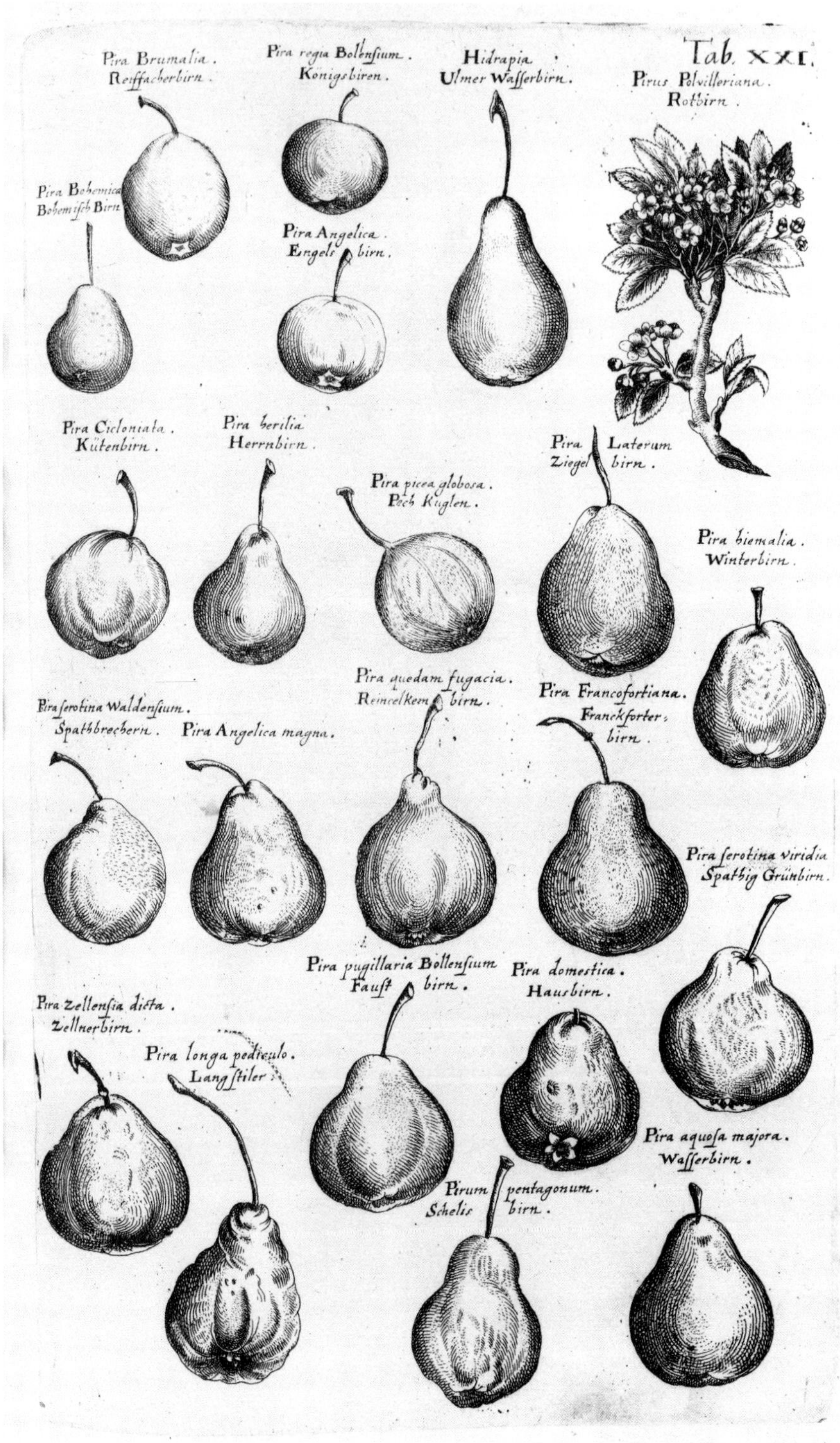

24 ▪ PEARS *Pyrus communis*

Engraving. In *Dendographias* by John Jonston (1662). ▪ In this work devoted to trees and their fruit, the English physician and botanist reminds us, at the distance of some three centuries, of the varieties of common fruit—today known to us denizens of supermarkets in three or four manifestations. Here he shows twenty-one different pears.

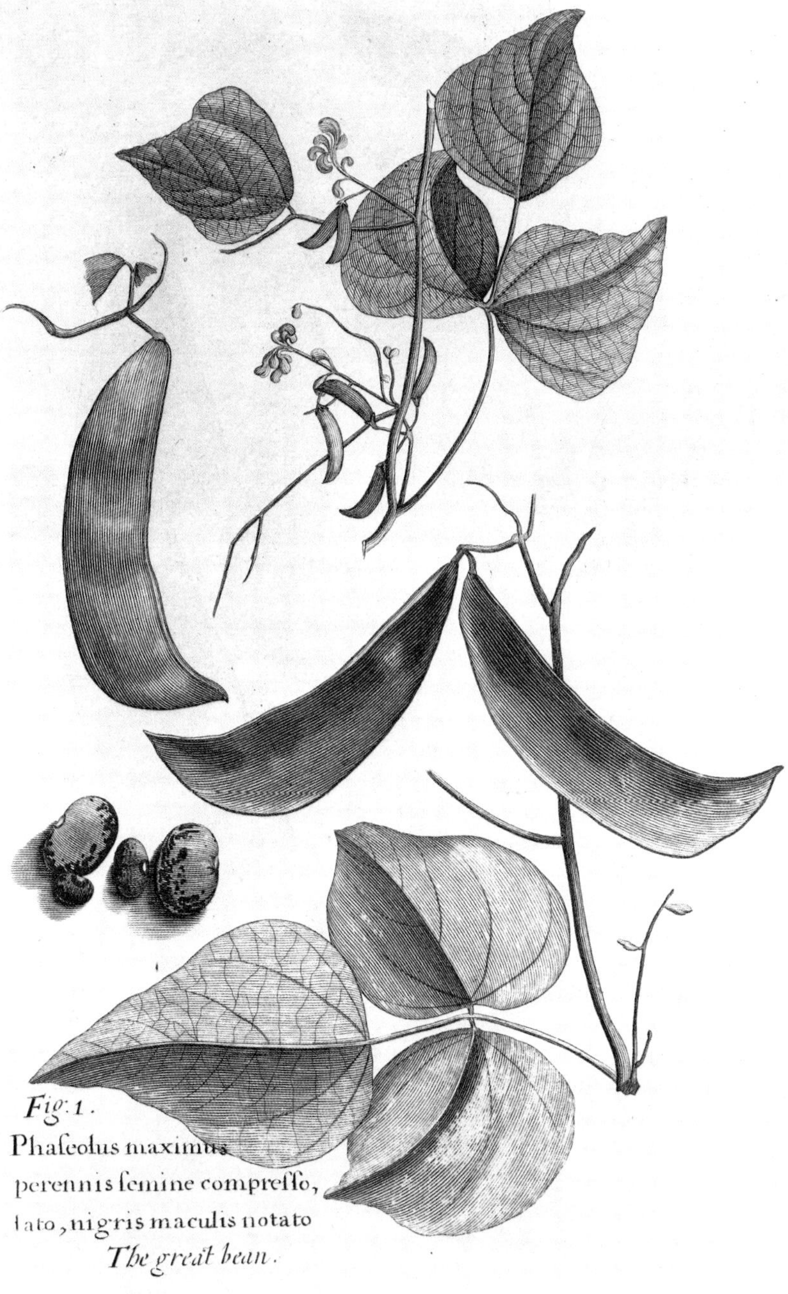

25 ▪ LIMA BEAN *Phaseolus lunatus*

"The Great Bean. Phaseolus maximus." Engraving, by M. van der Gucht from the drawing by E. Kickius. In *A Voyage to the Islands . . .* by Sir Hans Sloane (1707–25). ▪ The bulk of this work is concerned with the natural history of Jamaica. In the tradition of scientific travelers of the time, Sir Hans made minute descriptions of the plants he saw and collected, noting their gastronomical (he pronounced the great bean good to eat) as well as their botanical properties.

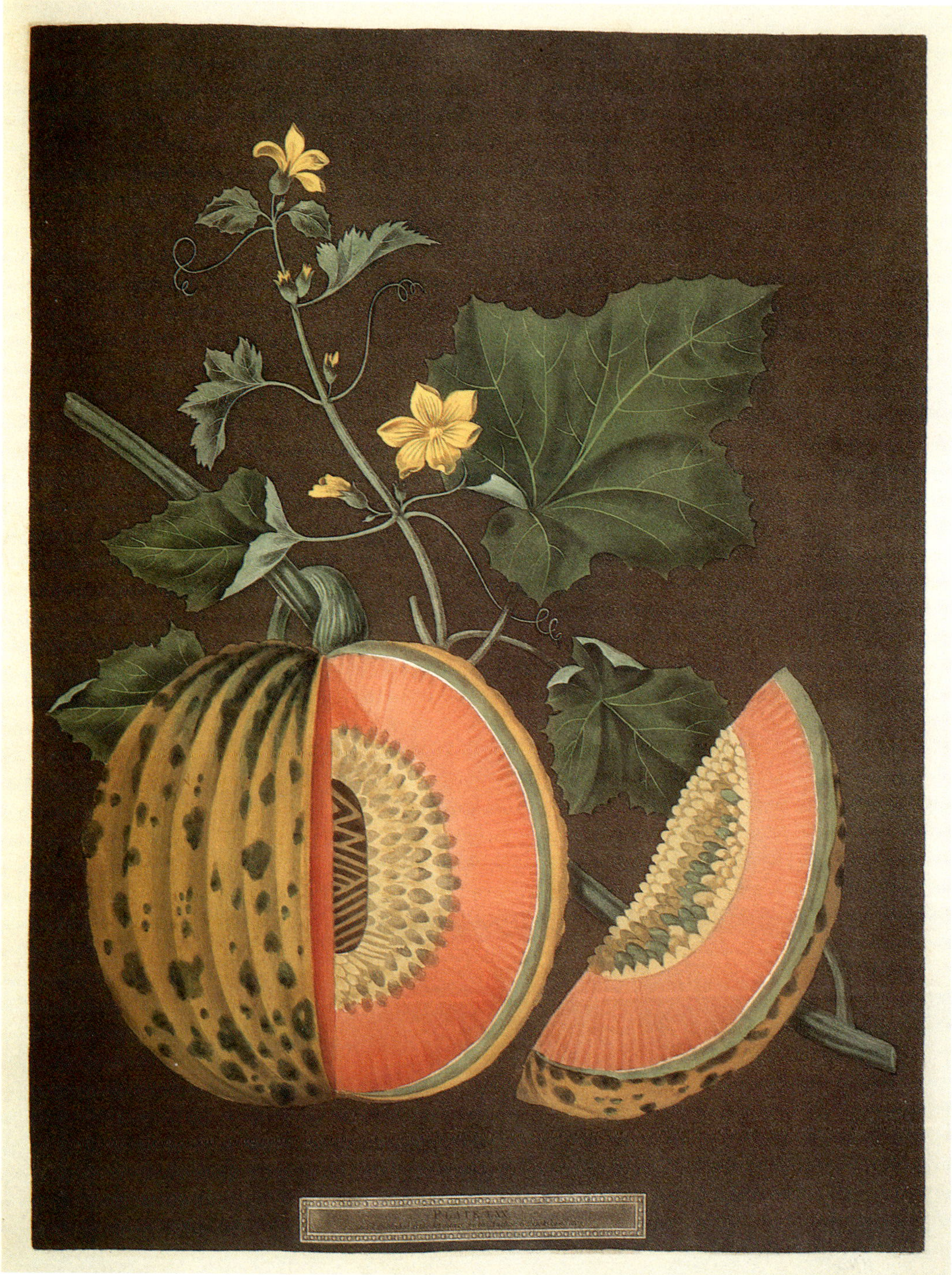

26 ▪ CANTALOUPE *Cucumis melo*

"Cantlope melon." Color-printed and hand-finished aquatint, by George Brookshaw. In *Pomona Britannica* by George Brookshaw (1804–12). ▪ The author's interest in the economic as well as the botanical aspects of growing fruit comes through in the plates that illustrate this book. Each fruit is shown at its peak of ripeness and delectability, as though waiting to tempt a customer at a fruitseller's stand.

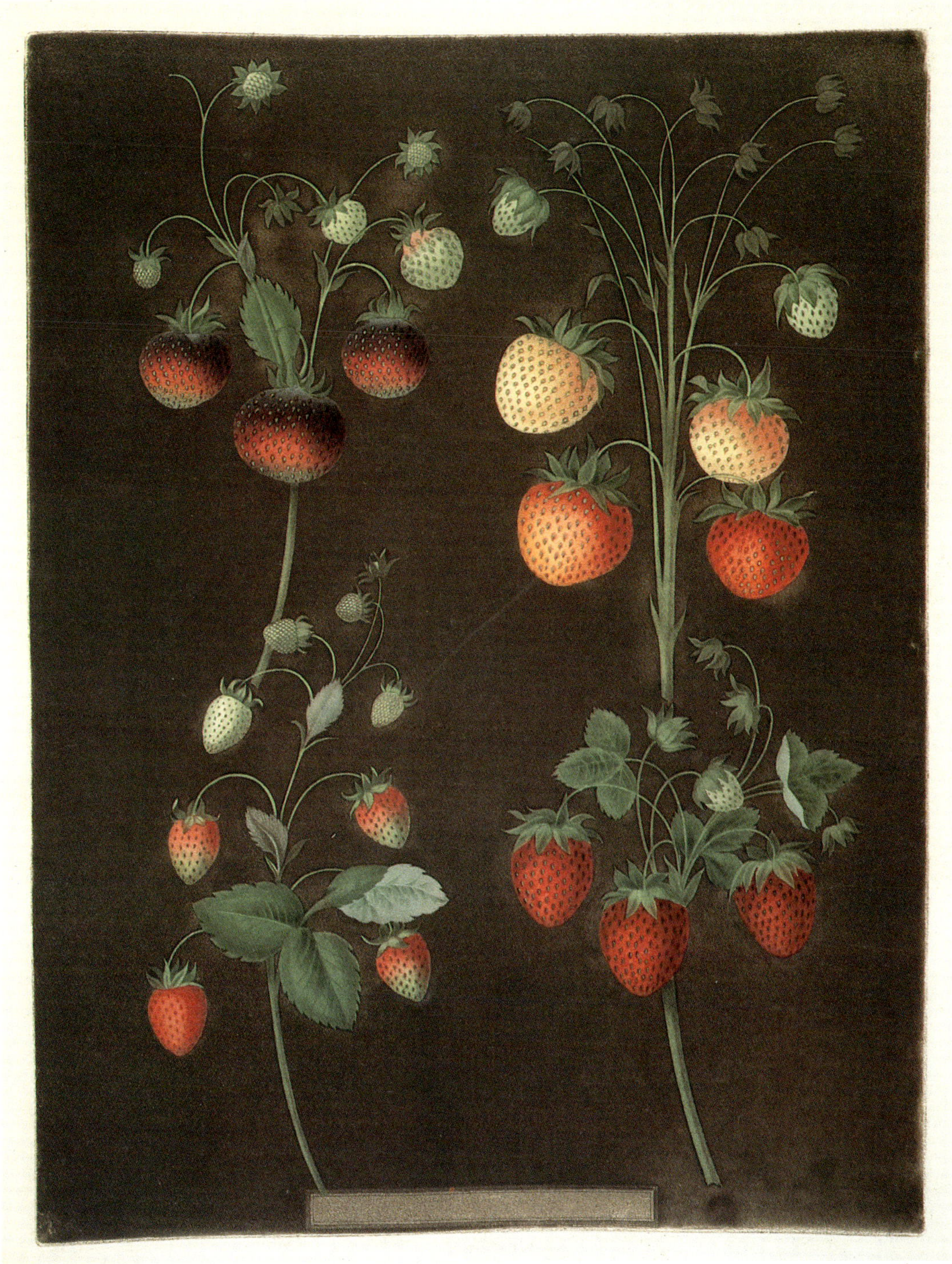

27 ▪ STRAWBERRIES *Fragaria spp.*

Color-printed and hand-finished aquatint, by George Brookshaw. In *Pomona Britannica* by George Brookshaw (1804–12). ▪ A total of fourteen varieties of strawberries are illustrated in this work. The four shown here include the Hoboy, the Chili strawberry, which the author notes, "is not worth cultivating in any gentleman's garden," the Scarlet Alpine, and the Scarlet-Flesh Pine.

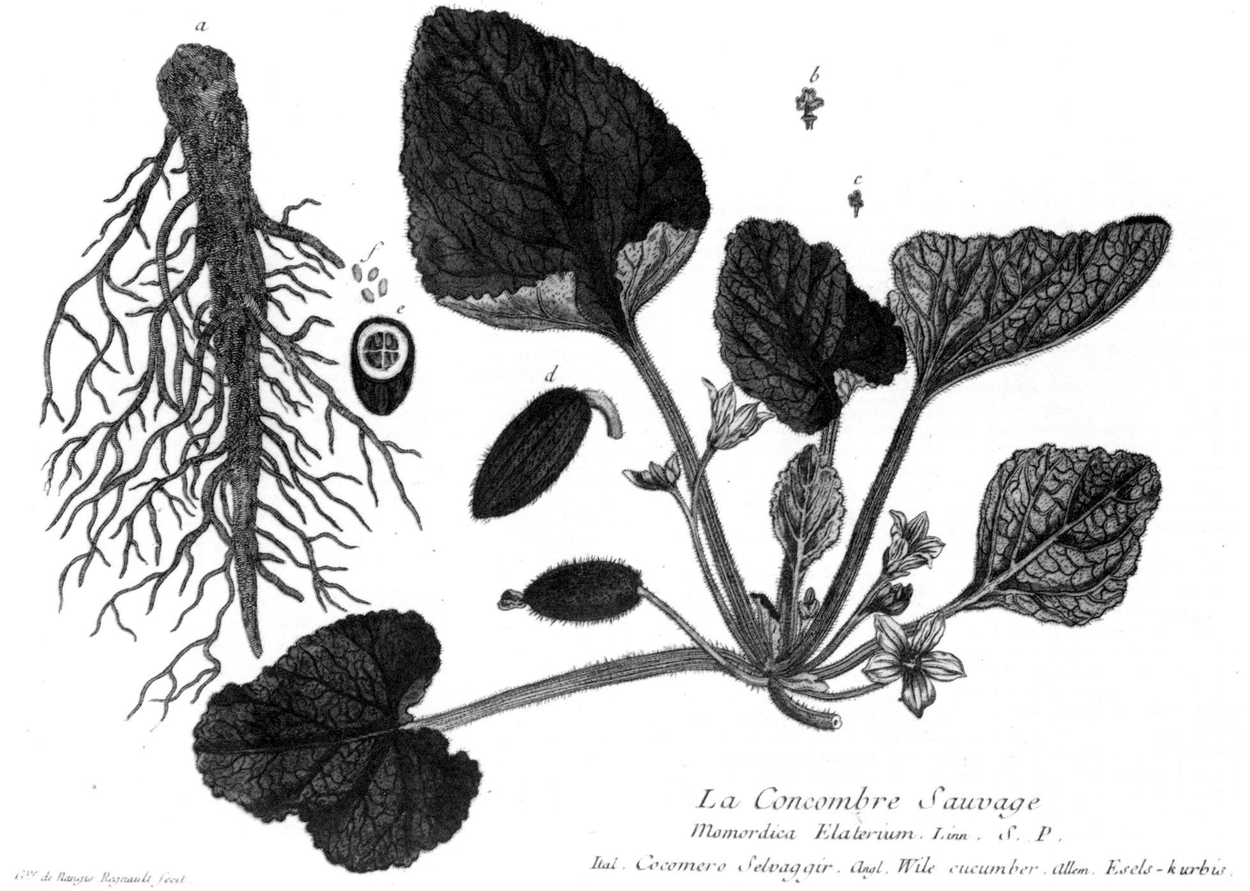

28 ▪ WILD CUCUMBER *Ecballium elaterium*

"La Concombre Sauvage." Color-printed and hand-colored engraving, from the drawing by Geneviève de Nangis-Regnault. In *La Botanique* . . . by Nicolas François Regnault (1774–80). ▪ Unlike the cucumber common to contemporary salads, this variety is described by Regnault as being "a violent purgative" suitable for removing from the body the most recalcitrant obstructions. It was also sometimes referred to as the squirting cucumber.

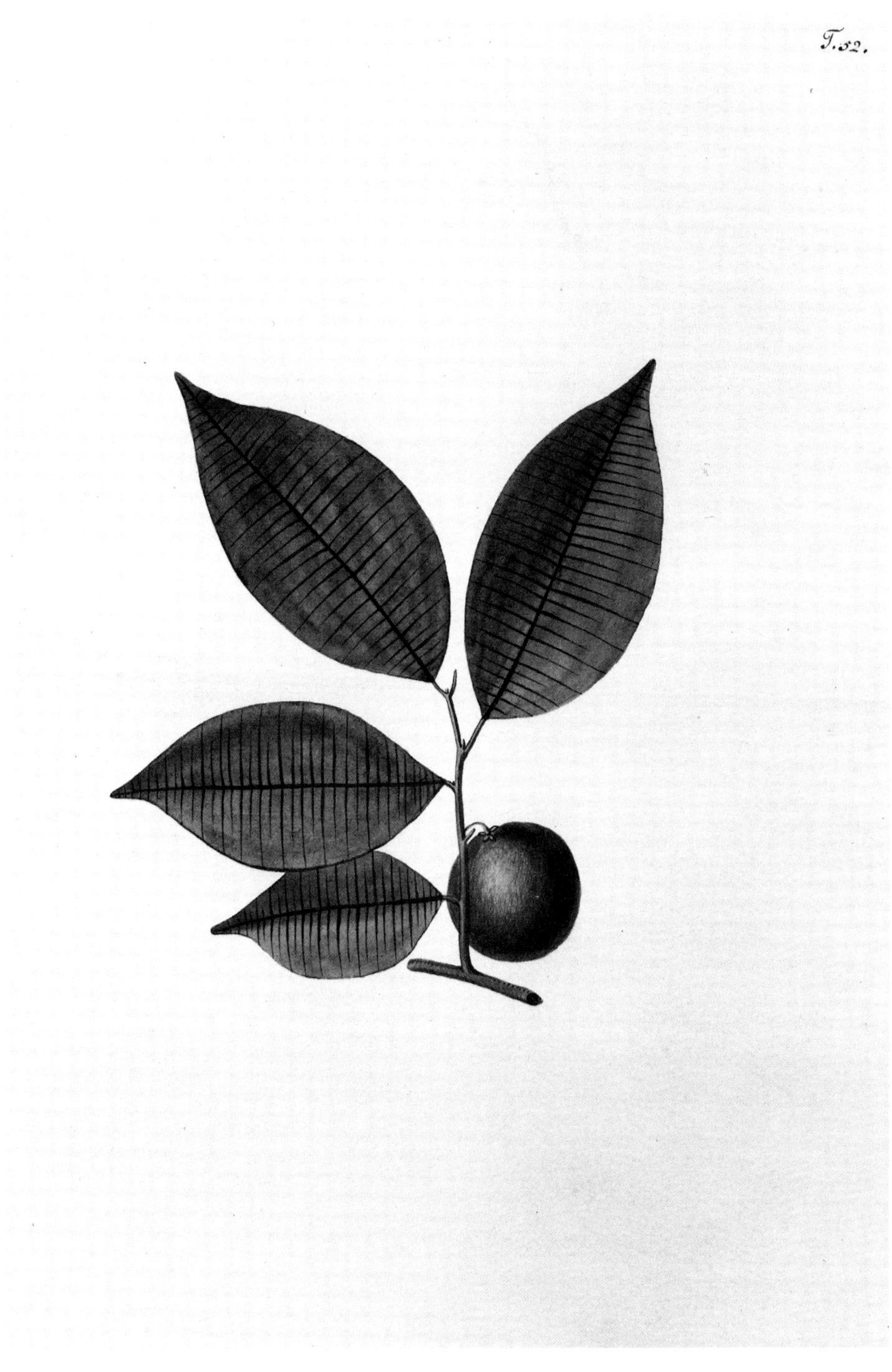

29 ▪ STAR APPLE *Chrysophyllum cainito*

Hand-colored engraving, from the drawing by Nikolaus Joseph Jacquin. In *Selectarum Stirpium Americanarum Historia* by Nikolaus Joseph Jacquin (1780–81). ▪ The author/artist traveled in the West Indies from 1754 to 1759, producing the first botanical record of his travels in 1763 and then this expanded version seventeen years later. Born in Holland, he moved to Austria in 1752 where he later became professor of botany and chemistry at the University of Vienna. Jacquin was made a baron in 1806.

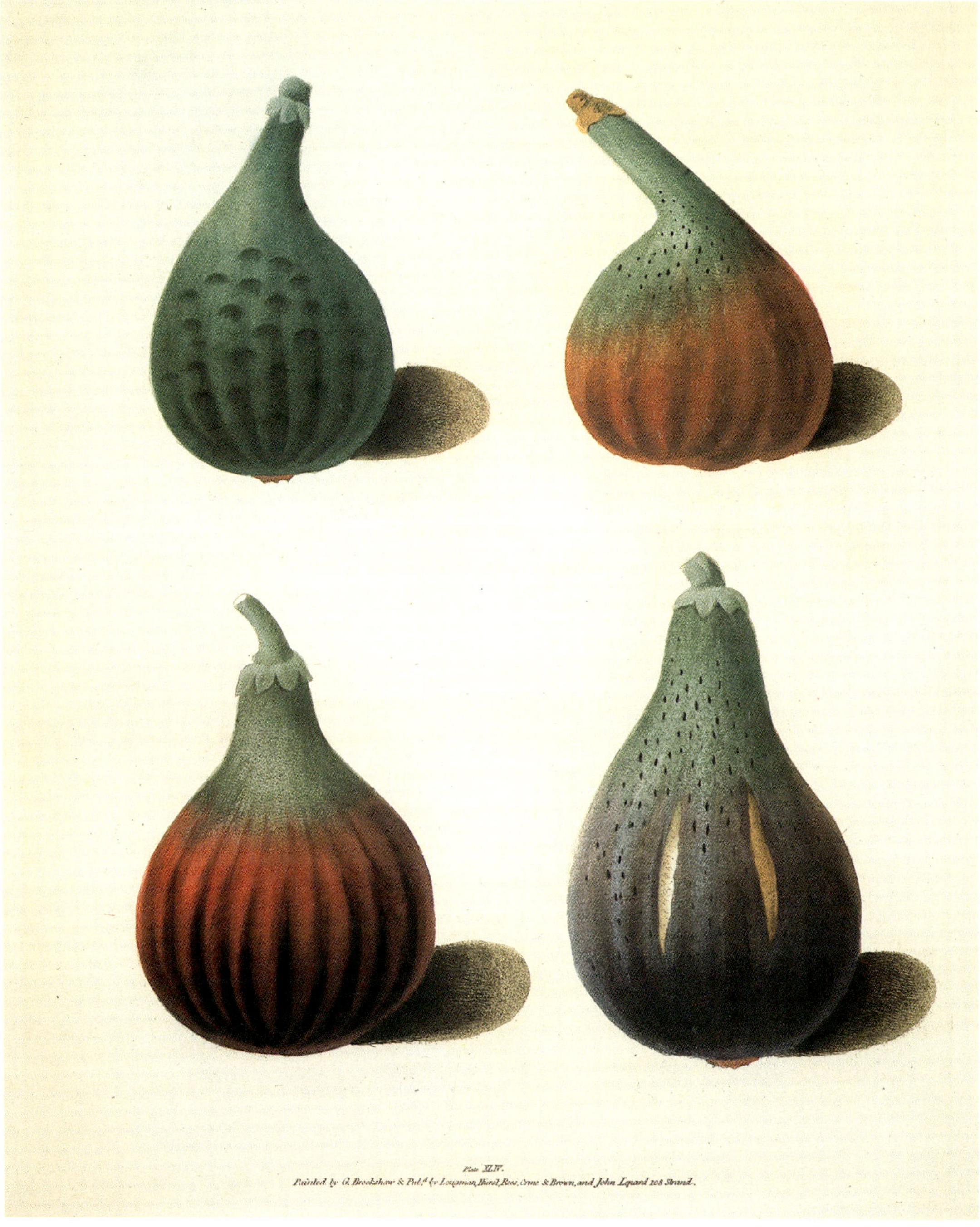

30 ▪ FIGS *Ficus carica*

Color-printed and hand-finished aquatint, by George Brookshaw. In *Pomona Britannica* by George Brookshaw (1816–17). ▪ In this second edition of his book on the fruits of England, Brookshaw has varied both the content and the method of printing of the plates. The number of fruits illustrated has been reduced and the dark backgrounds which served as a foil to the brilliant colors of the fruit are no longer used.

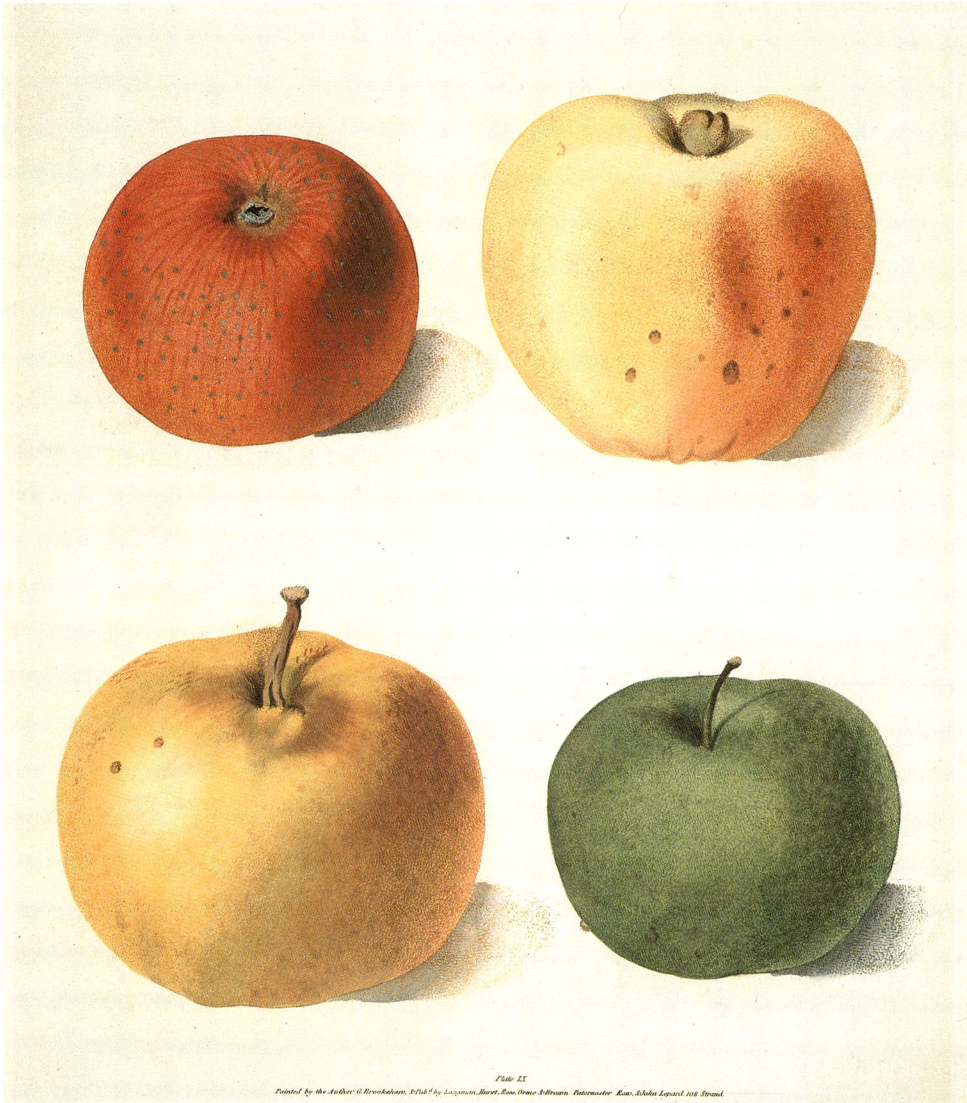

31 ▪ APPLES *Malus domestica*

Color-printed and hand-finished aquatint, by George Brookshaw. In *Pomona Britannica* by George Brookshaw (1816–17). ▪ The practical nature of Brookshaw's text comes through in his description of the apples pictured here, as when he notes that the apple in the upper right "is superior to all others for sauces, tarts and pies, as is its juice for cider."

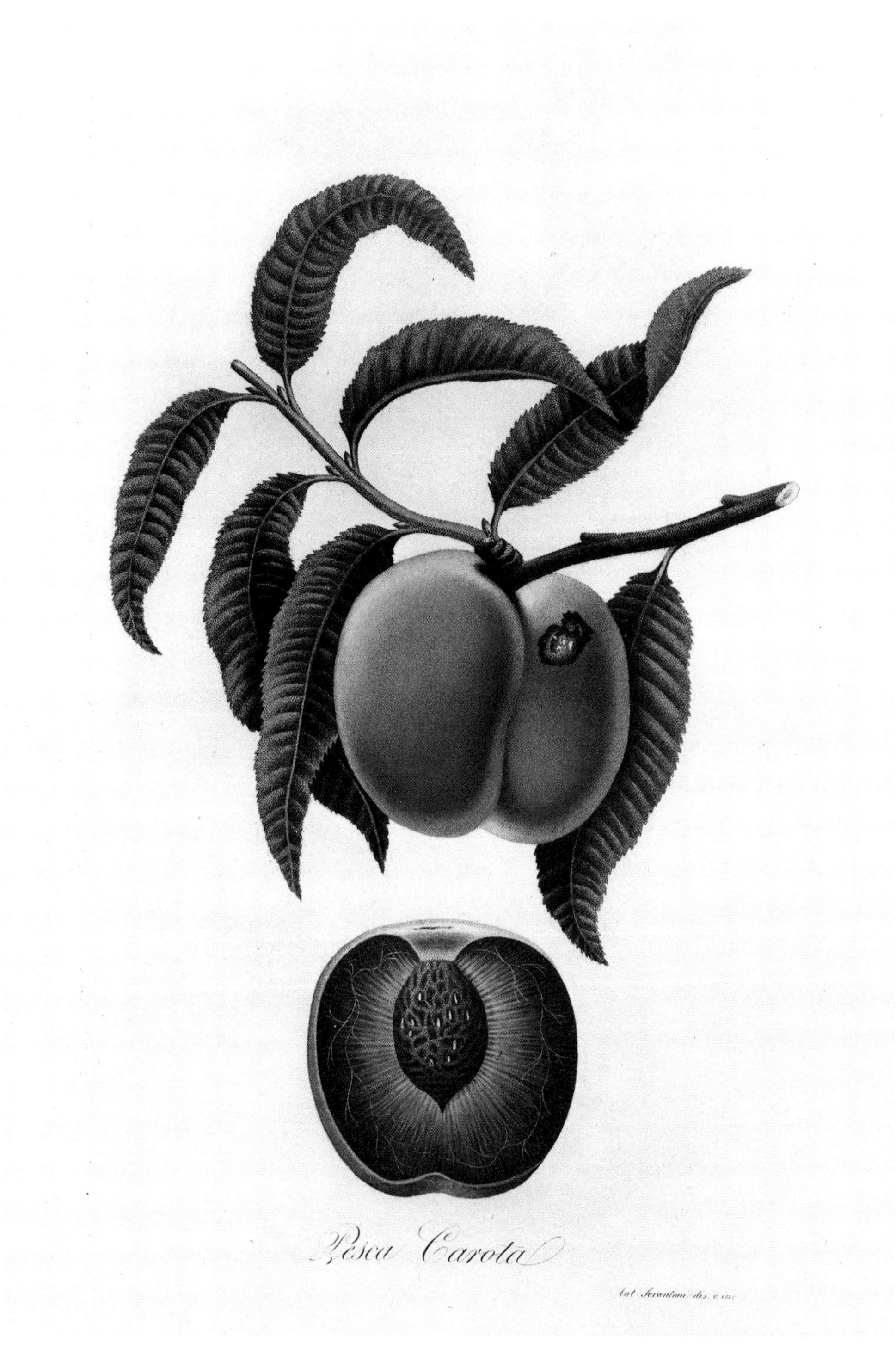

32 ▪ PEACH *Prunus persica*

"Pesca Carota." Stipple engraving, by Antonio Serantoni from his own drawing. In *Pomona Italiana* by Giorgio Gallesio (1817–39). ▪ This is the greatest Italian work on fruit. Unlike England and France in the eighteenth and nineteenth centuries, Italy had not developed a tradition of finely illustrated color-plate botanical books, so that Gallesio's work stands out not only for its beauty but also for its uniqueness in Italian publishing at that time.

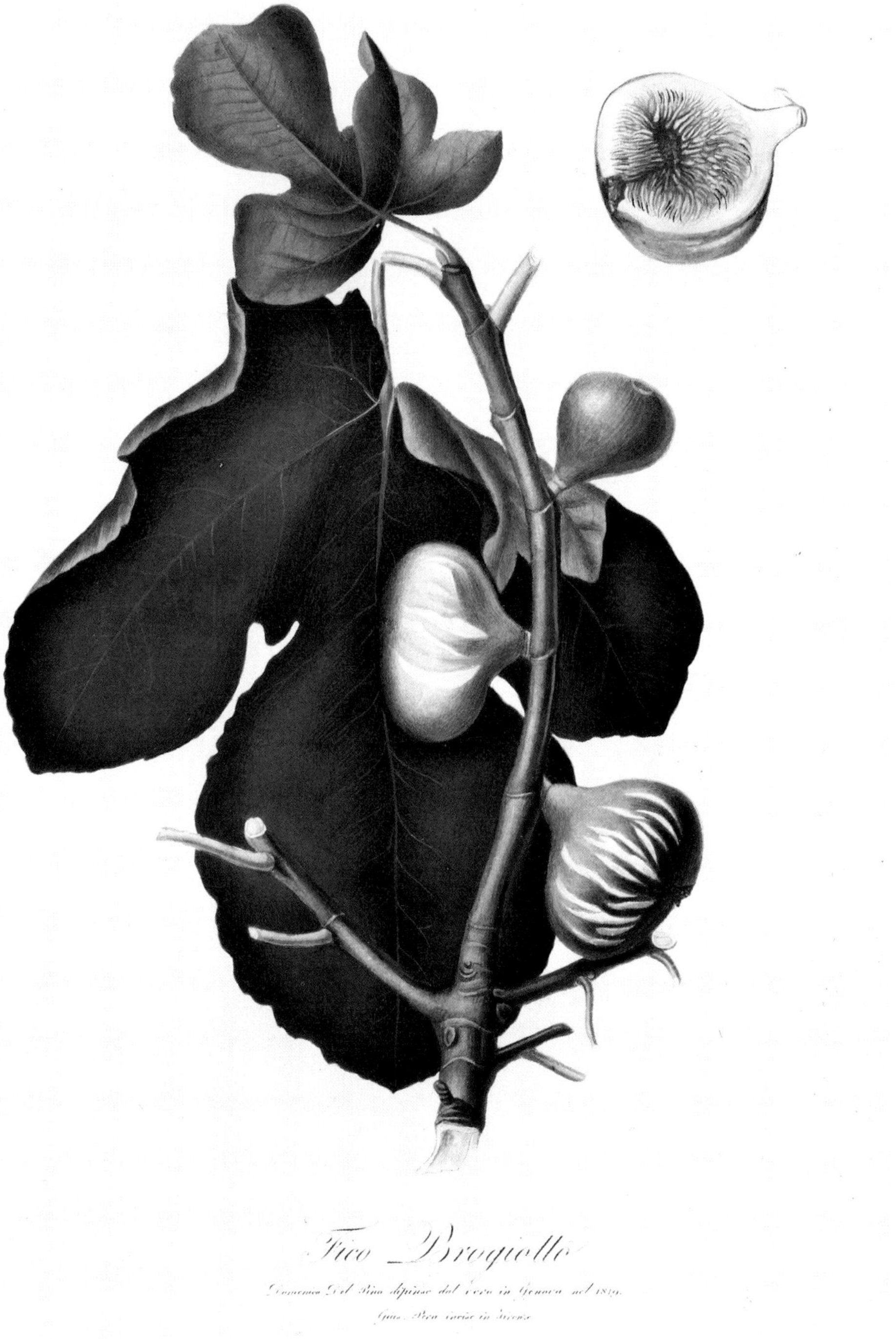

33 ▪ FIG *Ficus carica*

"Fico Brogiotto." Color-printed and hand-finished stipple engraving, by Giuseppe Pera from the drawing by Domenico del Pino. In *Pomona Italiana* by Giorgio Gallesio (1817–39). ▪ The author describes this fruit as the "king of figs" because of its large size and the splendor of its leaves. As with all the fruits he describes, he provides detailed information on the best ways and places in which to grow them.

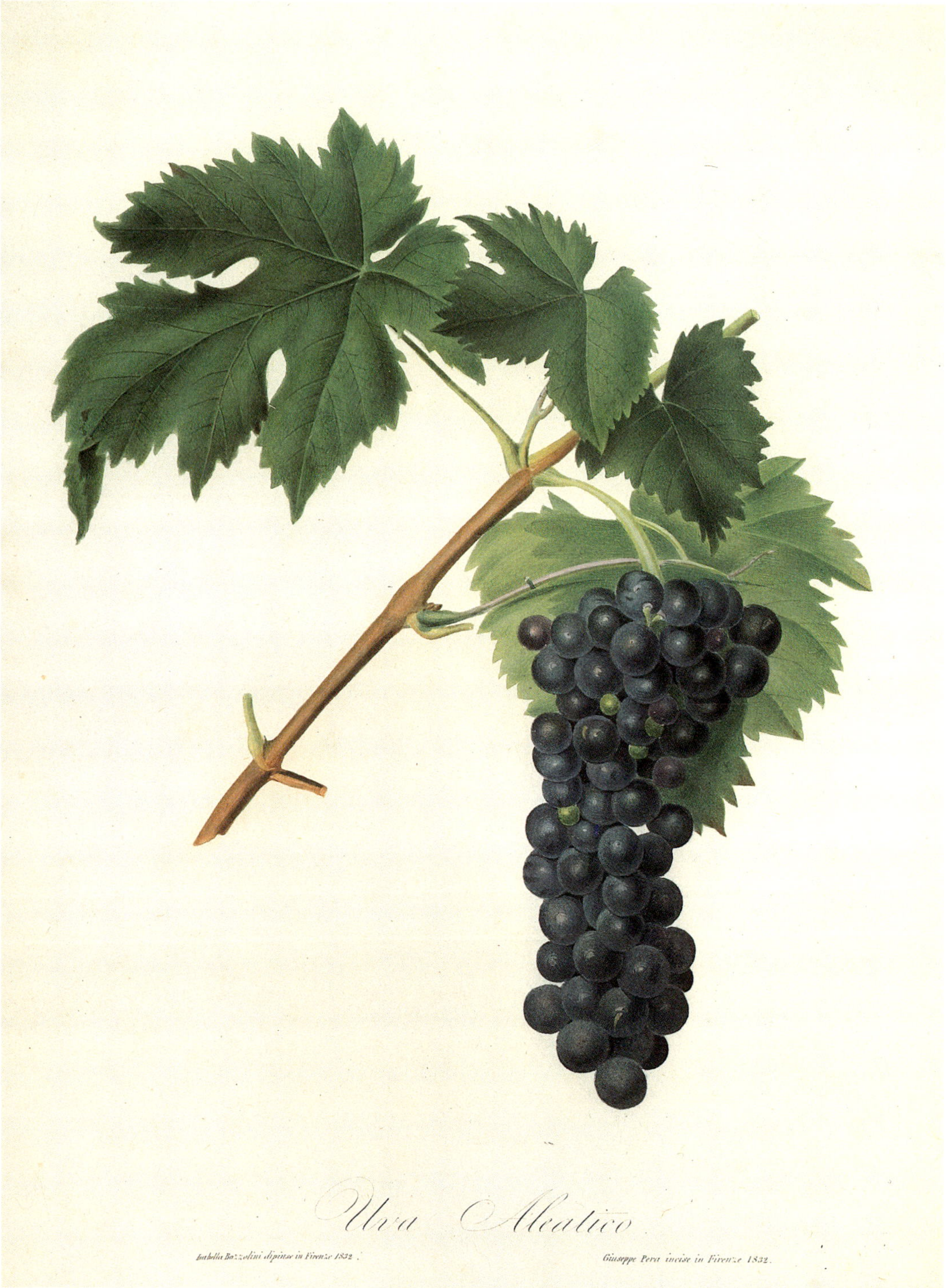

34 ▪ GRAPES *Vitis vinifera*

"Uva Aleatico." Stipple engraving, by Giuseppe Pera from the drawing by Isabella Bozzolini. In *Pomona Italiana* by Giorgio Gallesio (1817–39). ▪ This is a Tuscan grape, the author tells us, which, when mixed with other grapes, adds fragrance to wine.

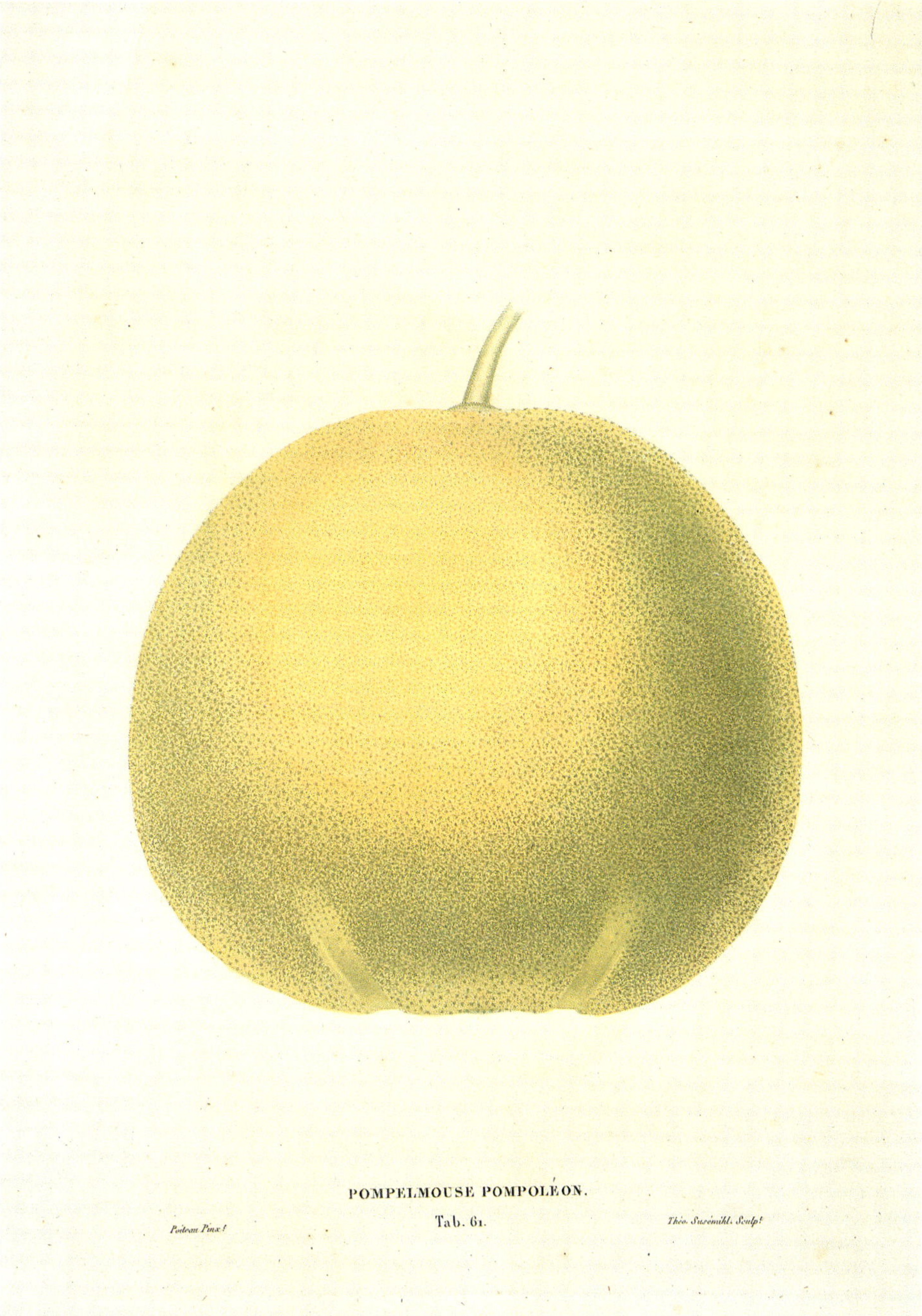

35 ▪ GRAPEFRUIT *Citrus x paradisi*

"Pompelmouse Pompoléon." Color-printed and hand-finished stipple engraving, by T. Susemihl from the drawing by Pierre Antoine Poiteau. In *Histoire Naturelle des Orangers* by Joseph Antoine Risso and Pierre Antoine Poiteau (1818–22). ▪ This is the most beautiful book ever produced devoted to the subject of citrus fruits. Its author was a pharmacist and botanist in Nice, in the south of France, and his special interest was the plants native to that region. Poiteau came by his knowledge of the tropical varieties of citrus fruits when he was sent to Haiti in 1796 by the Jardin des Plantes.

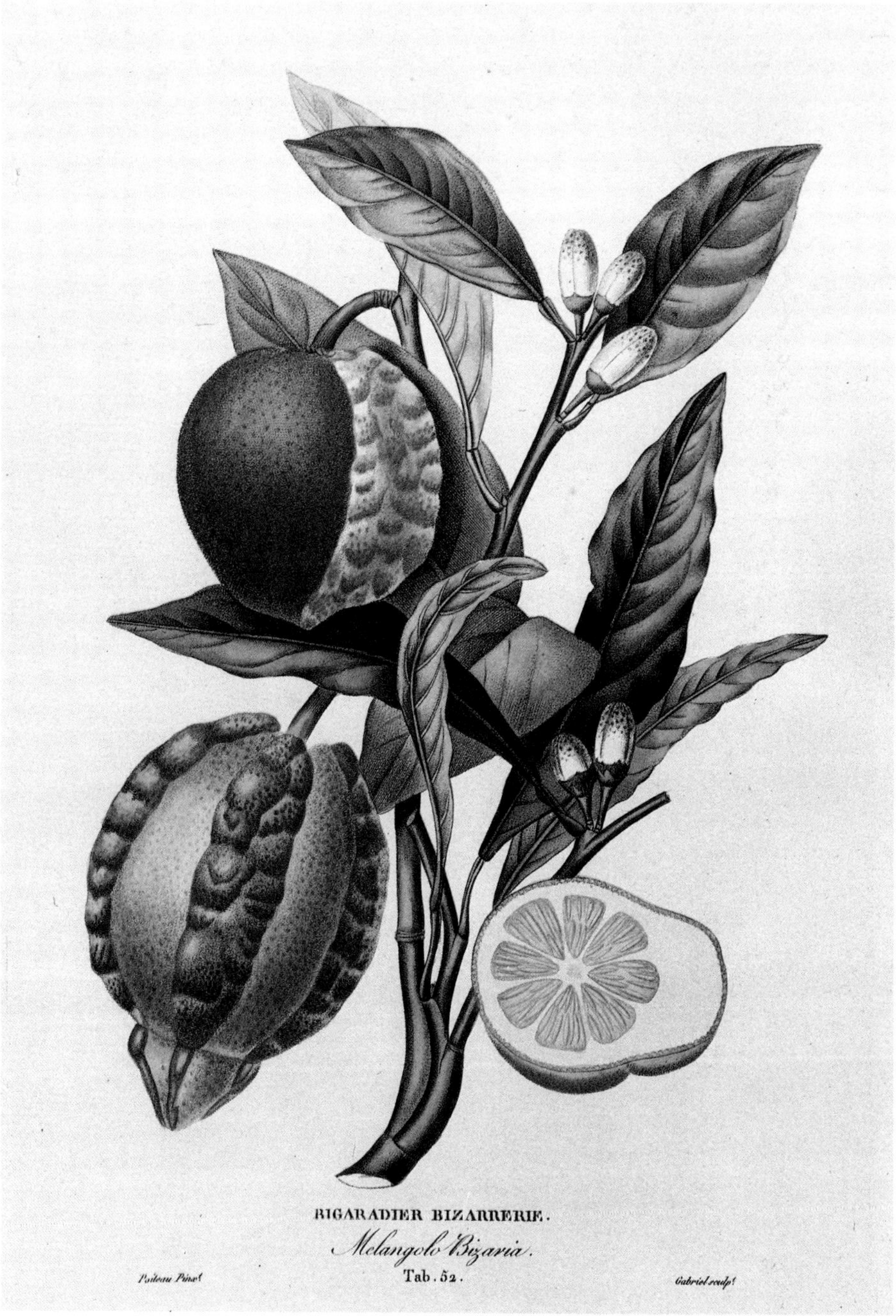

36 ▪ ORANGE *Citrus*

"Bigaradier Bizarrerie." Color-printed and hand-finished stipple engraving, by Gabriel from the drawing by Pierre Antoine Poiteau. In *Histoire Naturelle des Orangers* by Joseph Antoine Risso and Pierre Antoine Poiteau (1818–22). ▪ Poiteau based his drawings on particular specimens rather than as melded or ideal composites. In this case Risso tells us the orange was found in a garden in Nice.

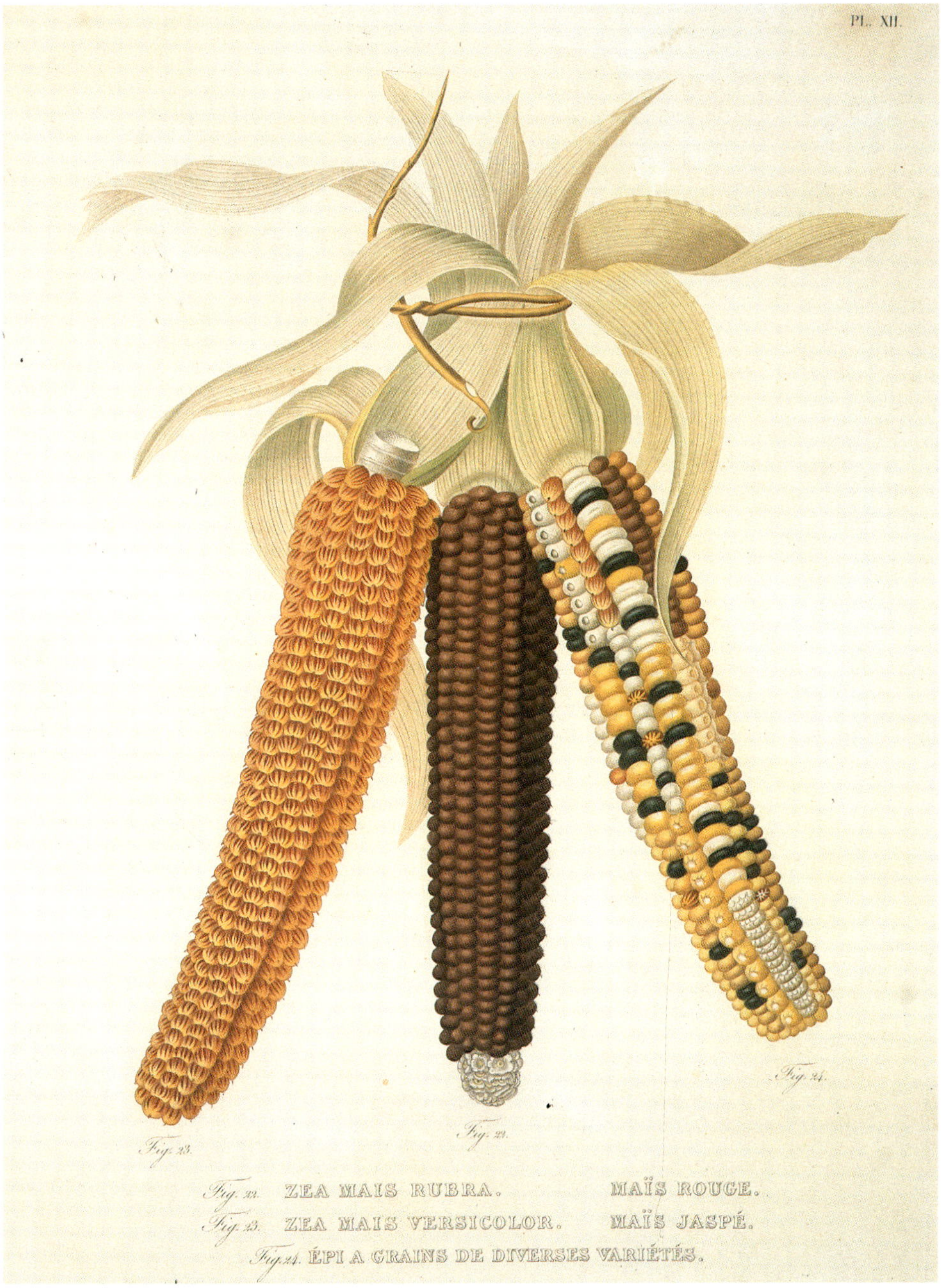

37 ▪ THREE VARIETIES OF CORN *Zea mays*

"Fig. 22. Zea mais rubra. Mais rouge; Fig. 23. Zea mais versicolor. Maïs jaspé; Fig. 24. Épi a grains de diverses variétés." Color-printed and hand-finished engraving, by Dupréel from the drawing by Anga Bottione-Rossi. In *Histoire Naturelle Agricole, et Économique du Mais* by Mathieu Bonafous (1836). ▪ The greatest illustrated book ever produced on the subject of corn, Bonafous's work establishes this vegetable, native to the Americas, within the mainstream of European agricultural activity and botanical documentation. It had been introduced into Europe in the sixteenth century when the plants of the New World were being documented and their uses investigated. By the time of this work by Bonafous, some twenty-two varieties of corn were in cultivation.

ORNAMENTAL FLOWERS AND FERNS

In the 1950s the English novelist C. P. Snow was moved to comment on the split that had developed in western society between science and the humanities. He described this loss of the unity of intellectual life as being characterized by a "two cultures" mentality, one in which the two realms of creativity proceeded along without any mutual awareness. Had he known something about the history of botanical science he might have modified his theory and tempered somewhat his despair over this loss. For the history of botany is also to a certain extent the history of art, one in which the progress in the systematic exploration of the natural world is matched by the advance in the quality of the means used to represent that world. ▪ The link between the advances in the science and the art of botanical documentation is the development of printing technology. Printing made possible the wide dissemination of information that had previously depended on the cumbersome and limited vehicle of handwritten and illustrated books. It also contributed to the rise of a secular intelligentsia, one whose concerns were increasingly devoted to science. None of this occurred overnight, of course; it was a cumulative process, which in the area of botany gathered steam in the sixteenth century, began to find its footing in the seventeenth century, and then, one is tempted to say, achieved its full flowering in the eighteenth and nineteenth centuries. ▪ It is in the literature of flowers where this advance is most dramatically represented. In the fifteenth and sixteenth centuries botanical illustration is represented by the dominant process of the woodcut. The flowers are simply delineated, most often their depictions remain uncolored. These images have a direct, practical quality, and insofar as one may use any aesthetic vocabulary in generalizing about their pictorial quality, their forthrightness has a certain elegance. ▪ The search for descriptive adjectives is unnecessary when one reaches the seventeenth century, however, for in this period many flower books are conceived of not merely as works of reference but as artistic monuments. The large folio volume of Basil Besler's *Hortus Eystettensis* (1613) was designed as a tribute to the greatness of the prince bishop of Eichstadt, Johann Conrad von Gemmingen, whose garden and its flowers it describes. Few people can hope for so great a monument. Through the artistry of Besler, the Nuremberg botanist in charge of the garden, and the skill of an anonymous engraver, images of flowers take on a significance beyond mere documentation. It is probably not entirely coincidental that in the painting of this period, the still-life genre is beginning to come into its own. ▪ In a late seventeenth-century album with an immodest title, *Beautiful Collection of Drawings of Flowers*, are some of the elements that fed the development of still-life painting. In this album, made up of finely prepared sheets of vellum, an anonymous artist has left us a record of the flowers which he or she had an occasion to observe and record. This is no mere note or sketchbook: each image is carefully laid out on the sheet and the drawing and coloring indicate a sensitivity not only to the demands of nature but also to the demands of art. ▪ Nature and art, those seemingly antithetical concepts, are united in the works of the greatest flower illustrators of the eighteenth and nineteenth centuries. The images they created speak to us not only of the incredible richness of beauty with which the natural world is endowed, but also of the skills that humankind (at one and the same time a participant and an observer of nature) has developed to adapt that beauty into the service of art. Among the first of the great artists who devoted themselves to the depiction of flowers in the eighteenth century is Georg Dionysius Ehret, whose work was first published in Johann Wilhelm Weinmann's *Phytanthoza Iconographia* (1737–45). Although a success for the artist in aesthetic terms, it was not a completely happy experience since Weinmann neither paid him well for his work nor acknowledged his contribution in the printed book. ▪ Such treatment would not have sat at all well with Pierre-Joseph Redouté, the "Rembrandt of Roses," the "Raphael of flowers," who worked in France in the late eighteenth and early nineteenth centuries. The series of books that he illustrated brought him great fame and the sort of social recognition that enabled him to enjoy the patronage of Marie Antoinette and Napoleon's second wife, the Empress Marie-Louise. Redouté has, in a sense, become almost too famous. His *Les Roses* (1817–24) is the Beethoven's Fifth Symphony of flower books, a work whose familiarity among connoisseurs breeds not so much contempt as a dismissive nod. But there is a reason for its fame: its quality of execution, which stands up to repeated scrutiny. The petals of the flowers have a diaphanous coloring and the leaves a delicacy of tint that exhibit a technical virtuosity and fluency still unmatched in the literature of botanical illustration. ▪ One of the few works contemporary with Redouté's career that can stand comparison with his art is Dr. Robert John Thornton's *New Illustration of the Sexual System of Carolus von Linnaeus* (1798–1807), better known for the subtitle of one of its parts, *The Temple of Flora.* Thornton himself drew only the rose depicted in this work, the other thirty plates were drawn by Peter Henderson, Philip Reinagle, and Sydenham Edwards. The flowers are shown against brooding romantic backgrounds, a device that encourages the multilevel approach to the contemplation of floral illustration as an aspect of both science and art. These backgrounds also reflect the literary fascination with flowers as symbolic things, a fascination which achieves its apotheosis in William Wordsworth's "crowd, a host of golden daffodils." ▪ The romantic attachment to flowers is not what invigorates Henry F. C. Sander's *Reichenbachia, Orchids Illustrated and Described* (1886–95). Orchids were Sander's business: he grew, hybridized, and sold them. He published his work of 192 chromolithograph plates in response to "the growing popularity of orchids, and the ever-increasing demand for information about them." From the crude woodcuts of the fifteenth century to the slick chromolithographs of the late nineteenth century one persistent theme endures that links floral illustration: a fascination with nature's endless variety and with man's capacity to translate that variety into art.

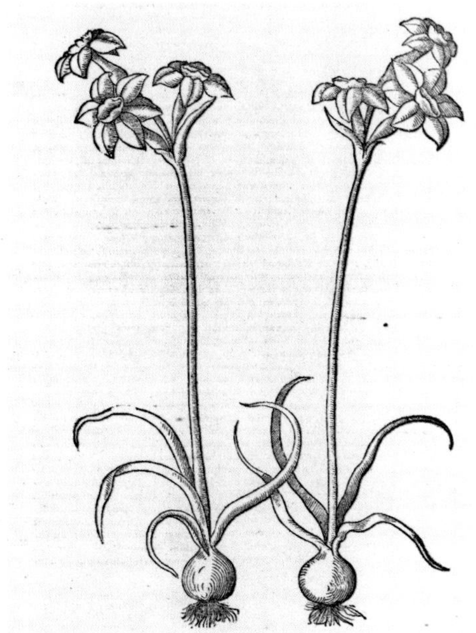

38 ▪ NARCISSUS *Narcissus sp.*

"Narcissus." Woodcut, by Wolfgang Meyerpeck or Giorgio Liberale. In *Commentarii in Sex Libros Dioscoridis* by Pier Andrea Matthioli (1565). ▪ The placement of the image is atypical of the general style the artist has chosen. Here the narcissus appears to "float" on the page, resisting the temptation, as it were, to fill the rectangular shape of the woodblock. The narcissus takes its name from the young man in a Greek myth who was cursed by the gods to fall in love with his own reflection. He died of this longing and was transformed into a flower.

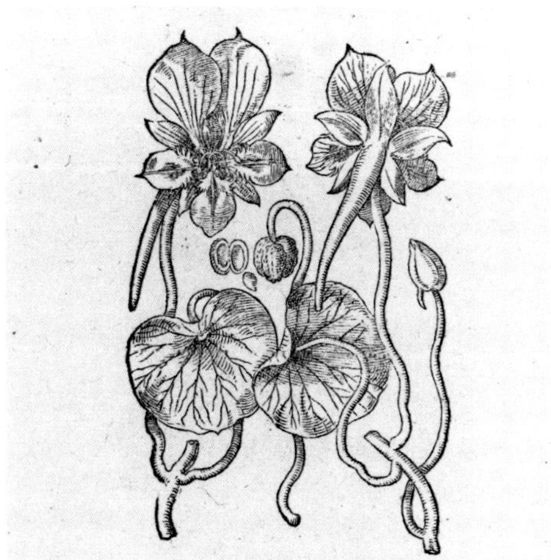

39 ▪ NASTURTIUM *Nasturtium indicum*

Woodcut. In *Hortus Medicus et Philosophicus* by Joachim Camerarius (1588). ▪ In 1586 the author, a German physician, published an edition of Matthioli's herbal. In his own book Camerarius is content merely to catalogue and describe the plants he illustrates, giving little or no medical advice about their use. Camerarius is also known for his important collection of emblems, which were published in his *Symbolorum et Emblematum* in 1605 and 1661.

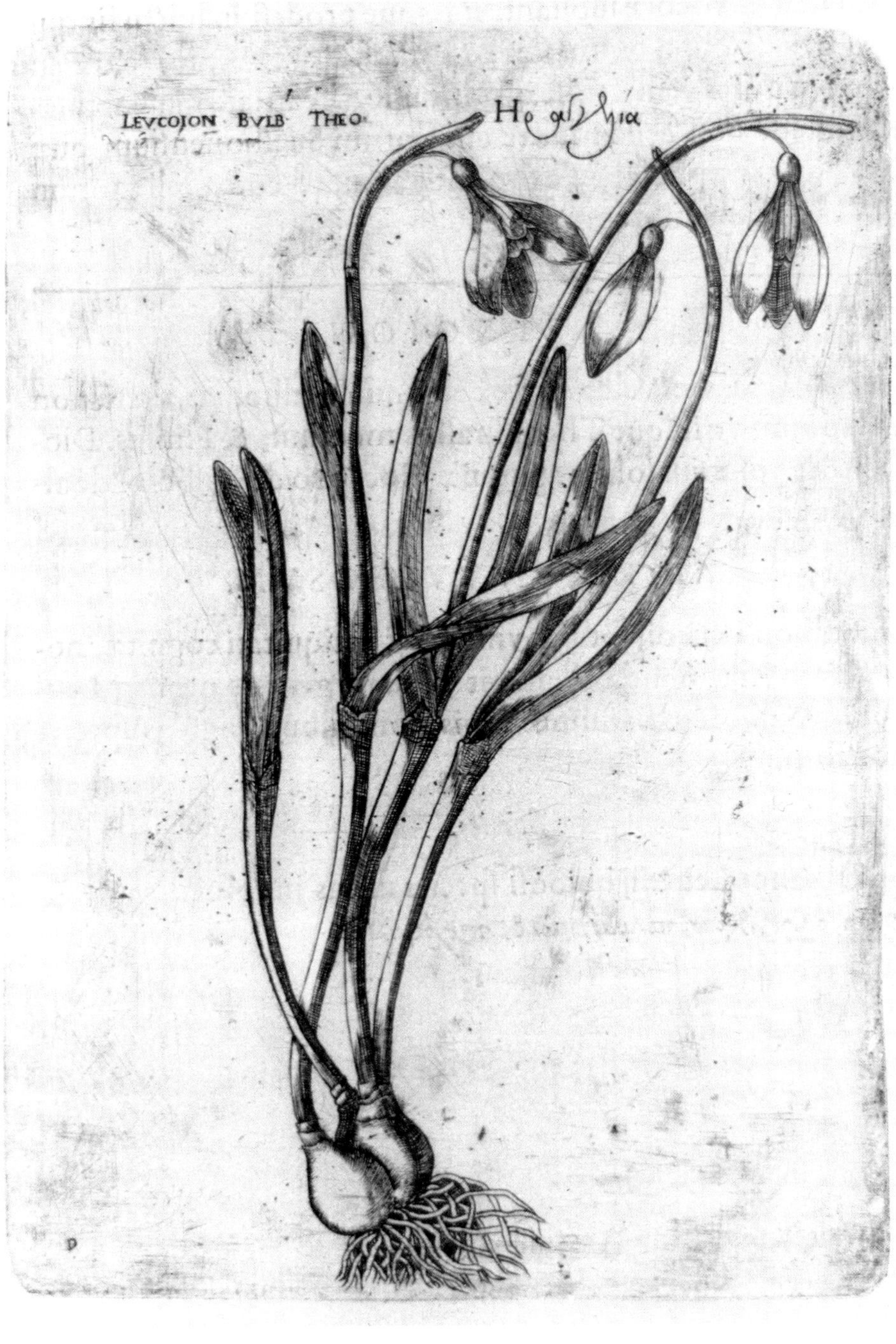

40 ▪ JONQUIL *Narcissus jonquilla*

Engraving. In *Specimen Historiae Plantarum* by Paul de Reneaulme (1611). ▪ For this book, the plants were all drawn from those in the royal gardens in Paris. The author, a physician as well as a botanist, created the Greek names he assigned to the flowers. In this way, Reneaulme's book set a precedent for the new formation of thousands of generic names of Greek derivation.

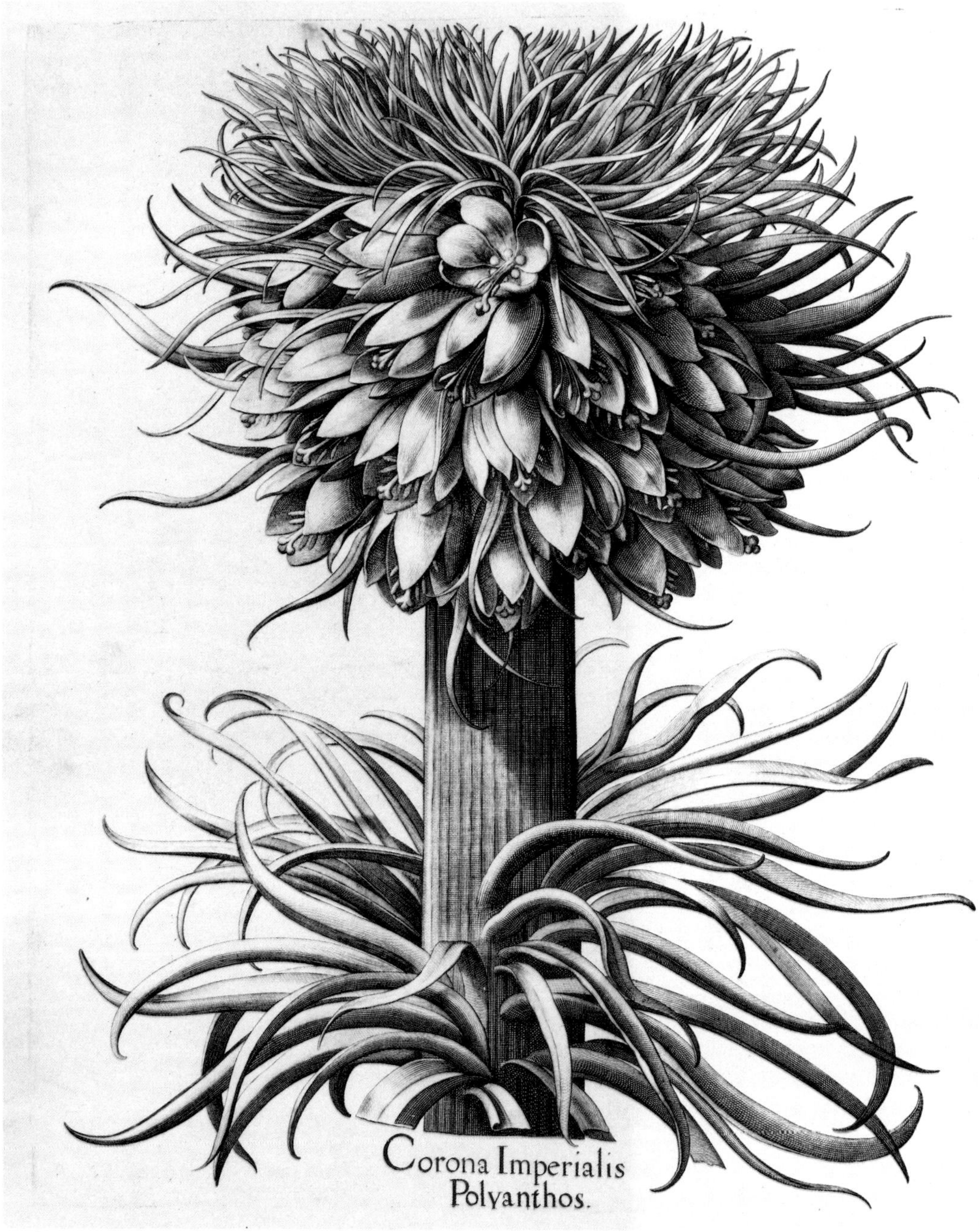

41 ▪ CROWN IMPERIAL *Fritillaria imperialis*

"Corona Imperialis Polyanthos." Engraving, from the drawing by Basil Besler. In *Hortus Eystettensis* by Basil Besler (1613). ▪ This magnificent work is widely regarded as the first great florilegium. Besler, a Nuremberg apothecary, documented the garden he was in charge of, that owned by Johann Conrad von Gemmingen, prince bishop of Eichstadt in Bavaria. The prince bishop subsidized the printing of this work, the only surviving evidence of his enthusiasm for flowers. So fine were the original copperplates for this book that they were used for printing all three editions: 1613, 1640, and 1713.

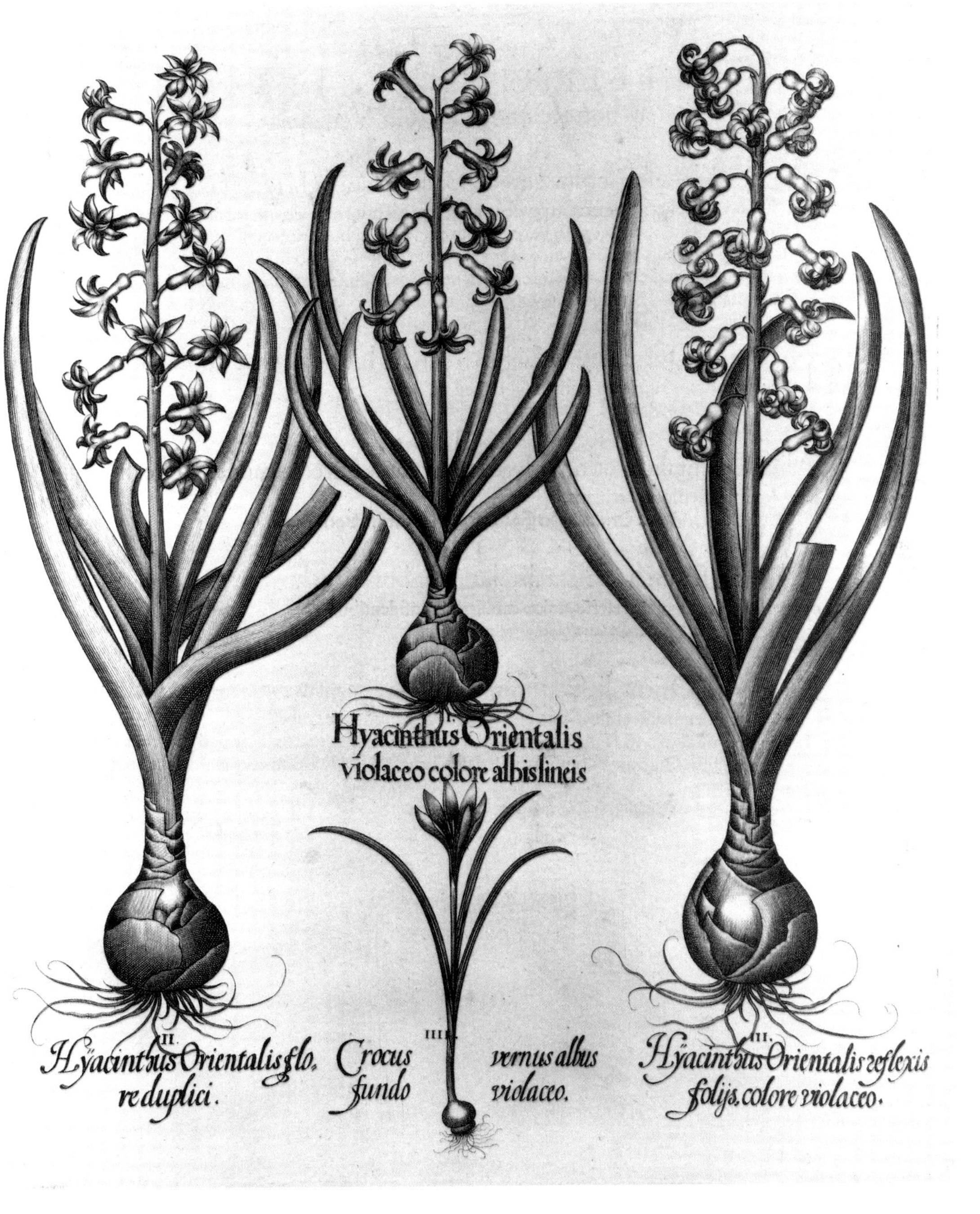

42 ▪ HYACINTHS *Hyacinthus orientalis*

"Hyacinthus Orientalis; Crocus." Engraving, from the drawing by Basil Besler. In *Hortus Eystettensis* by Basil Besler (1613). ▪ Organized according to the seasons in which flowers bloom, these hyacinths are from the spring garden. As with the other illustrations in this volume, the visual impact of the plates is not explainable merely by the large size of the plates. The forceful composition and strong use of dark and high contrast give these images a richness that transcends so-called documentary representation.

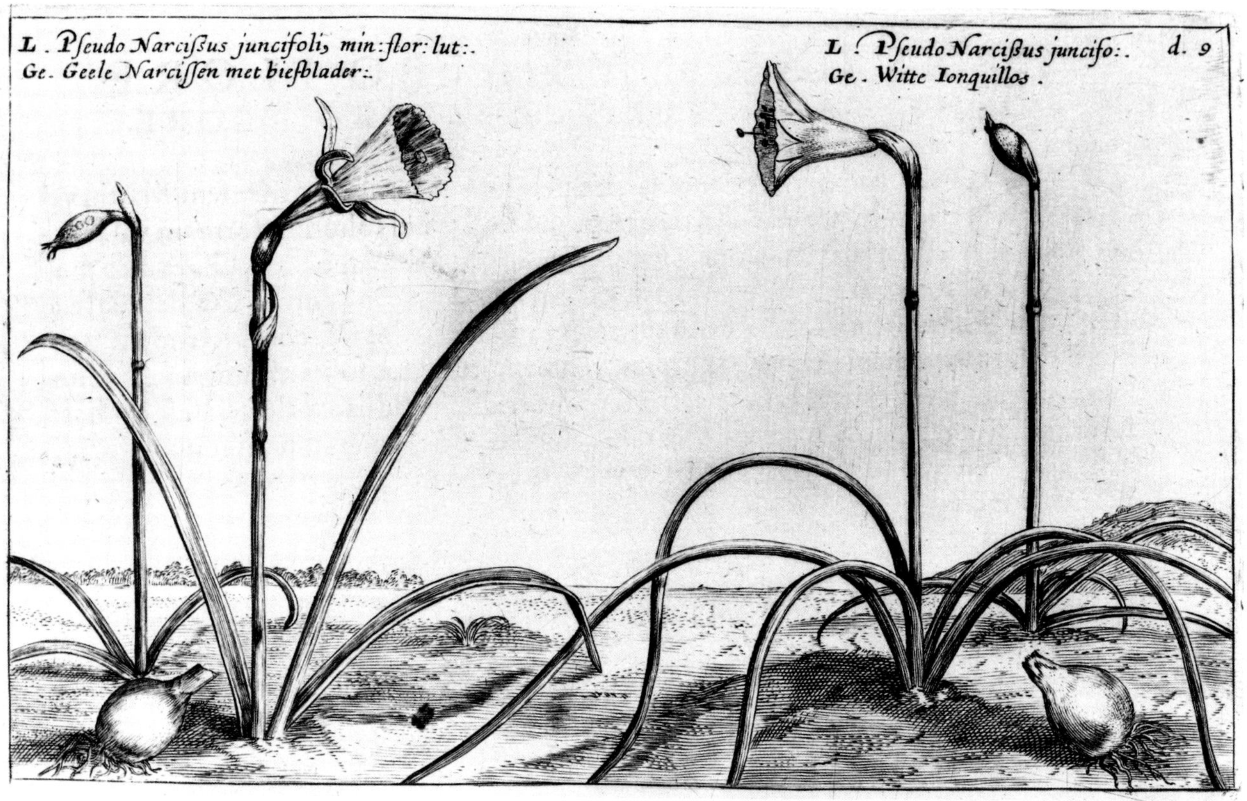

43 ▪ NARCISSUS *Narcissus pseudonarcissus*

"Pseudo Narcissus." Engraving, by Crispijn van de Passe. In *Hortus Floridus* by Crispijn van de Passe (1614–16). ▪ Among the greatest of those seventeenth-century Dutch artists who turned their attention to floral illustration was Crispijn van de Passe. His interest was less in botanical accuracy than in drawing and composition, a quality not surprising in someone whose profession was that of drawing master. The illustrations are notable for a "ground-level" perspective, typical of Dutch landscape painting. Although the mania for tulips reached its apogee in Holland in 1634–36, Van de Passe's rendering anticipates this enthusiasm.

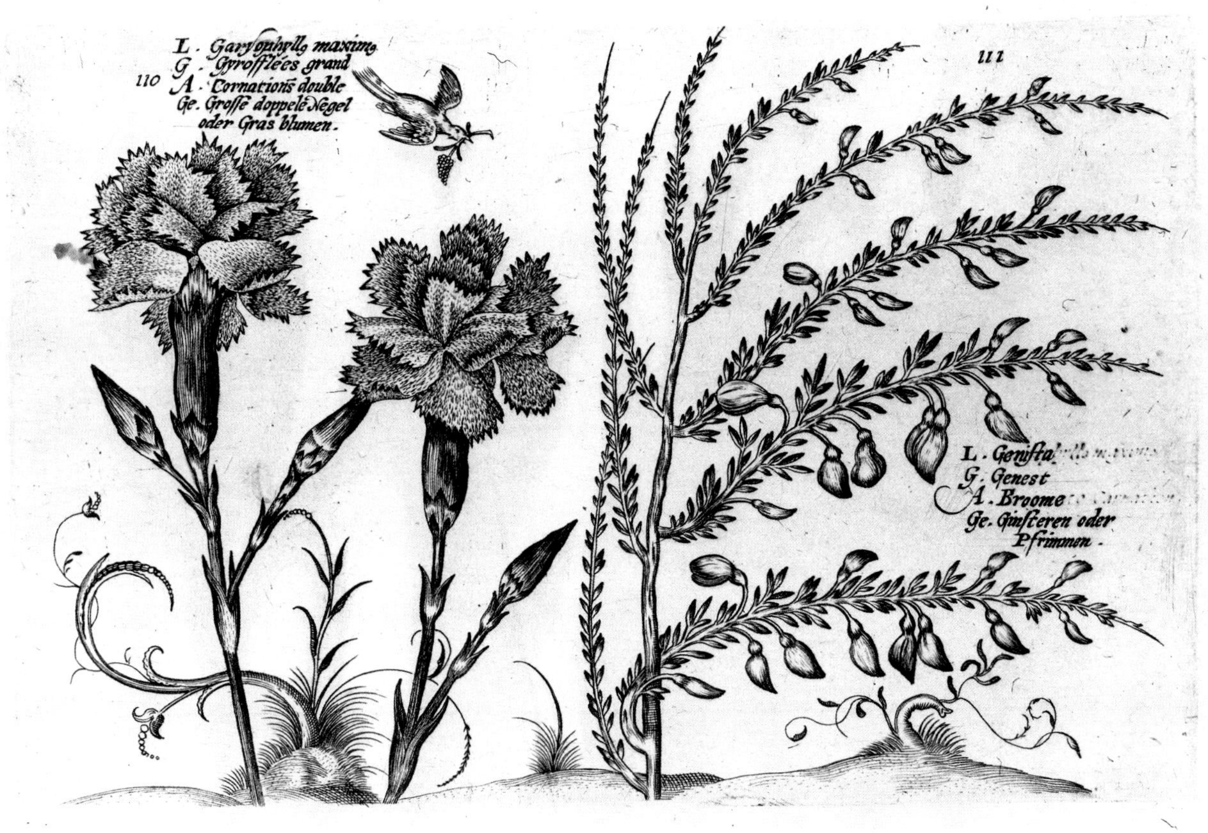

44 ▪ DOUBLE CARNATIONS *Dianthus sp.* ▪ BROOM *Cytisus sp.*

Engraving, by Crispijn van de Passe. In *Hortus Floridus* by Crispijn van de Passe (1614–16). ▪ The playful and painterly approach that Van de Passe brought to floral illustration was largely without precedent. While early herbalists included fanciful illustrations of plants in their works—some based on lore, others based on hearsay—Van de Passe's addition of a bird flying through the sky showed his predeliction for more decorative, atmospheric elements.

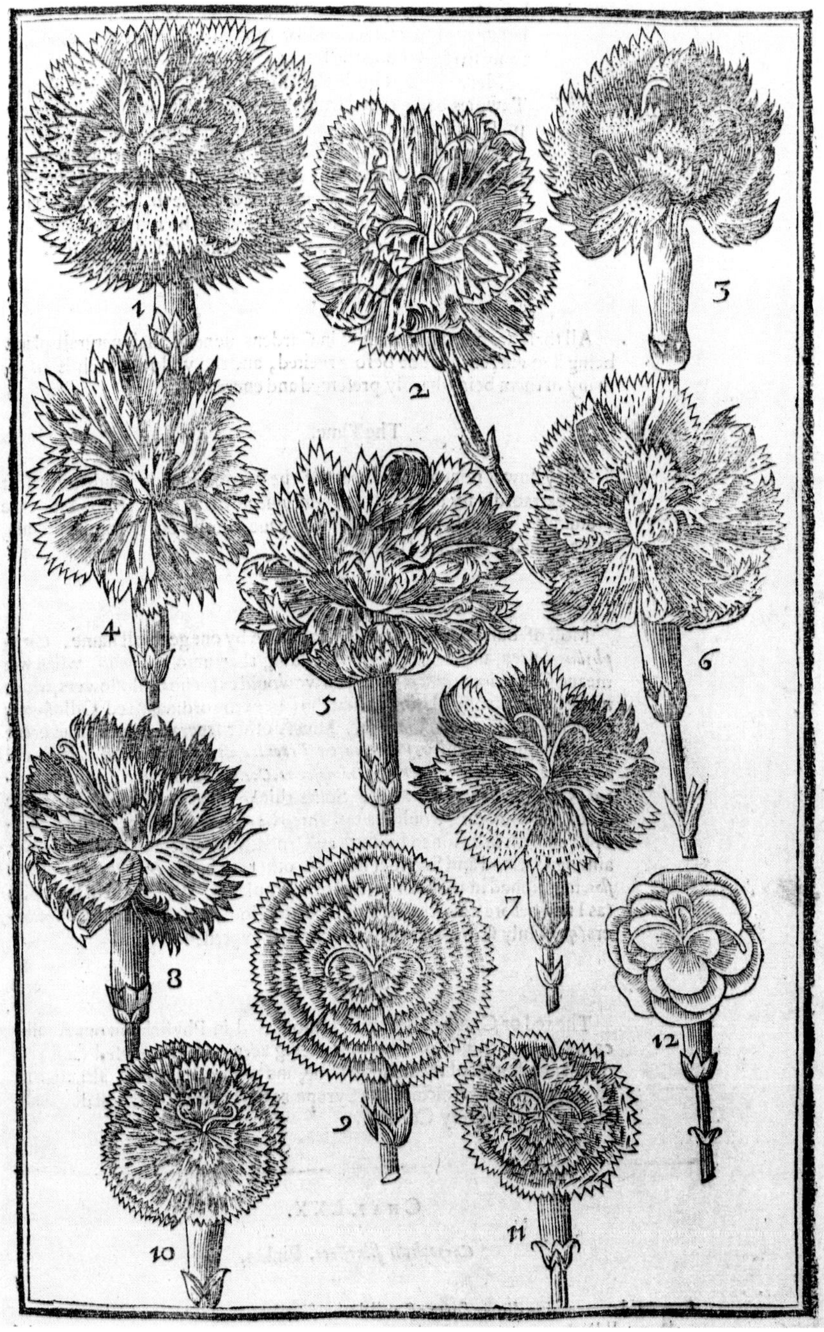

45 ▪ CARNATIONS AND OTHER FLOWERS *Dianthus spp.*

"The Garden of Pleasant Flowers." Woodcut. In *Paradisi in Sole* by John Parkinson (1635). ▪ Parkinson, herbarist to Charles I, intended this work as a practical gardening book rather than a traditional herbal. His nomenclature offers a rather more personal touch, as for example that of the flower pictured, top left, named "Master Tuggie his Princess," after a plantsman of the day. Parkinson's chapter on carnations contains descriptions of some nineteen varieties, descriptions that concern themselves more with the color and size of the flower than with its botanical properties as such.

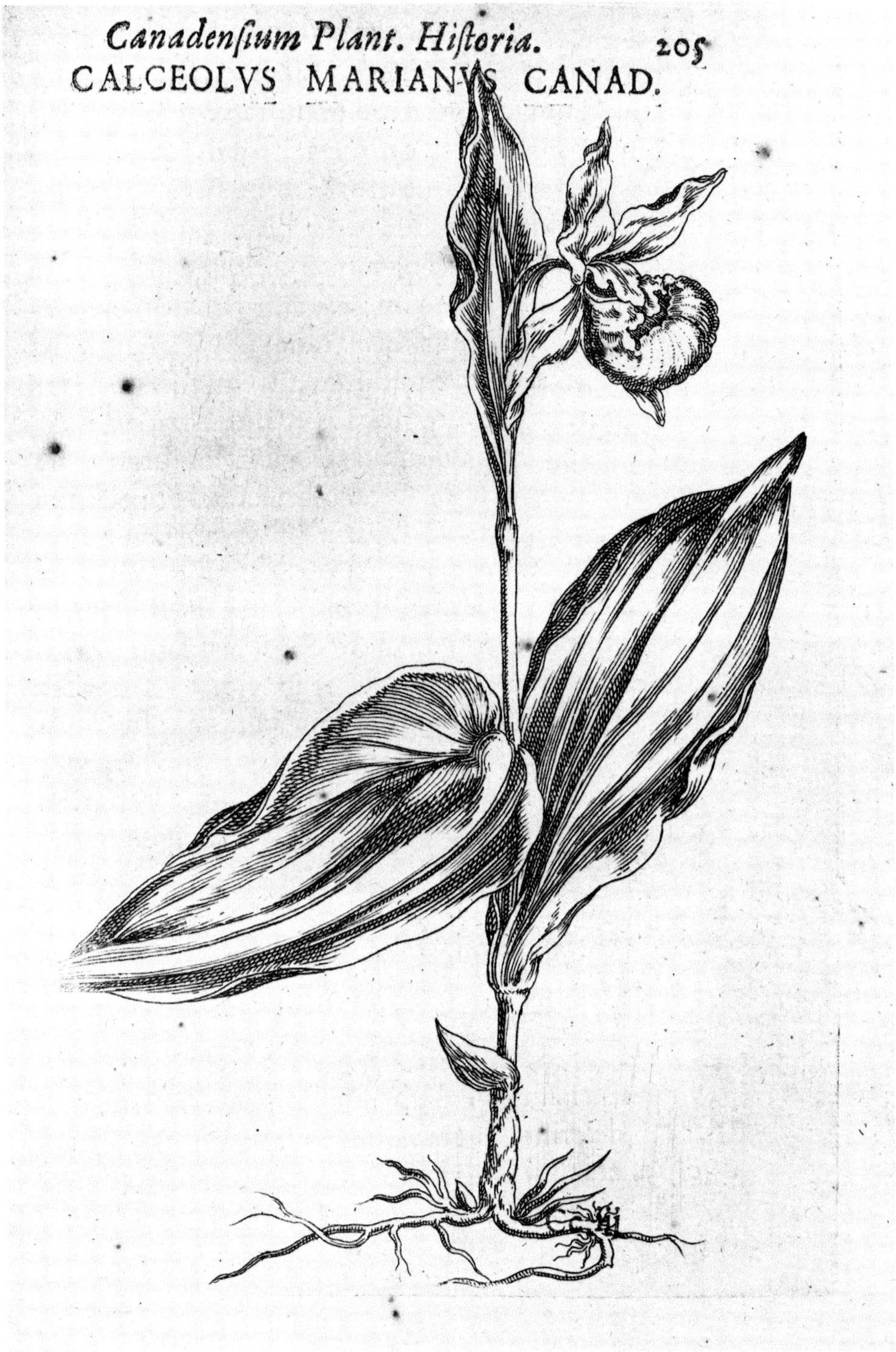

46 ▪ THE LADY'S SLIPPER ORCHID *Cypripedium sp.*

"Calceolus Marianus Canad." Etching. In *Canadensium Plantarum . . . Historia* by Jacques Cornut (1635). ▪ This is the first flora of the French colony of Canada. The French botanist based his work on specimens brought by explorers returning from the New World. About thirty Northeast American plants are described and illustrated for the first time in European botanical literature in this volume.

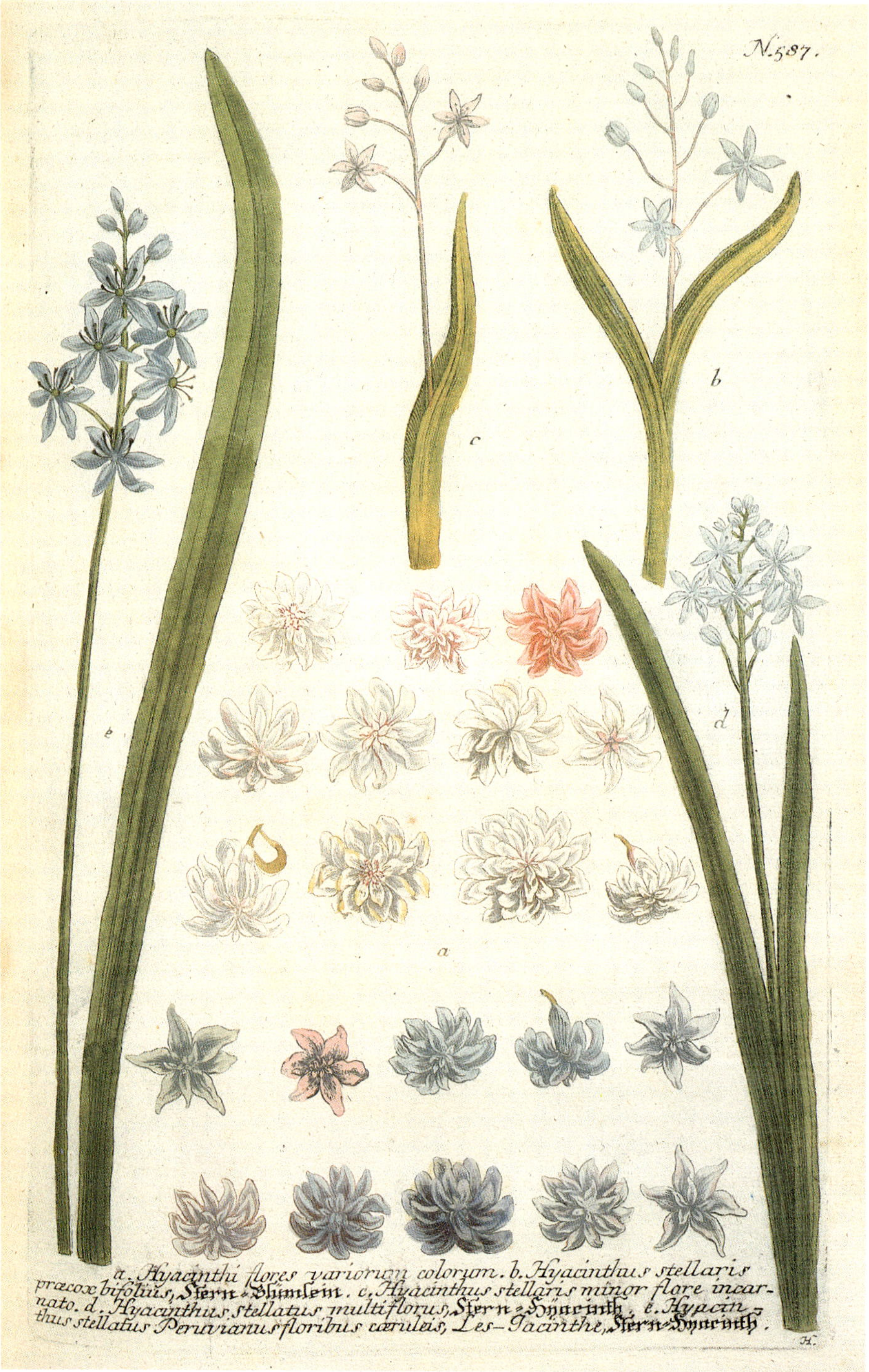

47 ▪ HYACINTHS *Hyacinthus spp.*

Color-printed and hand-finished engraving, from the drawing by Georg Dionysius Ehret. In *Phytanthoza Iconographia. . . .* by Johann Wilhelm Weinmann (1737–45). ▪ This work contains Ehret's first appearance as a botanical illustrator, and it is one of the first botanical books with illustrations printed using color and printed mezzotint, with some additional watercolor touch-up done by hand.

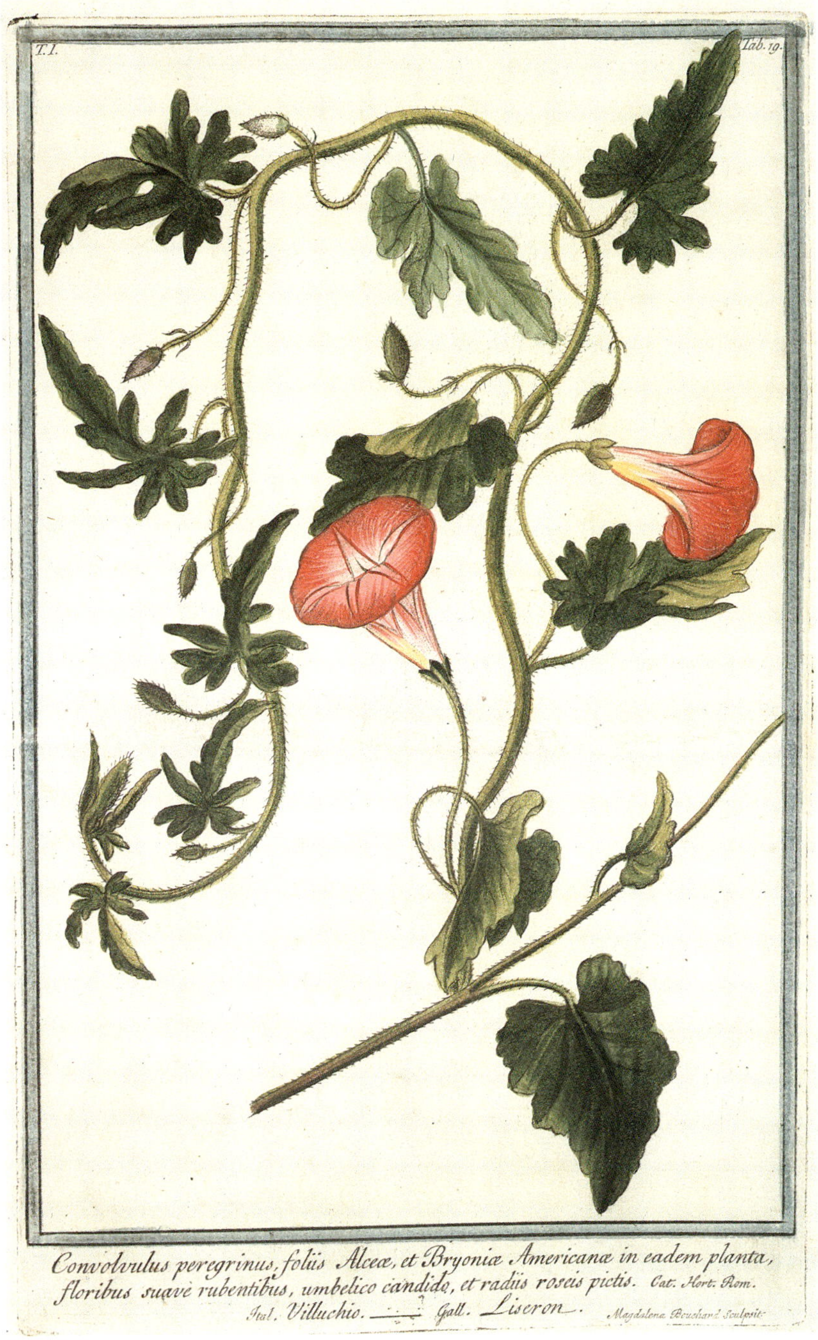

48 ▪ CONVOLVULUS PEREGRINUS *Convolvulus althaeoides*

"Convolvulus peregrinus." Hand-colored engraving, from the drawing by Cesare Ubertini. In *Hortus Romanus* by Giorgio Bonelli and others (1772–93). ▪ This is one of the few Italian efforts at the publication of color-plate botanical books in the eighteenth century. This should not, however, be attributed to any lack of skill in the art of engraving or printing on the part of Italian publishers, for magnificent illustrated books were being published in this period. Rather it may be owing to the absence of botanical investigation on a par with the countries of northern Europe.

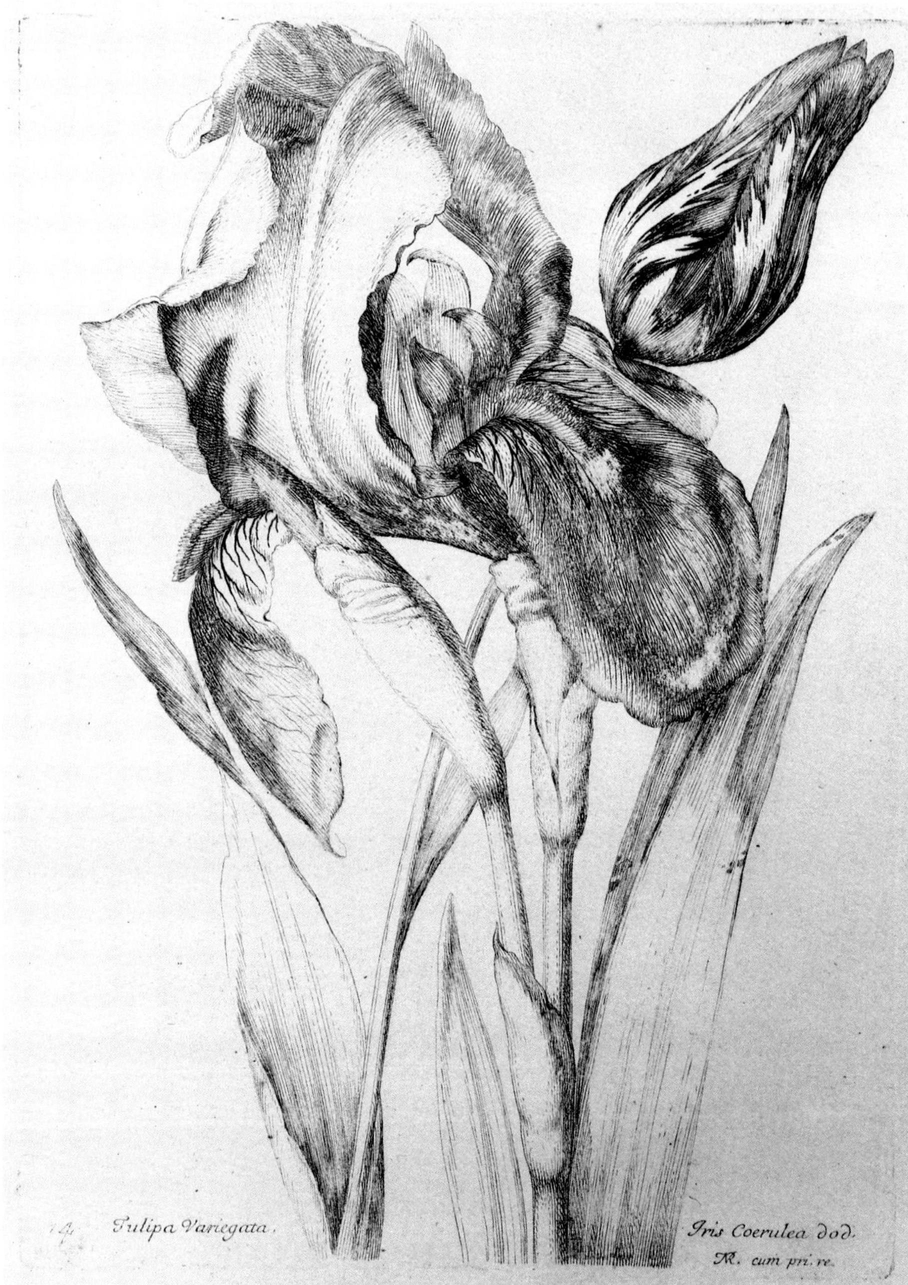

49 ▪ TULIP *Tulipa sp.* ▪ IRIS *Iris pumila*

"Tulipa Variegata and Iris Coerulea." Engraving, by Nicolas Robert from his own drawing. In *Diverses Fleurs Dessinées et Gravées d'Après Le Naturel* by Nicolas Robert (1660). ▪ Like Crispijn van de Passe, by whose work he may well have been influenced, Robert was an artist rather than a botanist. In his engravings are echoes of seventeenth-century flower painting with its emphasis on dramatic composition and luxuriant textures.

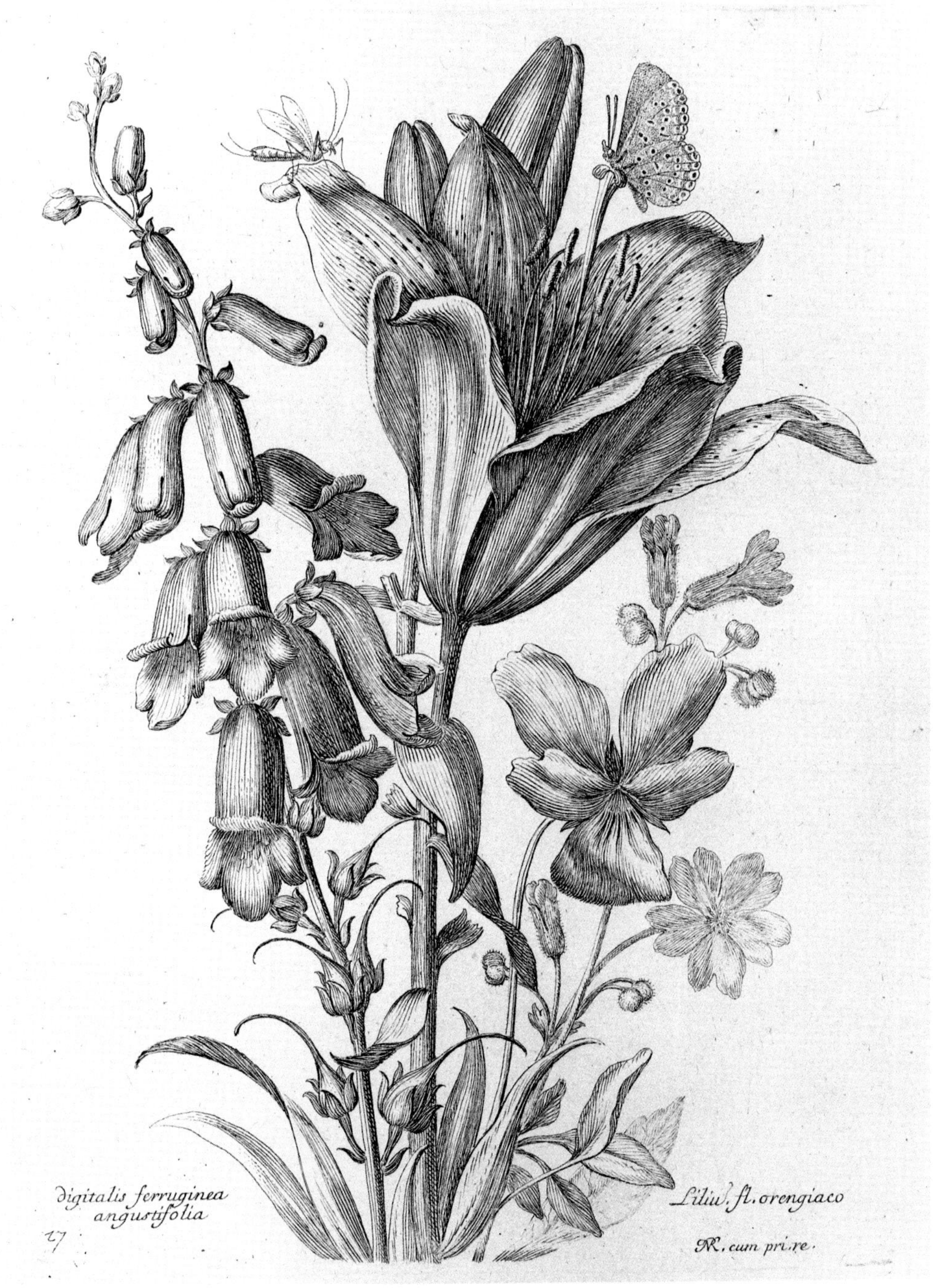

50 ▪ DIGITALIS *Digitalis purpurea* ▪ LILY *Lilium sp.*

"Digitalis ferruginea angustifolia and Liliu[m] fl. orengiaco." Engraving, by Nicolas Robert from his own drawing. In *Diverses Fleurs Dessinées et Gravées d'Après Le Naturel* by Nicolas Robert (1660). ▪ The butterfly resting on the lily should be noted; where this mixture of botanical and natural history subject matter in the same image is one that is seen more frequently in the work of eighteenth century artists such as Maria Sibylla Merian and Mark Catesby to provide ecological information, Robert's butterflies were intended more as decoration.

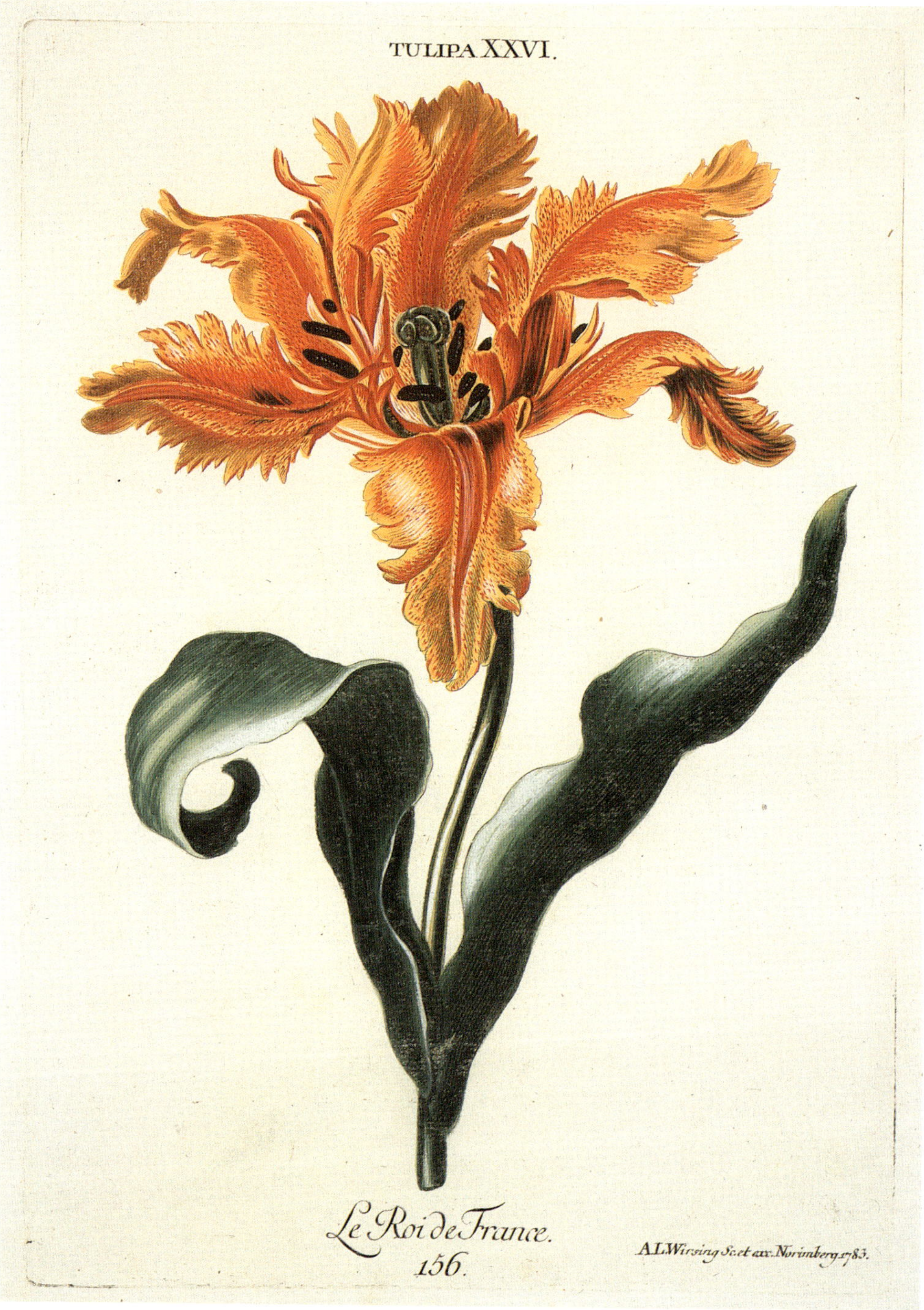

51 ▪ PARROT TULIP *Tulipa gesneriana*

"Le Roi de France." Hand-colored engraving, by A. L. Wirsing. In *Hortus Nitidissimus. . . .* by Christoph Jacob Trew (1750–86). ▪ Although Trew had a serious interest in botanical science the illustrations in this work, such as this image of the tulip known as the "Roi de France," seem to speak of a basic love of the visual glory of flowers. This interest in lush imagery would seem to be a reflection of the rococo love of ornament which flourished in the decorative arts in the early eighteenth century.

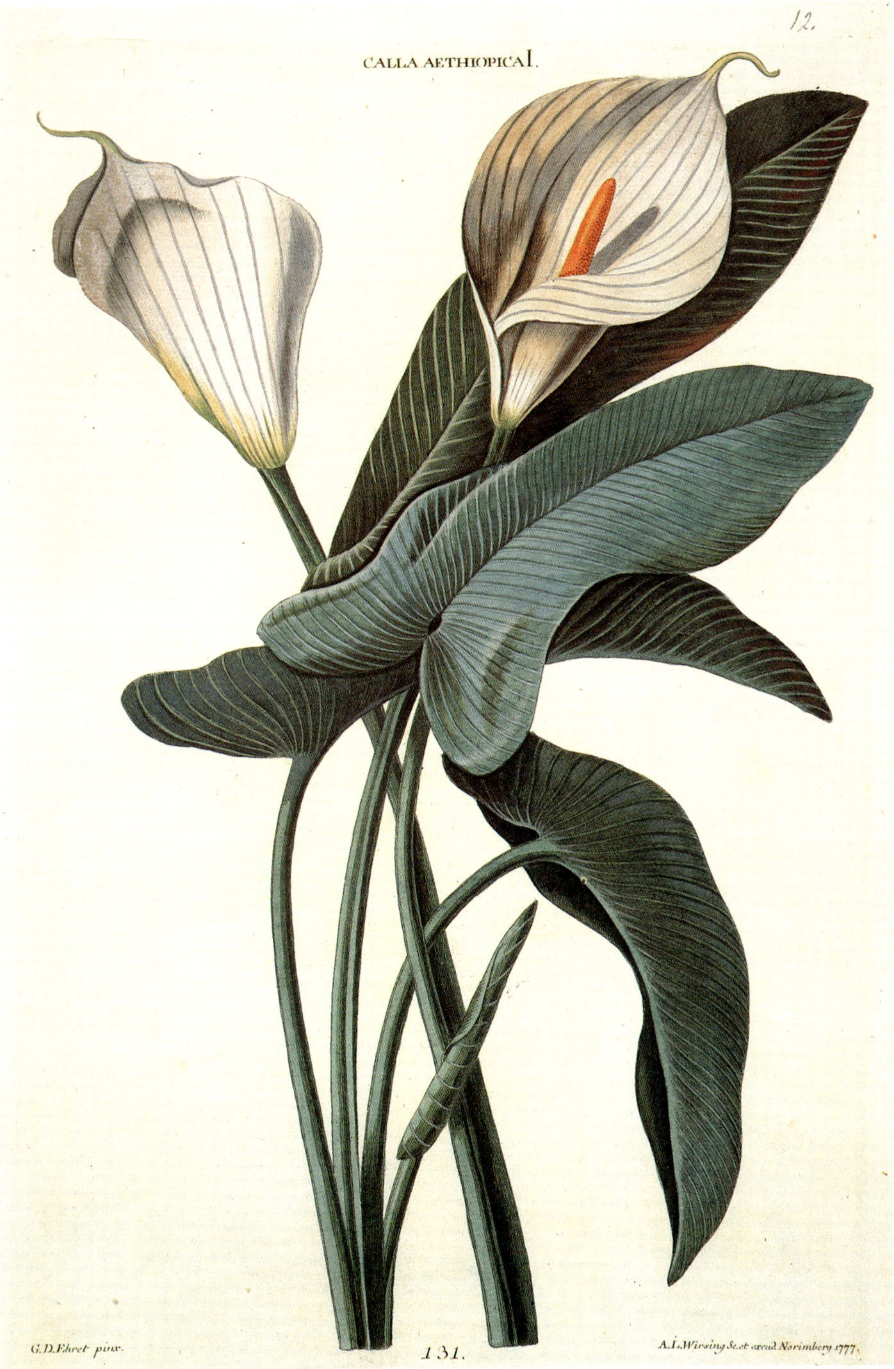

52 ▪ CALLA LILY *Zantedeschia aethiopica*

"Calla aethiopica." Hand-colored engraving, by A. L. Wirsing from the drawing by Georg Dionysius Ehret. In *Hortus Nitidissimus. . . .* by Christoph Jacob Trew (1750–86). ▪ Ehret, the greatest of botanical artists before Redouté's time, collaborated on a number of works with Trew, a Nuremberg physician with a strong interest in botany, who was his patron. Of Ehret's consummate artistry one observer has remarked that he "achieves realism, majesty, ineffable color, all in one breathtaking look."

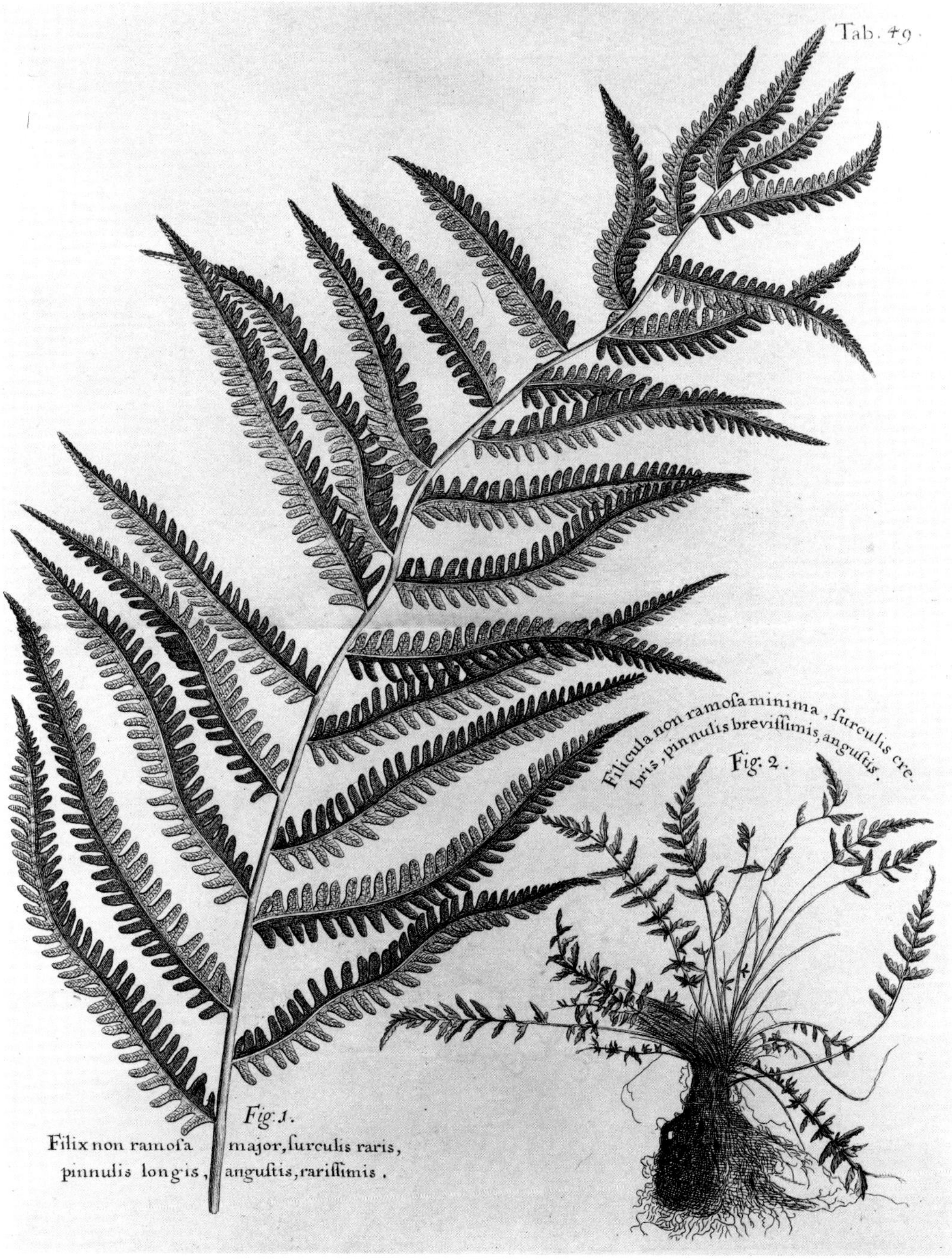

53 ▪ FERNS *Thelypteris sp.* ▪ *Asplenium sp.*

Engraving, by M. van der Gucht from the drawing by E. Kickius. In *A Voyage to the Islands. . . .* by Sir Hans Sloane (1707–25). ▪ More than one hundred different types of ferns are described by the author in this impressive work. Their presentation is quite distinctive owing to the accompanying text, which sometimes curves around the image like a protective skin. Sir Hans was a distinguished figure in eighteenth-century English intellectual life. A physician by training, he succeeded Sir Isaac Newton as president of the Royal Society and founded the Chelsea Physic Garden, in which his friend, Elizabeth Blackwell, made her drawings.

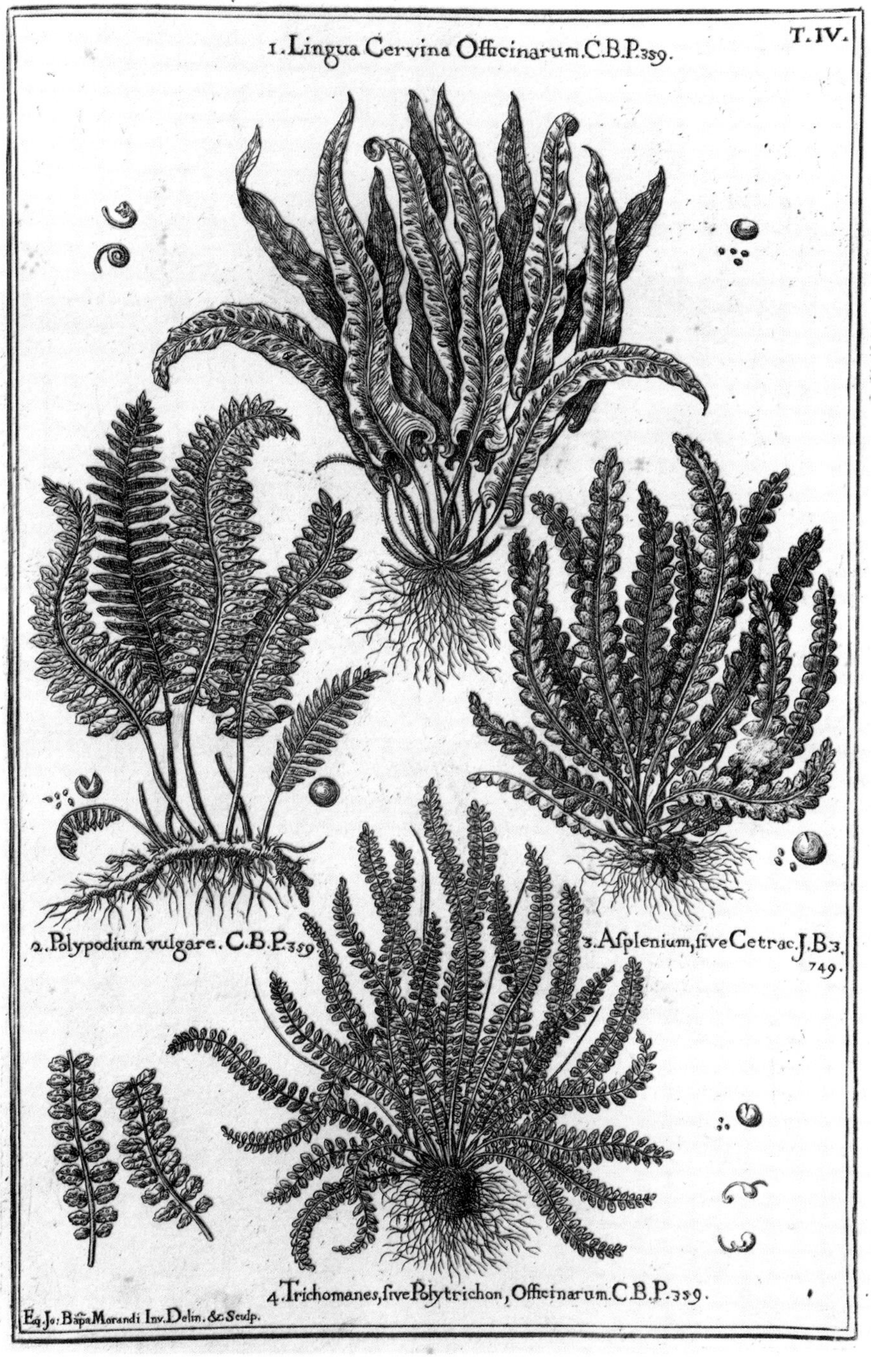

54 ▪ HART'S TONGUE FERN *Phyllitis scolopendrium* ▪ *Polypodium vulgare* ▪ MAIDENHAIR FERN *Asplenium trichomanes* ▪ RUSTY-BACK FERN *Ceterach officinarum*

Etching by Giambattista Morandi, from his own drawing. In *Historia Botanica-Practica* by G. B. Morandi (1744). ▪ The "practical botany" of the title of this work relates to the author's interest, comparable to that of earlier herbalists, in the medicinal properties of the plants he describes. Polypodium vulgare, he notes, is good for curing gout; Morandi bolsters his claim with references to Dodoens, among others.

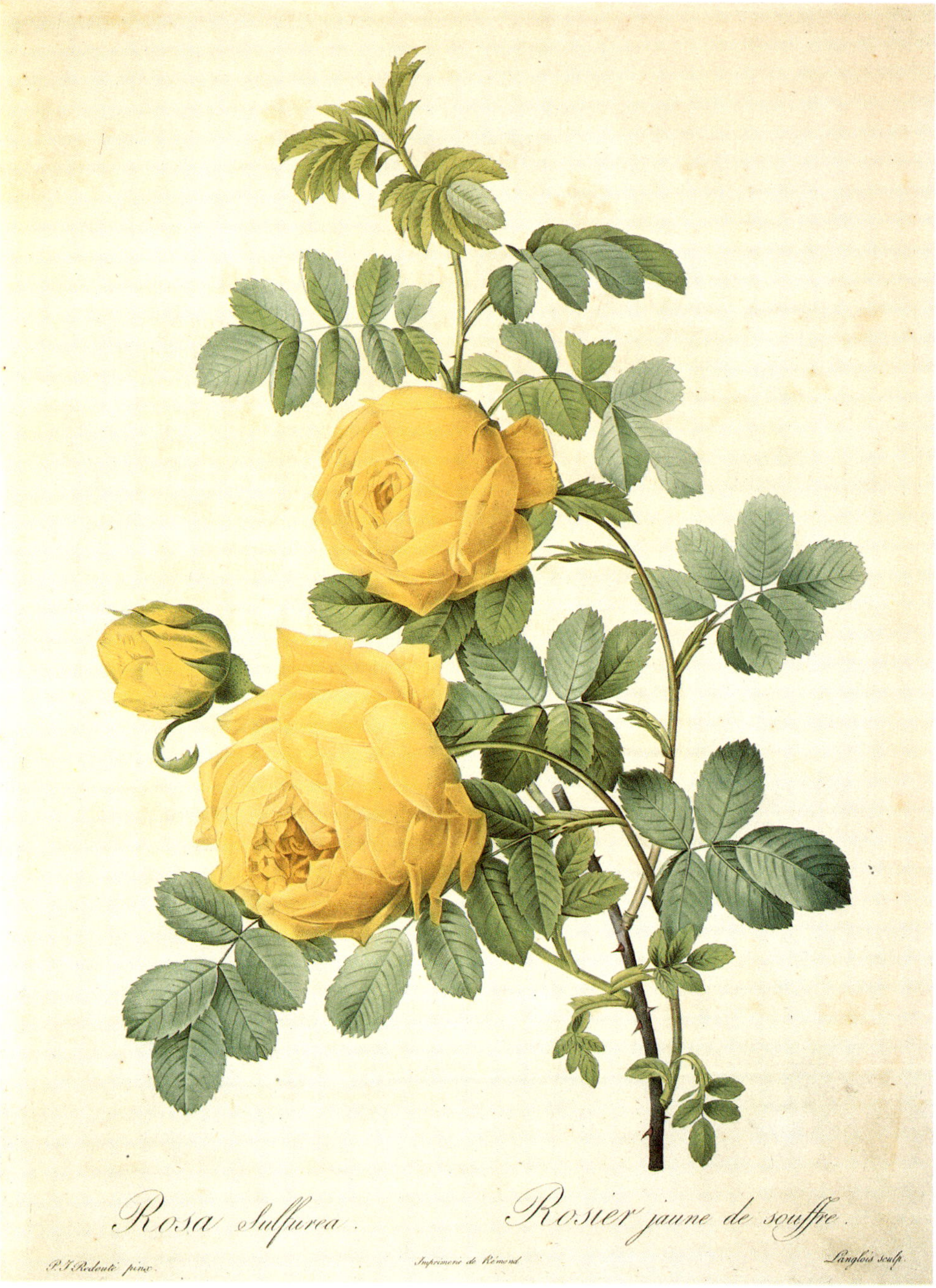

55 ▪ SWEETBRIAR *Rosa eglanteria*

"Rosa sulfurea. Rosier jaune de souffre." Color-printed and hand-finished stipple engraving, by Langlois from the drawing by Pierre-Joseph Redouté. In *Les Roses* by Pierre-Joseph Redouté and Claude Antoine Thory (1817–24). ▪ The consummate statement of Redouté's art as well as his most familiar book, *Les Roses*, is in the breathtaking delicacy of its depiction of petals and leaves, a work of documentary as well as artistic significance. Almost all of the roses known at that time were described and reproduced, including some varieties that are no longer available in cultivation.

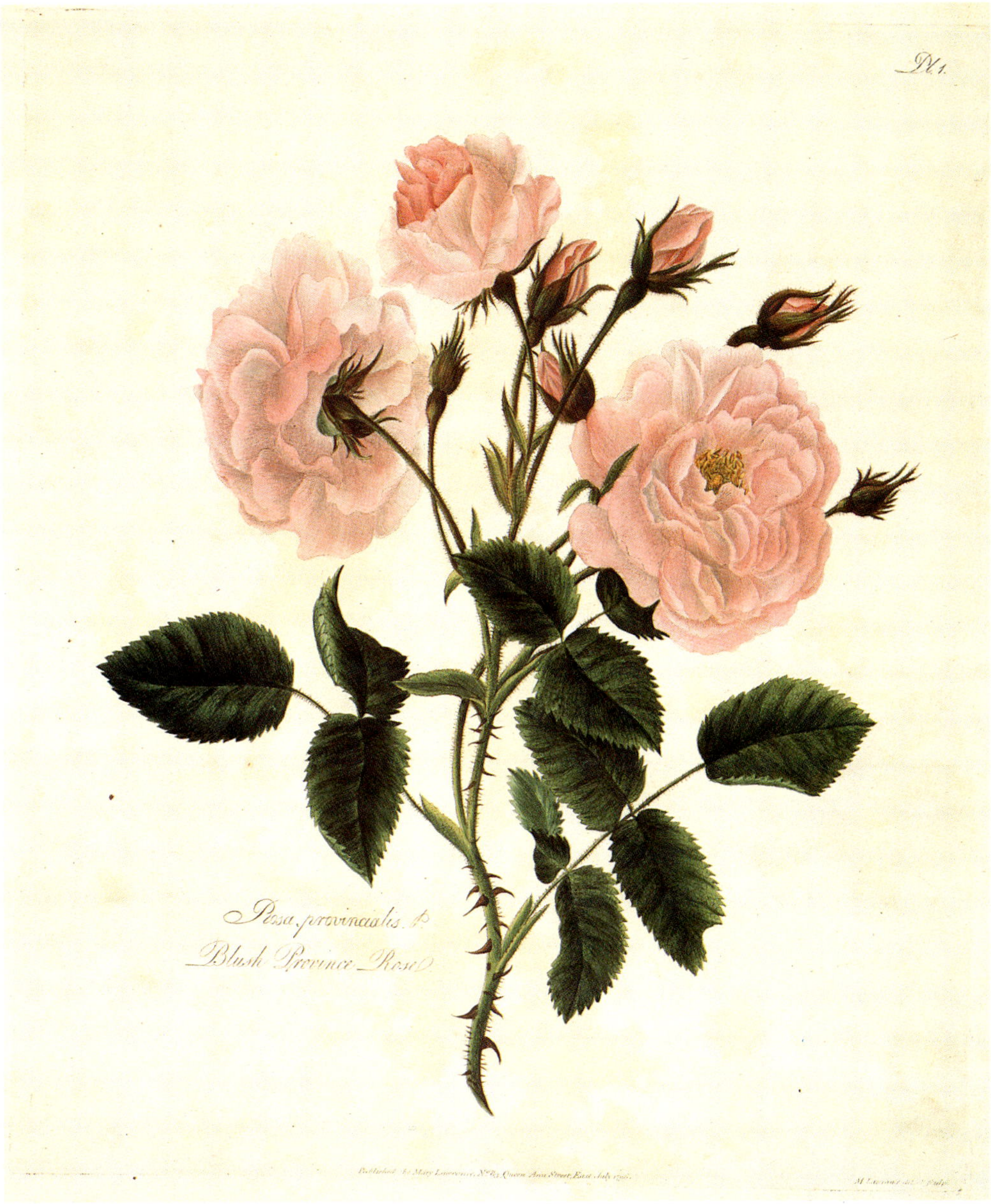

56 ▪ BLUSH PROVINCE ROSE *Rosa centifolia*

Hand-colored engraving, by Mary Lawrance from her own drawing. In *A Collection of Roses from Nature* by Mary Lawrance (1799). ▪ Preceding Redouté's more famous work by some twenty years, this book drew on the newfound popularity of roses as an element in English gardens. Less delicate in drawing and coloring than *Les Roses*, Mrs. Lawrance's *Collection* has about it a certain charm and prettiness that one associates with the efforts of a particularly English type of amateur.

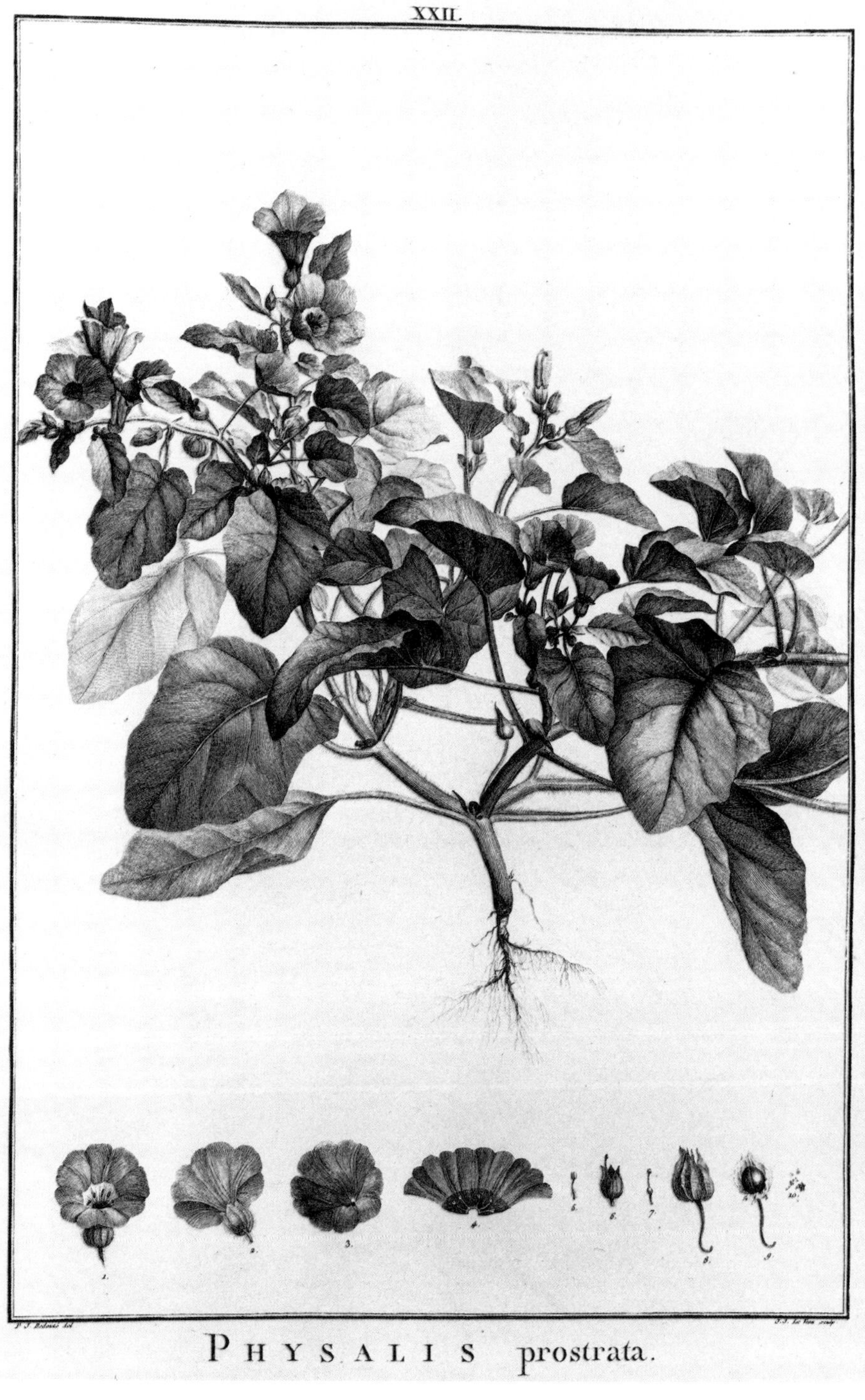

57 ▪ GROUND CHERRY *Physalis prostrata*

"Physalis prostrata." Engraving, by J. J. Le Veau from the drawing by Pierre-Joseph Redouté. In *Stirpes Novae. . . .* by Charles Louis L'Héritier de Brutelle (1784–91). ▪ This is the first major book to which Redouté contributed illustrations. L'Héritier was an amateur botanist who had taken the twenty-five-year-old artist under his wing and given him his first commission.

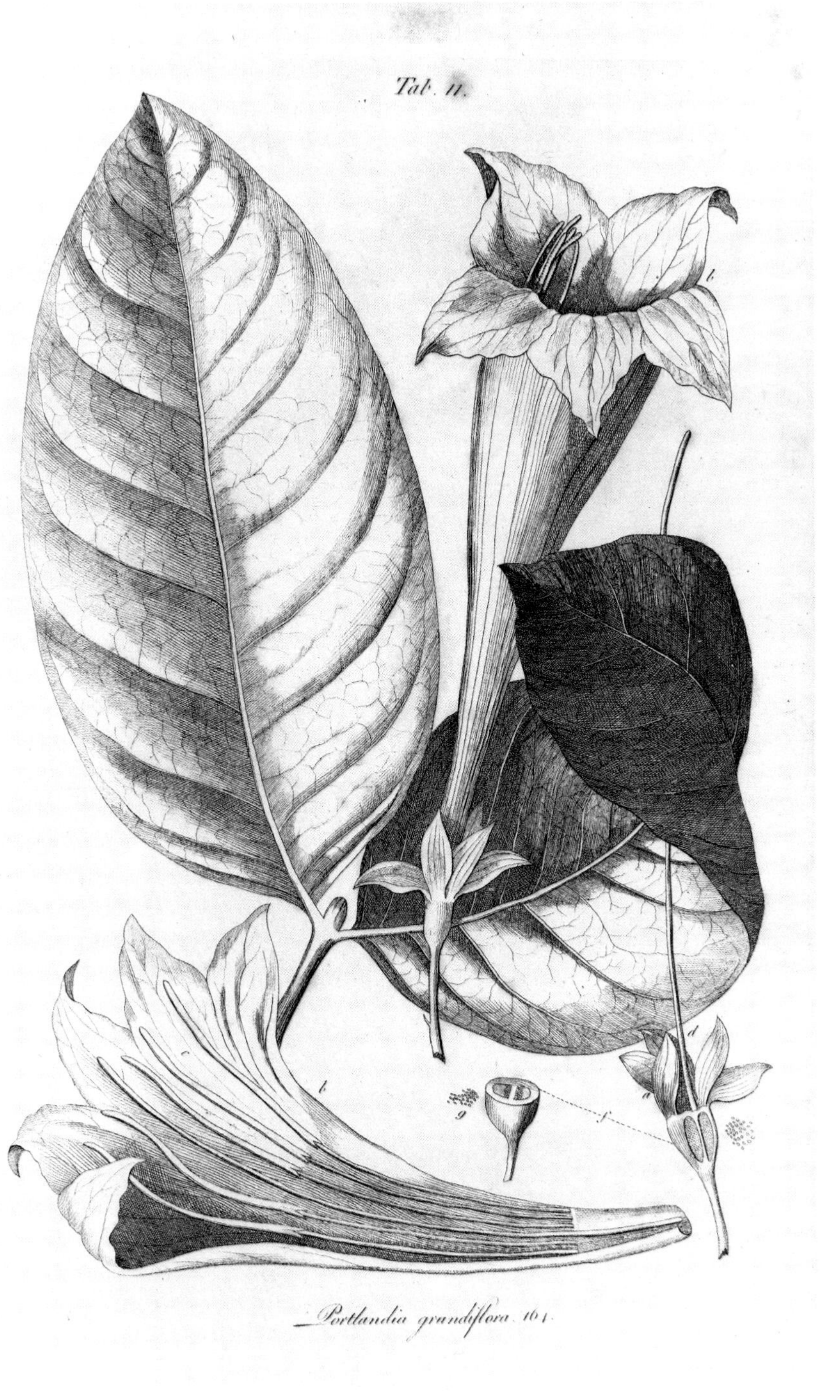

58 ▪ PORTLANDIA *Portlandia grandiflora*

"Portlandia Grandiflora." Engraving, from the drawing by Georg Dionysius Ehret. In *The Civil and Natural History of Jamaica* by Patrick Browne (1789). ▪ Ehret married the sister-in-law of Philip Miller, curator of the Chelsea Physic Garden, which he frequented to find subjects for his illustrations of rare or newly introduced plants. This work by the English physician Browne was published some nineteen years after the artist's death.

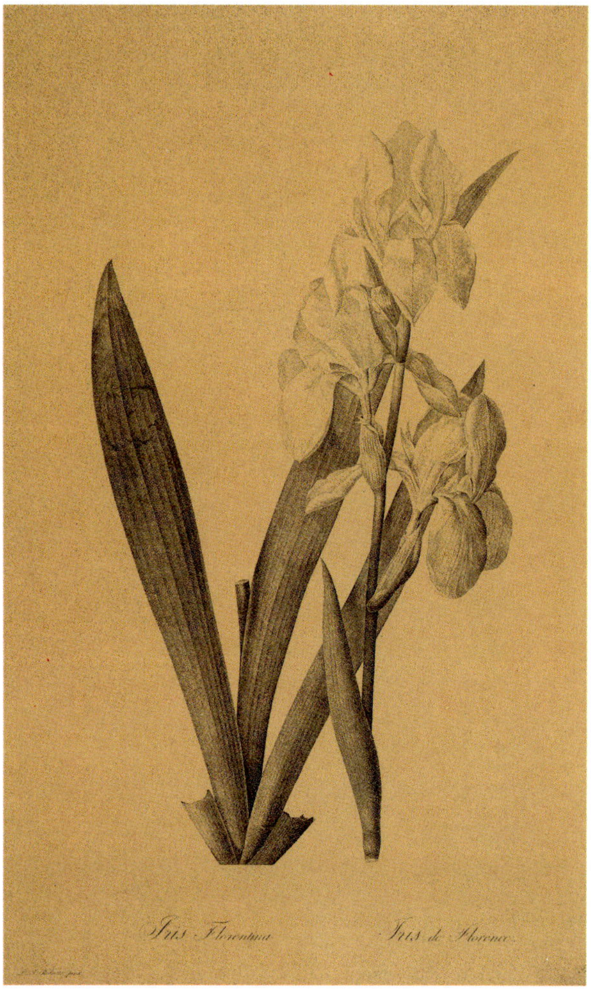

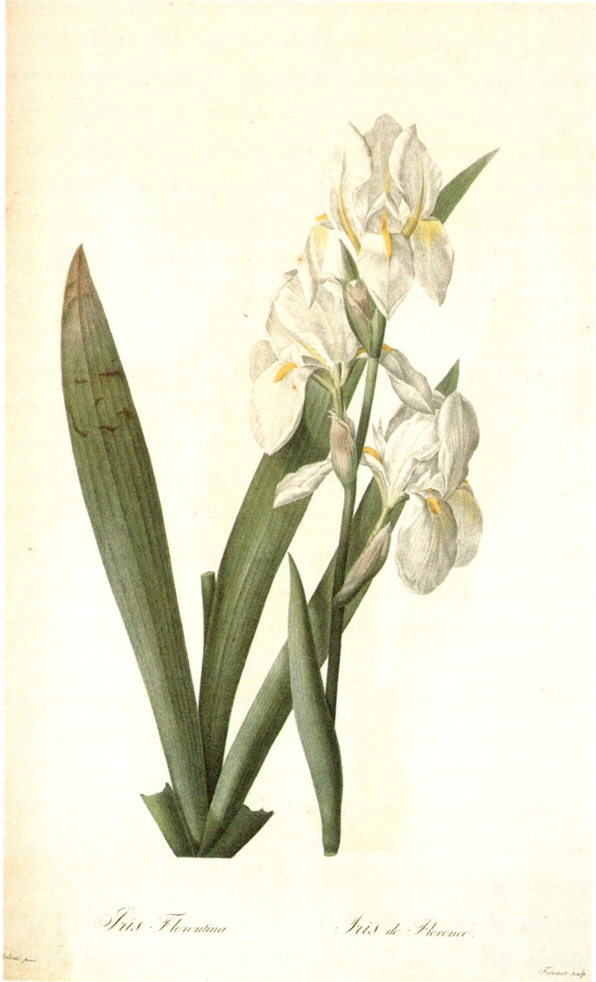

59 ▪ IRIS *Iris florentina*

"Iris Florentina. Iris de Florence." Color-printed and hand-retouched stipple engraving, by Tassaert from the painting by Pierre-Joseph Redouté. In *Les Liliacées* by Pierre-Joseph Redouté (1802–16). ▪ Called the "Raphael of Flowers" and the "Rembrandt of Roses," Redouté is often considered the greatest of botanical artists and *Les Liliacées* his greatest work. Produced under the patronage of the Empress Josephine, Napoleon's first wife, its illustrations reveal most clearly Redouté's mastery of precise botanical description, composition, engraving, and color printing.

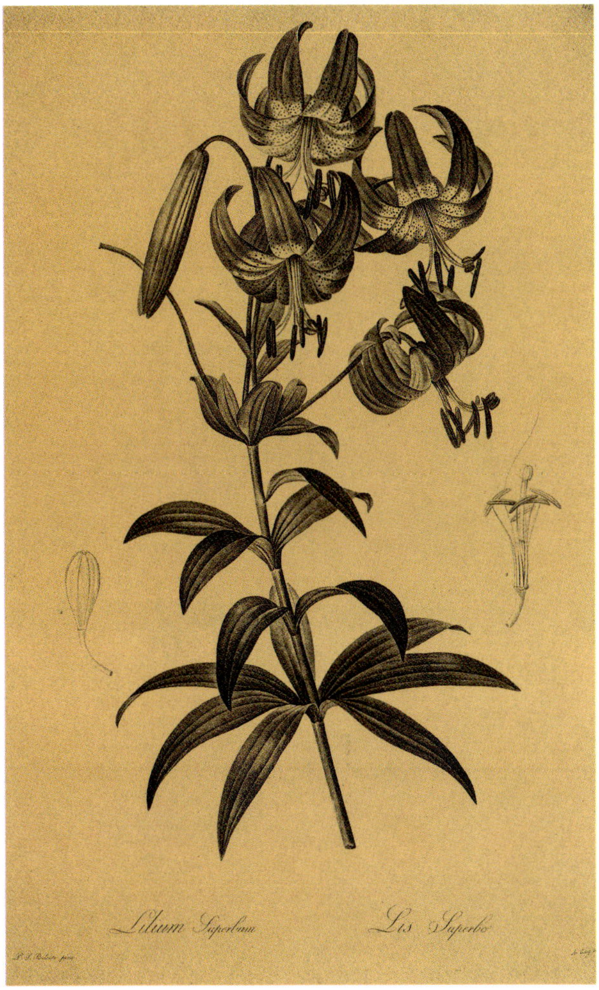

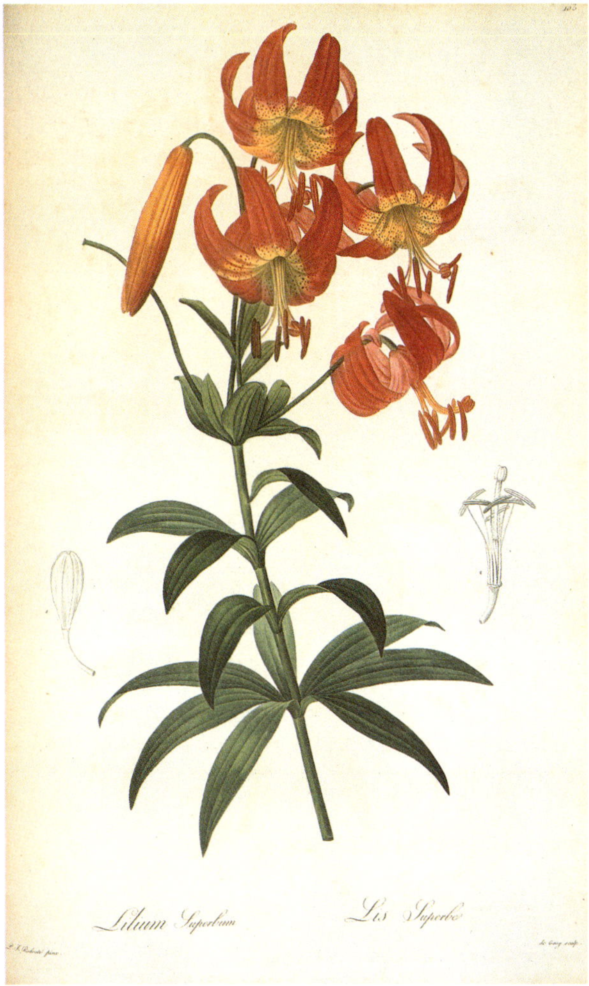

60 ▪ SUPERB LILY *Lilium superbum*

"Lilium Superbum. Lis Superbe." Color-printed and hand-retouched stipple engraving, by De Gouy from the painting by Pierre-Joseph Redouté. In *Les Liliacées* by Pierre-Joseph Redouté (1802–16). ▪ The Library's copy of this work is rare, having the plates in both colored and uncolored states, the latter being printed on tan paper. This offers the observer the opportunity of observing at close hand the clarity of Redouté's depictions and the effects of his (or his assistants') coloring on that depiction.

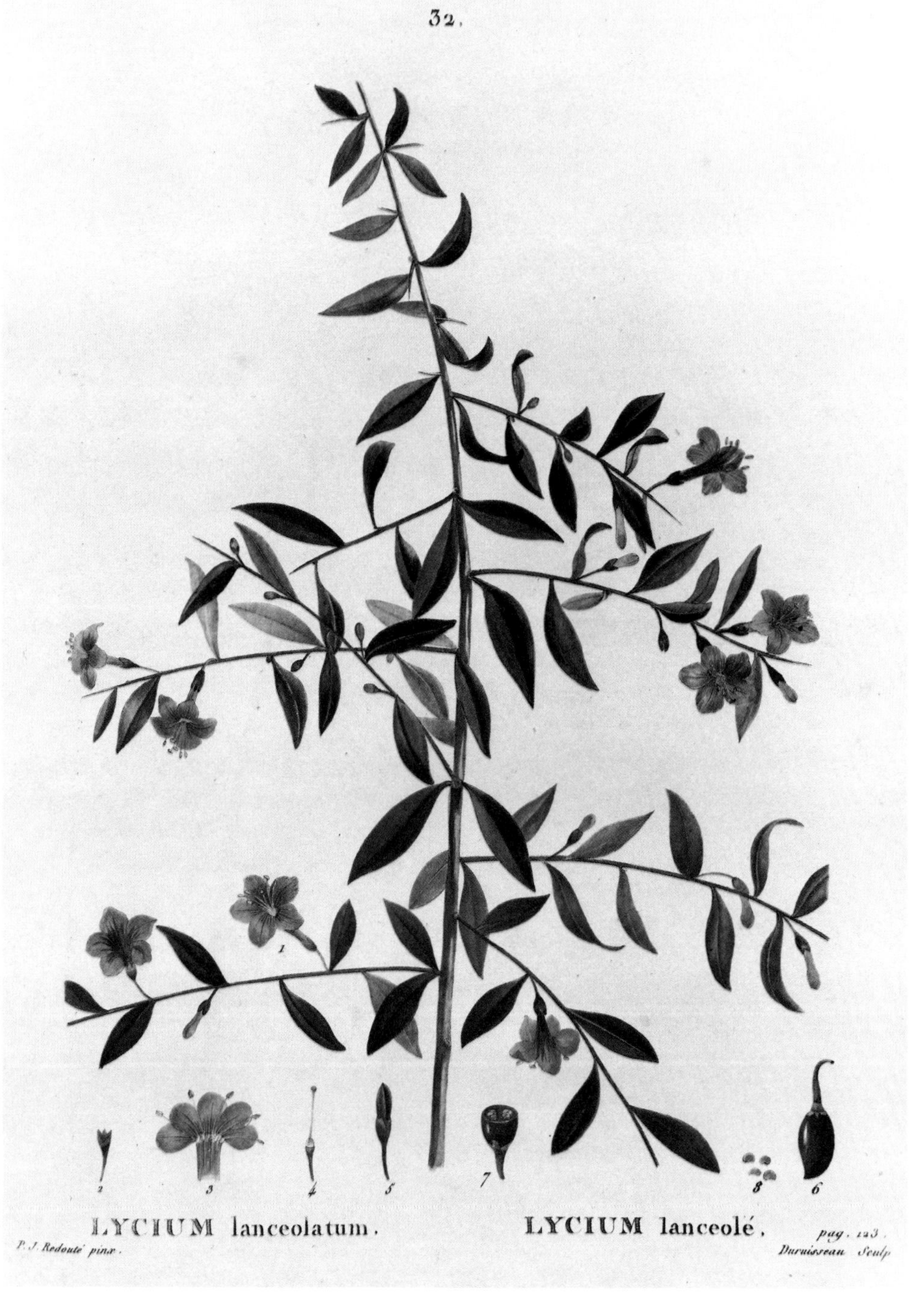

61 ▪ CHINESE MATRIMONY VINE *Lycium chinense*

"Lycium lanceolatum." Hand-colored engraving, by Duruisseau from the drawing by Pierre-Joseph Redouté. In *Traité Des Arbres et Arbustes Que L'On Cultive en France en Pleine Terre* by Henri Louis Duhamel du Monceau (1800–19). ▪ Duhamel du Monceau owned the large woodblocks that had been put to such fine use in the herbals by Matthioli, and so used them for the first edition of this work, published in 1755. The later edition of this French dendrologist's work was updated with illustrations by Redouté.

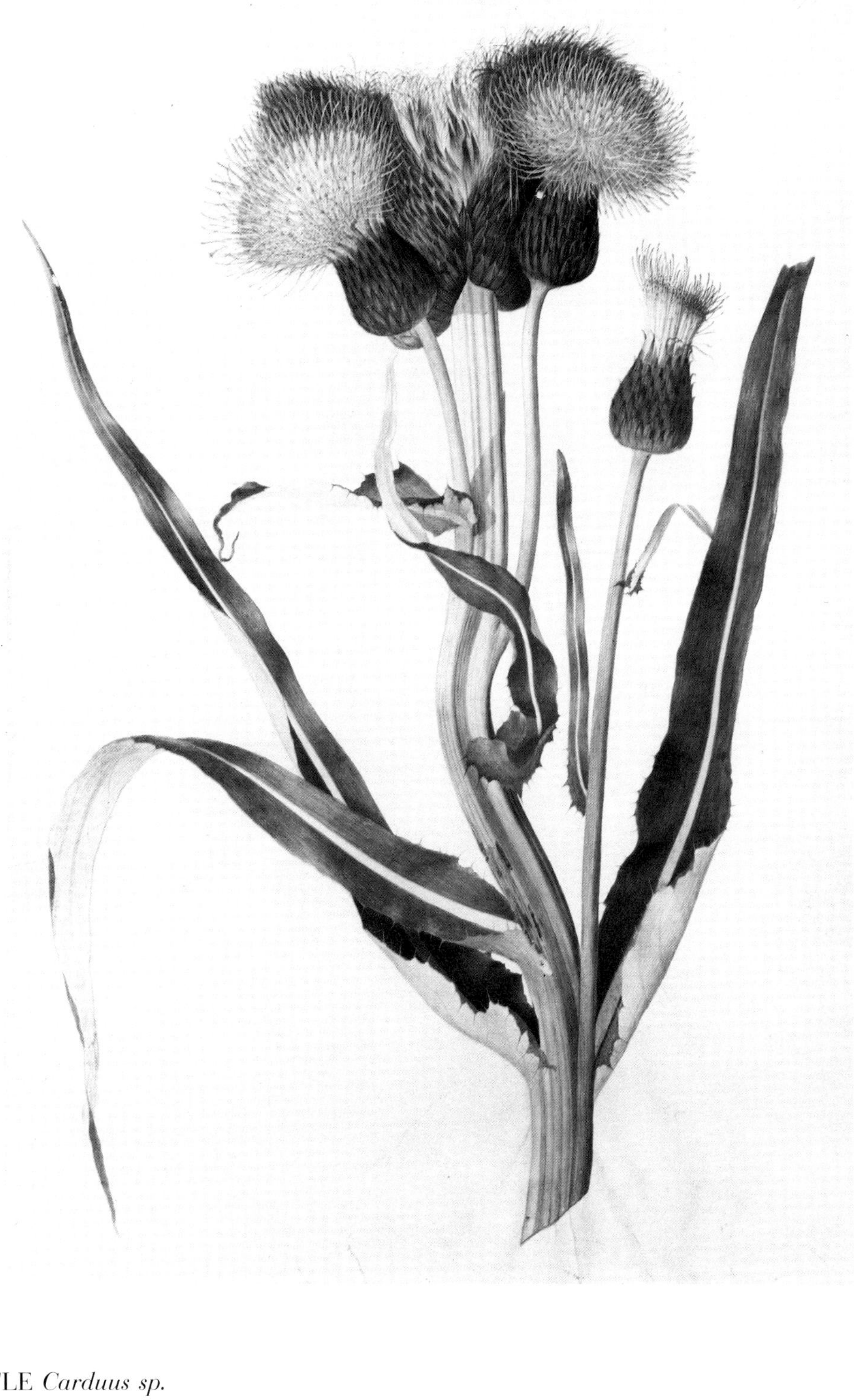

62 ▪ THISTLE *Carduus sp.*

Watercolor on vellum. In *Beautiful Collection of Drawings of Flowers* (c. 1700?). ▪ This anonymous work comes from an album of 131 original watercolors on vellum which were bound together in the eighteenth century. It reveals one of the most striking aspects of early botanical illustration: the degree to which artistic abilities in both execution and design are combined with an intense interest in the scientific documentation of plants.

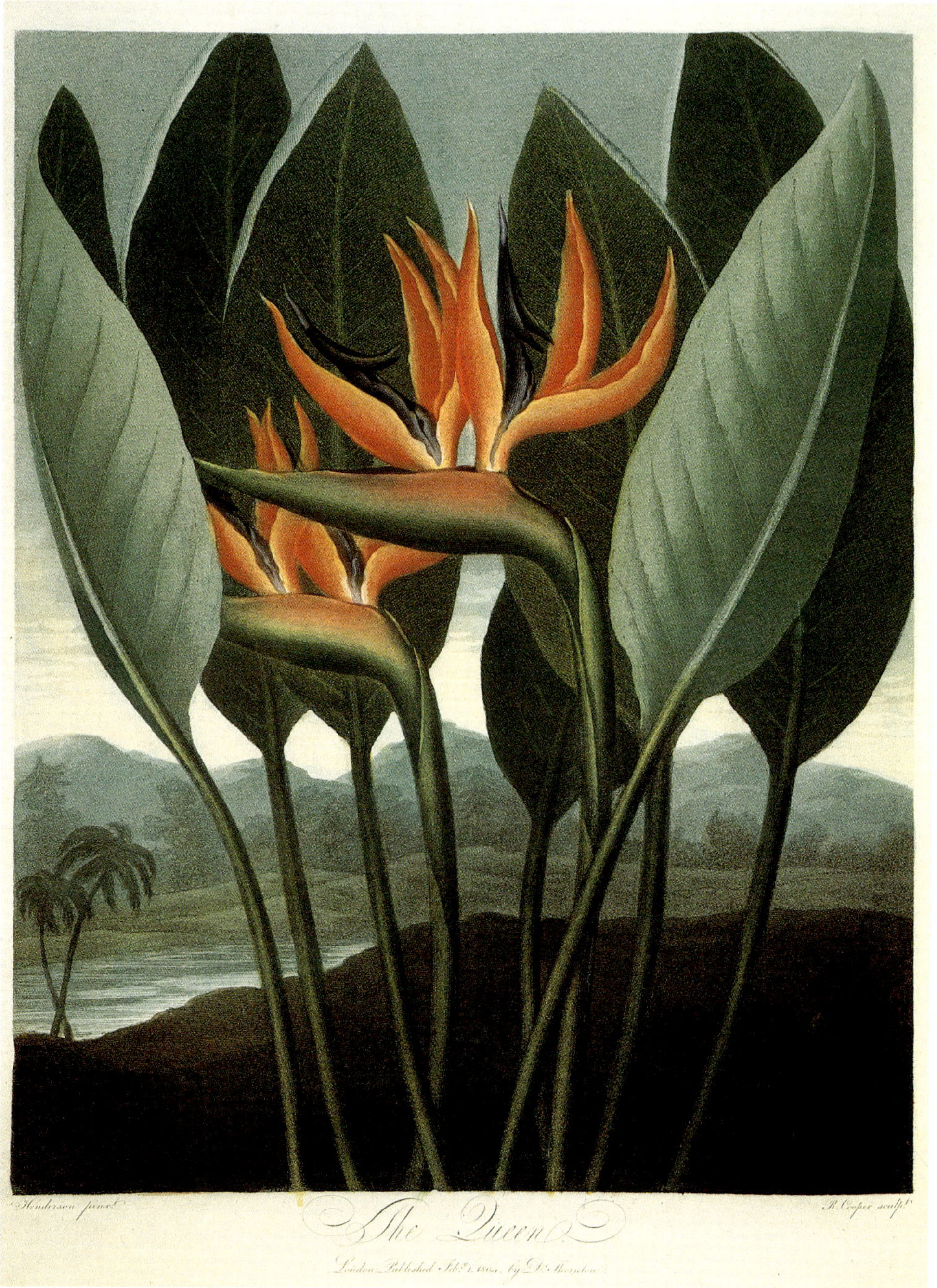

63 ▪ BIRD OF PARADISE *Strelitzia reginae*

"The Queen." Color-printed aquatint, by Peter Henderson from the engraving by R. Cooper. In *New Illustration of the Sexual System of Carolus von Linnaeus . . . The Temple of Flora, or Garden of Nature* by Dr. Robert John Thornton (1798–1807). ▪ The Queen commemorated in the name of this plant is Charlotte of Mecklenburg-Strelitz, queen to George III. This is the first plate of the *Strelitzia*, existing in one state only. Thornton's book was originally issued in parts from 1798 to 1807, when it finally appeared in book form. When the book was reissued in 1812 another plate was substituted for that of the queen-plant.

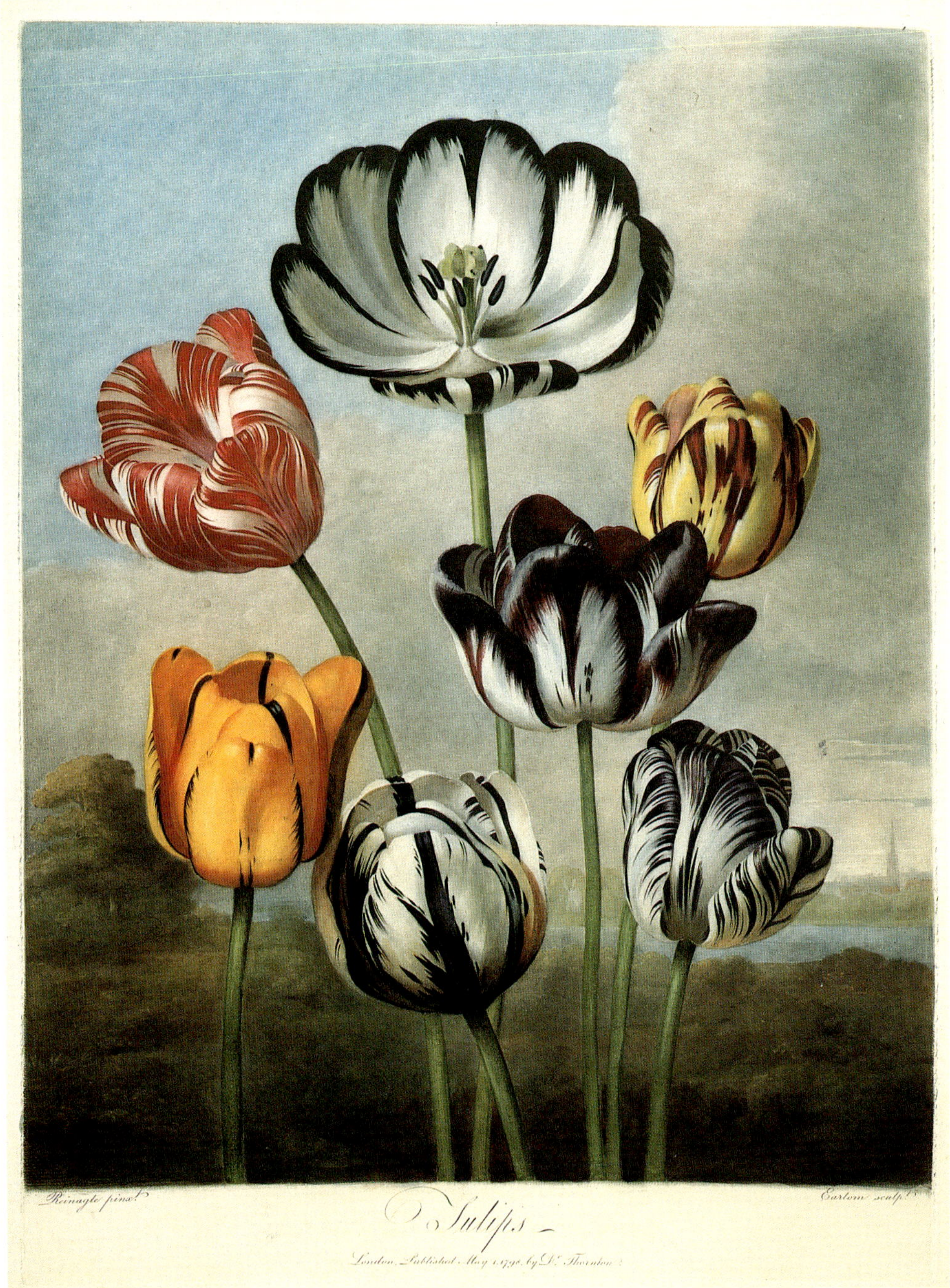

64 ▪ TULIPS *Tulipa spp.*

"Tulips." Color-printed aquatint engraving, by Earlom from the painting by Philip Reinagle. In *New Illustration of the Sexual System of Carolus von Linnaeus . . . The Temple of Flora, or Garden of Nature* by Dr. Robert John Thornton (1798–1807). ▪ Of these flowers Thornton notes that they are a "striking display of the wonderful power of the beneficient Creator, who has placed these beautiful objects before us, for our recreation, and admiration." Indeed they also show the influence of the Romantic sensibility on botanical illustration, with the strong and swaying tulips drawn against the evocative poetic background.

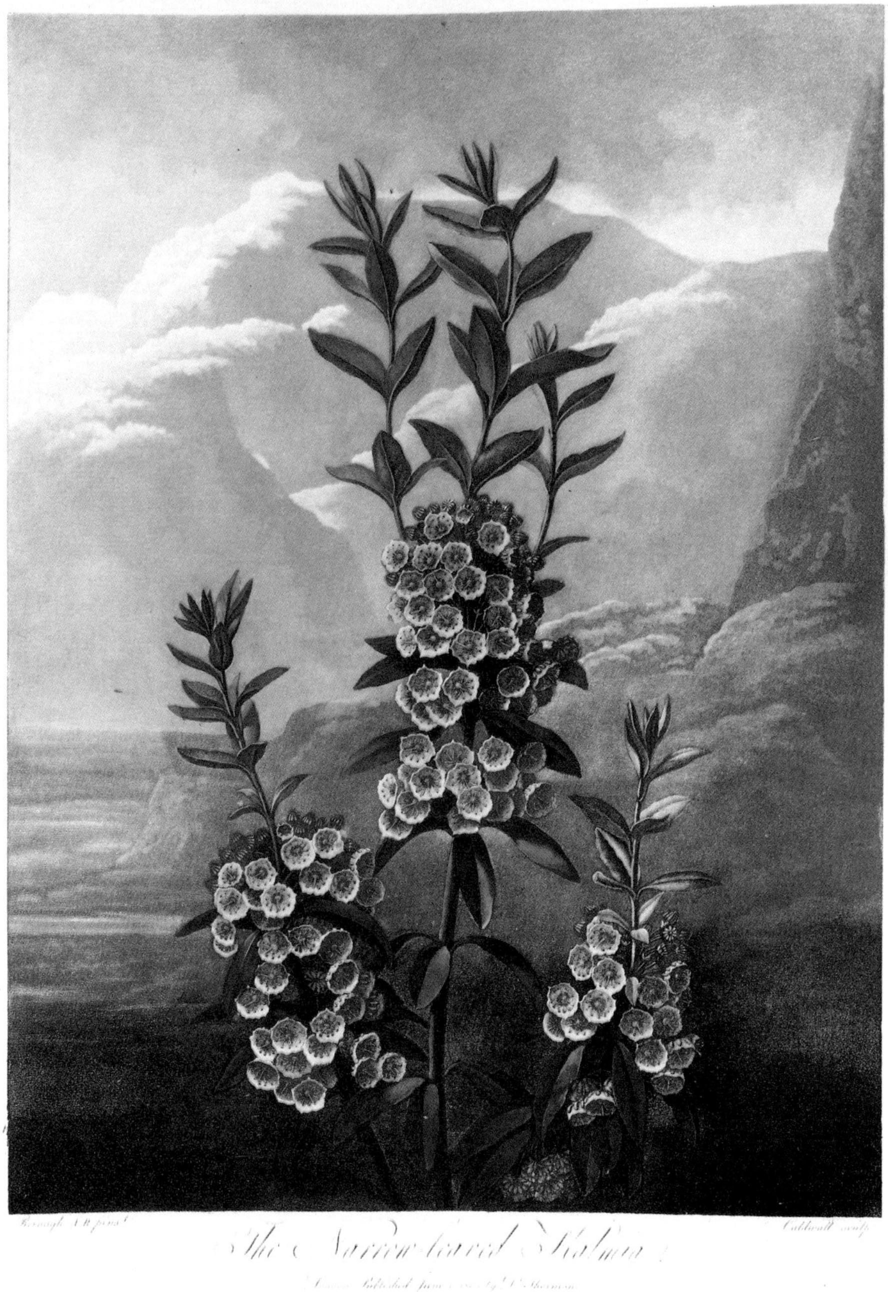

65 ▪ SHEEP LAUREL *Kalmia angustiflora*

"The Narrow-Leaved Kalmia." Color-printed aquatint engraving, by Caldwall from the painting by Philip Reinagle. In *New Illustration of the Sexual System of Carolus von Linnaeus . . . The Temple of Flora, or Garden of Nature* by Dr. Robert John Thornton (1798–1807). ▪ The dramatic illustrations in this work are often accompanied by poetry of a sort. For Kalmia, the chosen text begins: "High rise the cloud-capp'd hills where Kalmia glows/With dazzling beauty, 'mid a waste of snows."

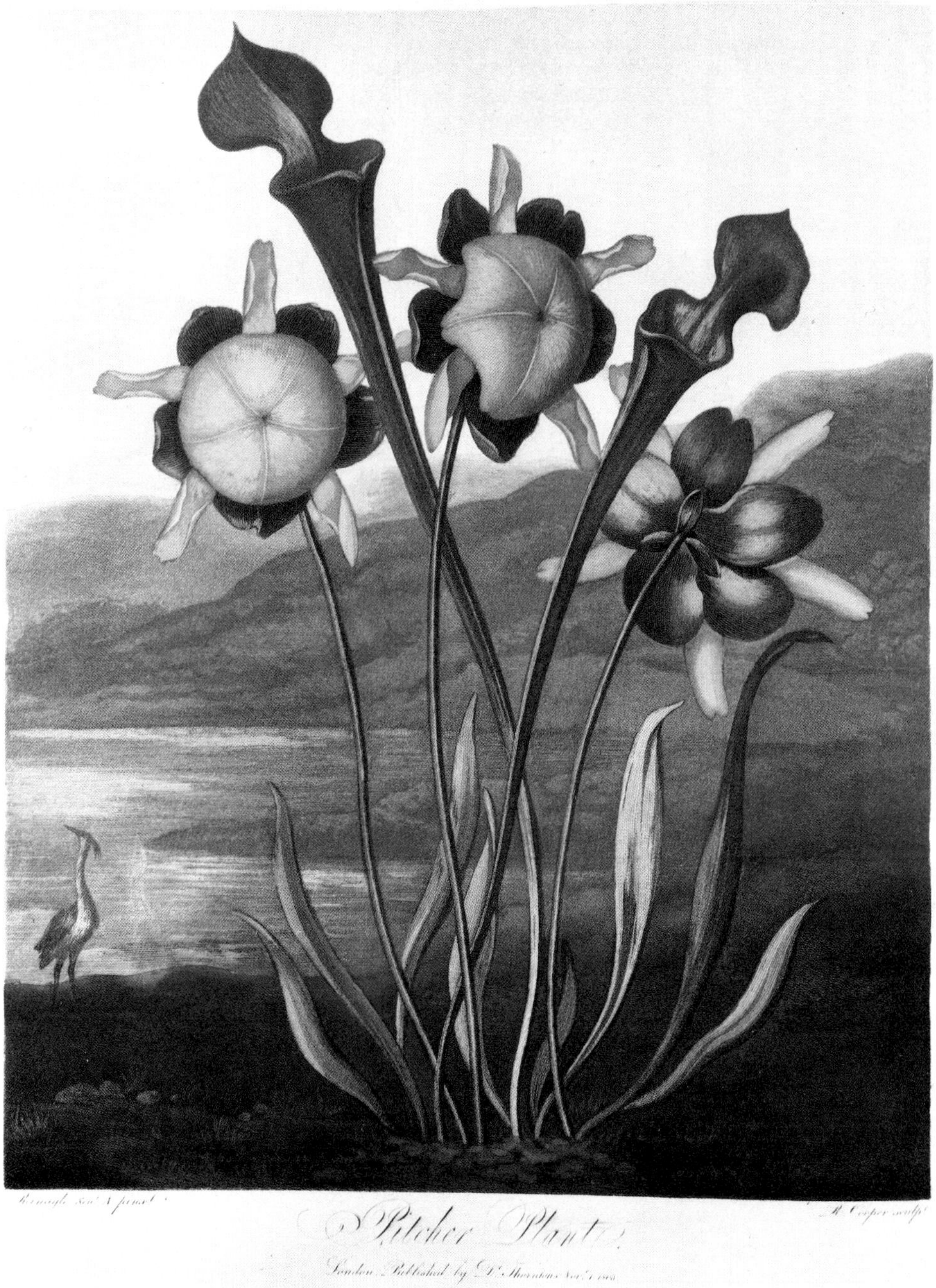

66 ▪ PITCHER PLANT *Sarracenia flava*

"Pitcher plant." Color-printed aquatint engraving, by R. Cooper from the painting by Philip Reinagle. In *New Illustration of the Sexual System of Carolus von Linnaeus . . . The Temple of Flora, or Garden of Nature* by Dr. Robert John Thornton (1798–1807). ▪ Although it was an aesthetic success, this book was not a financial one and Thornton had to struggle to avoid bankruptcy. He blamed his commercial failure on the ruinous taxes that the British public was forced to pay to finance the war with Napoleon; Thornton's addition of an anti-war poem into his text may have mitigated somewhat his displeasure with the government.

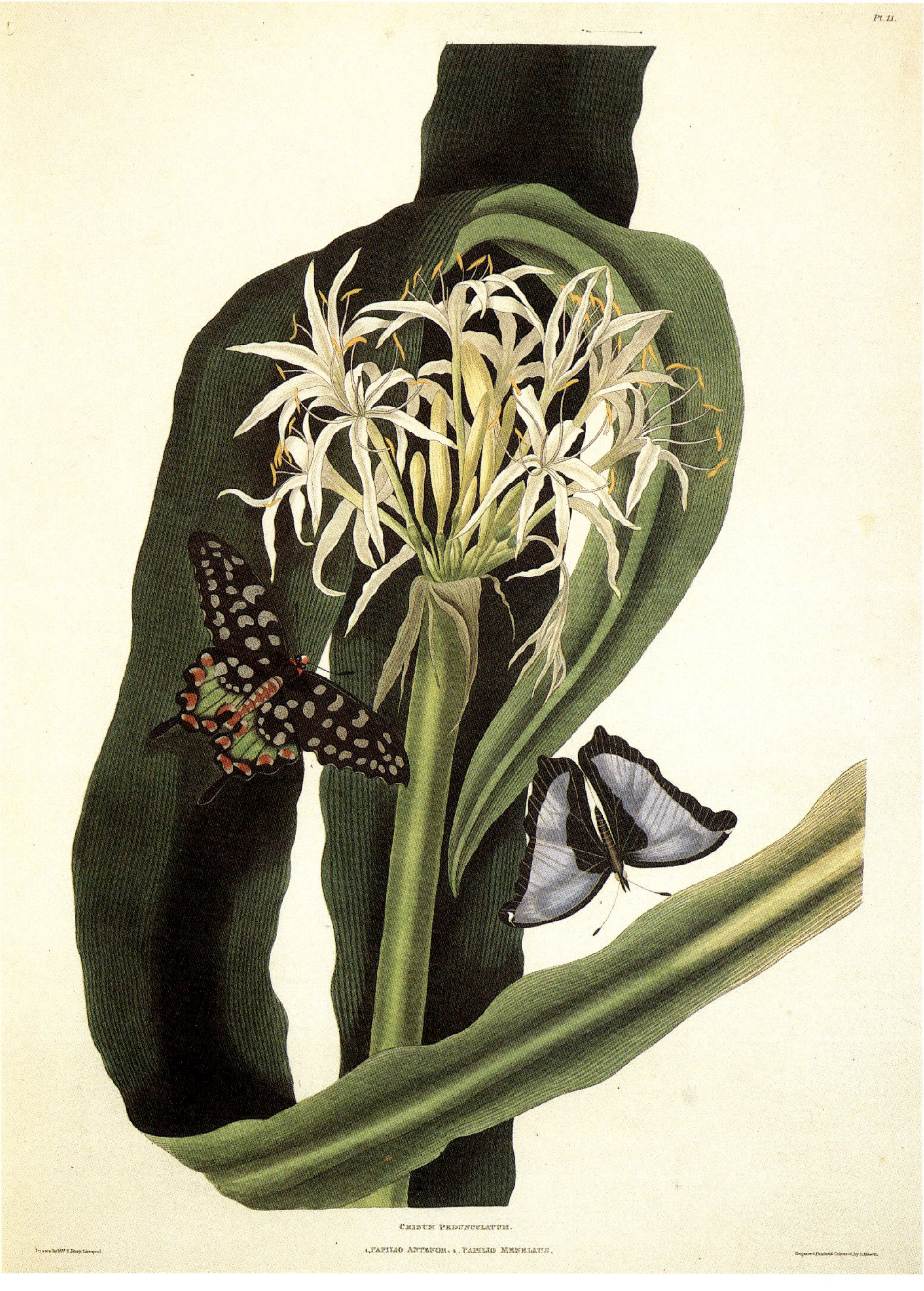

67 ▪ SPIDER LILY *Crinum pedunculatum*

"Crinum pedunculatum." Color-printed and hand-finished aquatint engraving, by Robert Havell from the drawing by Priscilla Susan Bury. In *A Selection of Hexandrian Plants* by Mrs. Edward Bury (1831–34). ▪ This work grew out of the author-artist's "favorite recreation," which as the Preface notes was "to preserve some memorial of the brilliant and fugitive beauties, of a particularly splendid and elegant tribe of plants." The engraver was also employed by J. J. Audubon for his monumental *Birds of America.*

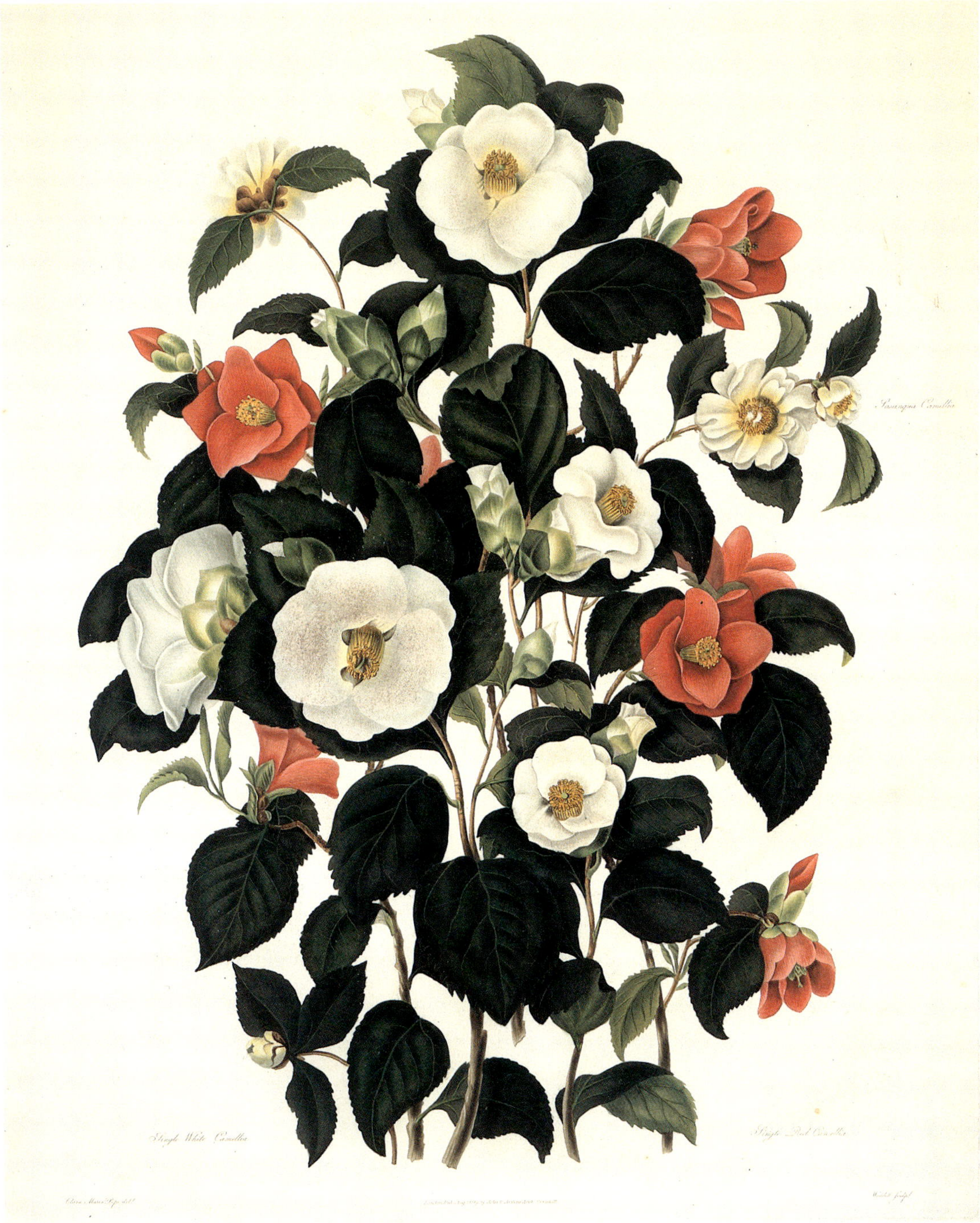

68 ▪ CAMELLIAS *Camellia spp.*

"Single White Camellia; Single Red Camellia; Lasangua Camellia." Hand-colored aquatint engraving, by Weddell from the drawing by Clara Maria Pope. In *A Monograph on the Genus Camellia* by Samuel Curtis (1819). ▪ Curtis, an English nurseryman, was an important figure in English horticultural life of the early nineteenth century through his control of *Curtis's Botanical Magazine;* information in the journal was based on plants Curtis actually grew. The magazine, now known as *The Kew Magazine*, is the oldest continually published horticultural journal.

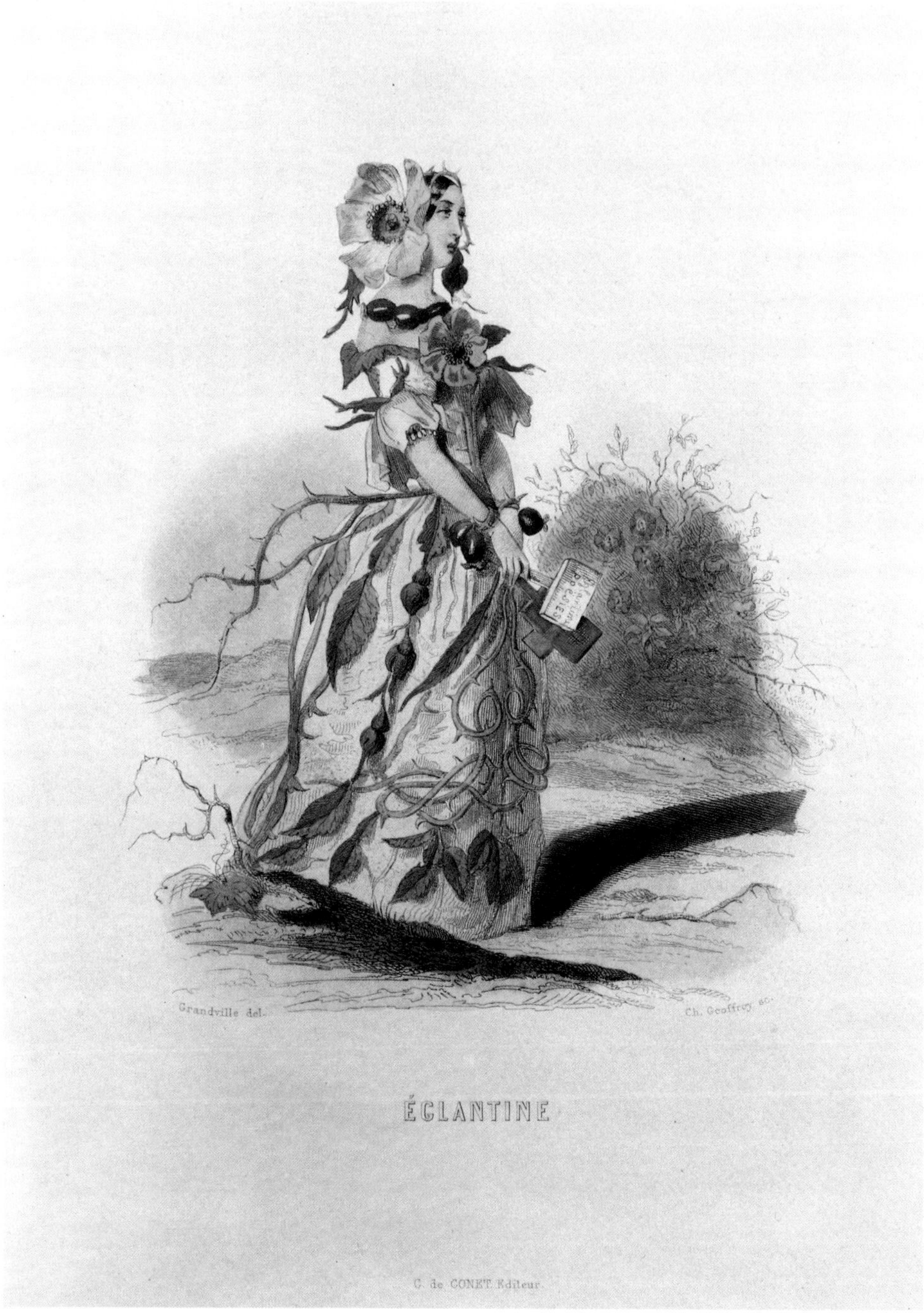

69 ▪ ÉGLANTINE *Rosa eglanteria*

"Églantine." Color-printed engraving, by C. M. Geoffroy from the drawing by J. J. Grandville (Jean Ignace Isidore Gérard). In *Les Fleurs Animées* by J. J. Grandville (1847). ▪ The fascination with floral culture that characterized the early nineteenth century was taken to its logical, that is, bizarre extreme by this French caricaturist. His image here is a play on the name of a character in a French medieval romance, the story of Orson and Valentine, whose wife was Églantine. In this proto-surreal work women are not merely dressed up to represent flowers, but in some sense become flowers or vice versa.

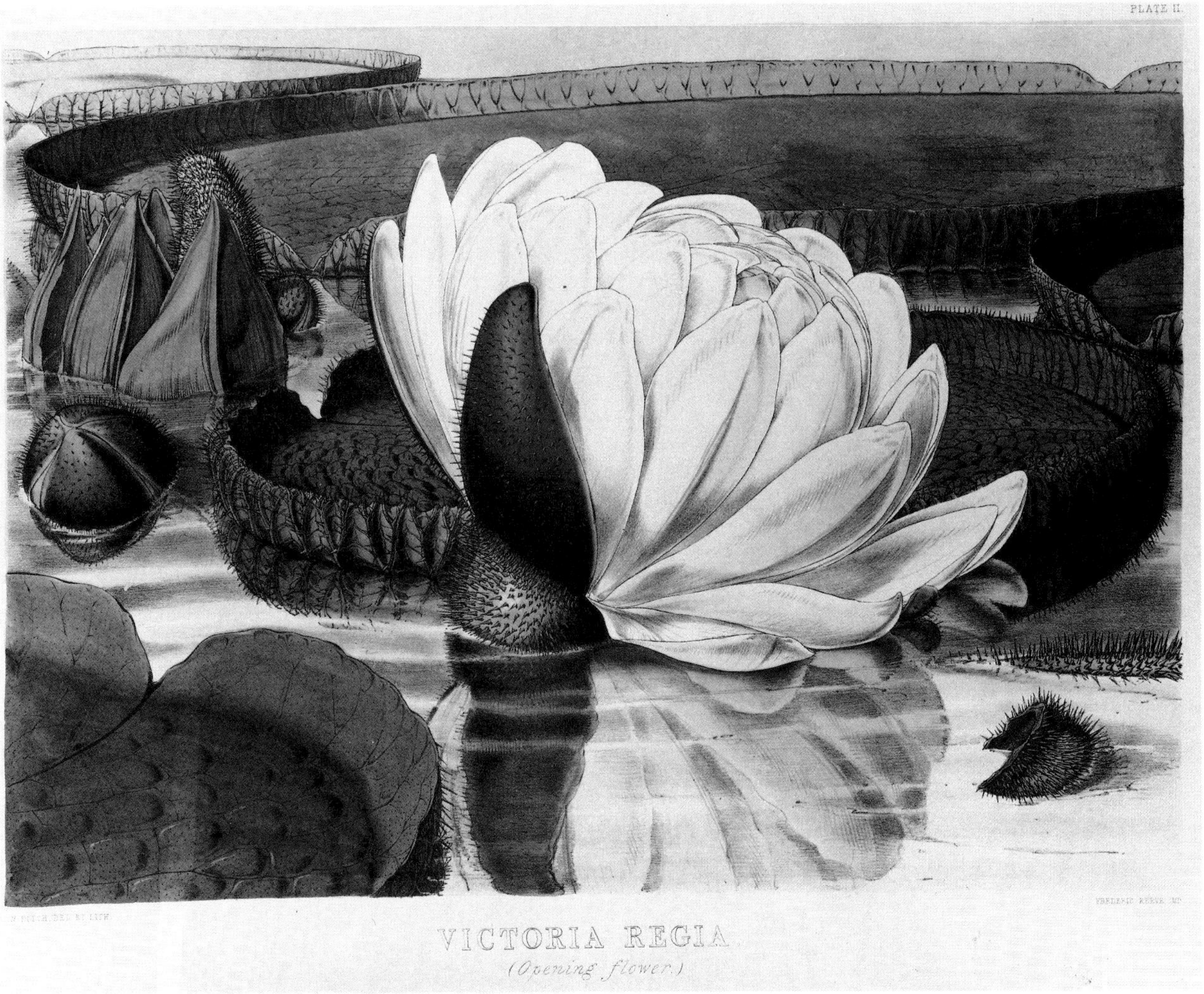

70 ▪ ROYAL WATER LILY *Victoria amazonica*

"Victoria Regia." Color-printed lithograph, by Walter Fitch from his own drawing. In *Victoria Regia: or Illustrations of the Royal Water-Lily* by Sir W. J. Hooker (1851). ▪ This gigantic water lily, native to Central America, was discovered by Europeans in the early nineteenth century; it was later named for Queen Victoria.

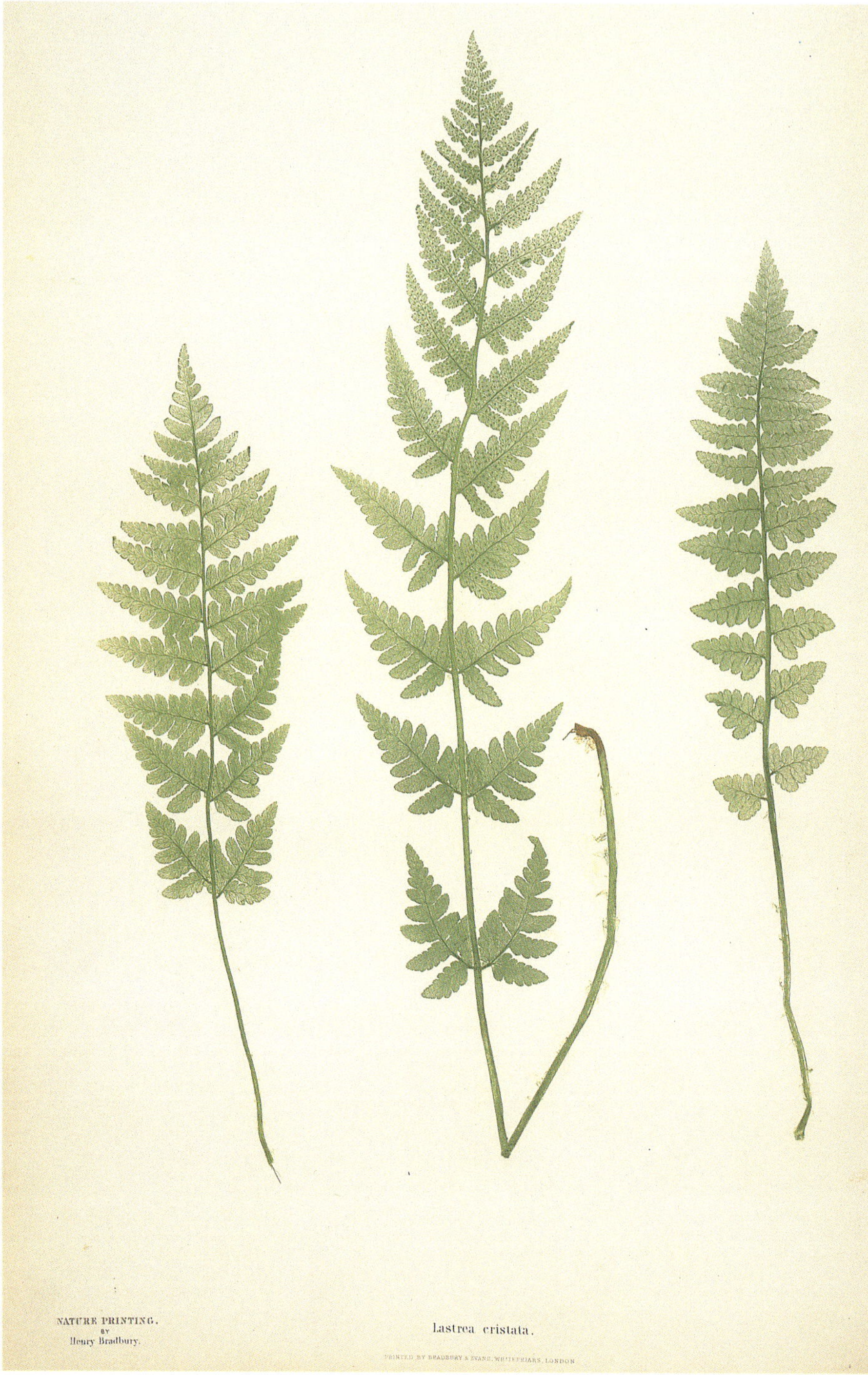

71 ▪ CRESTED BUCKLER FERN *Dryopteris cristata*

"Lastrea cristata." Nature printing, by Henry Bradbury. In *The Ferns of Great Britain and Ireland* by Thomas Moore (1857). ▪ Curator of the Chelsea Physic Garden in London and an active contributor to English gardening magazines, Moore produced this work in response to the fashion for ferns which gripped the English gardening public in the mid-nineteenth century.

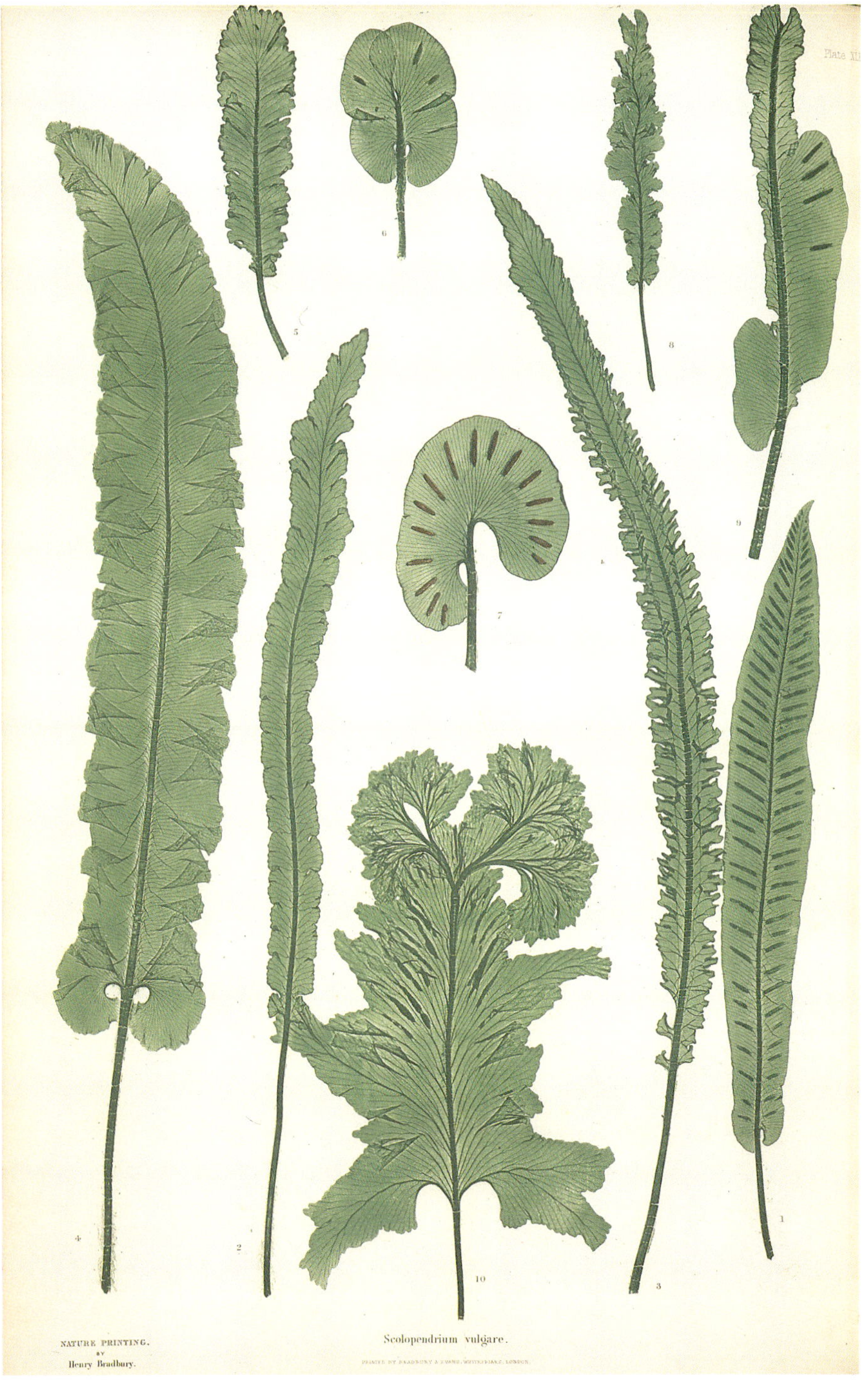

72 ▪ COMMON HART'S TONGUE FERN *Asplenium scolopendrium*

Nature printing, by Henry Bradbury. In *The Ferns of Great Britain and Ireland* by Thomas Moore (1857). ▪ The process by which the plates in this book were reproduced was originally developed by the Imperial Printing Office in Vienna. The ferns were used to produce an intaglio plate which was then printed like an engraving. This provided the "absolute accuracy" that the author required.

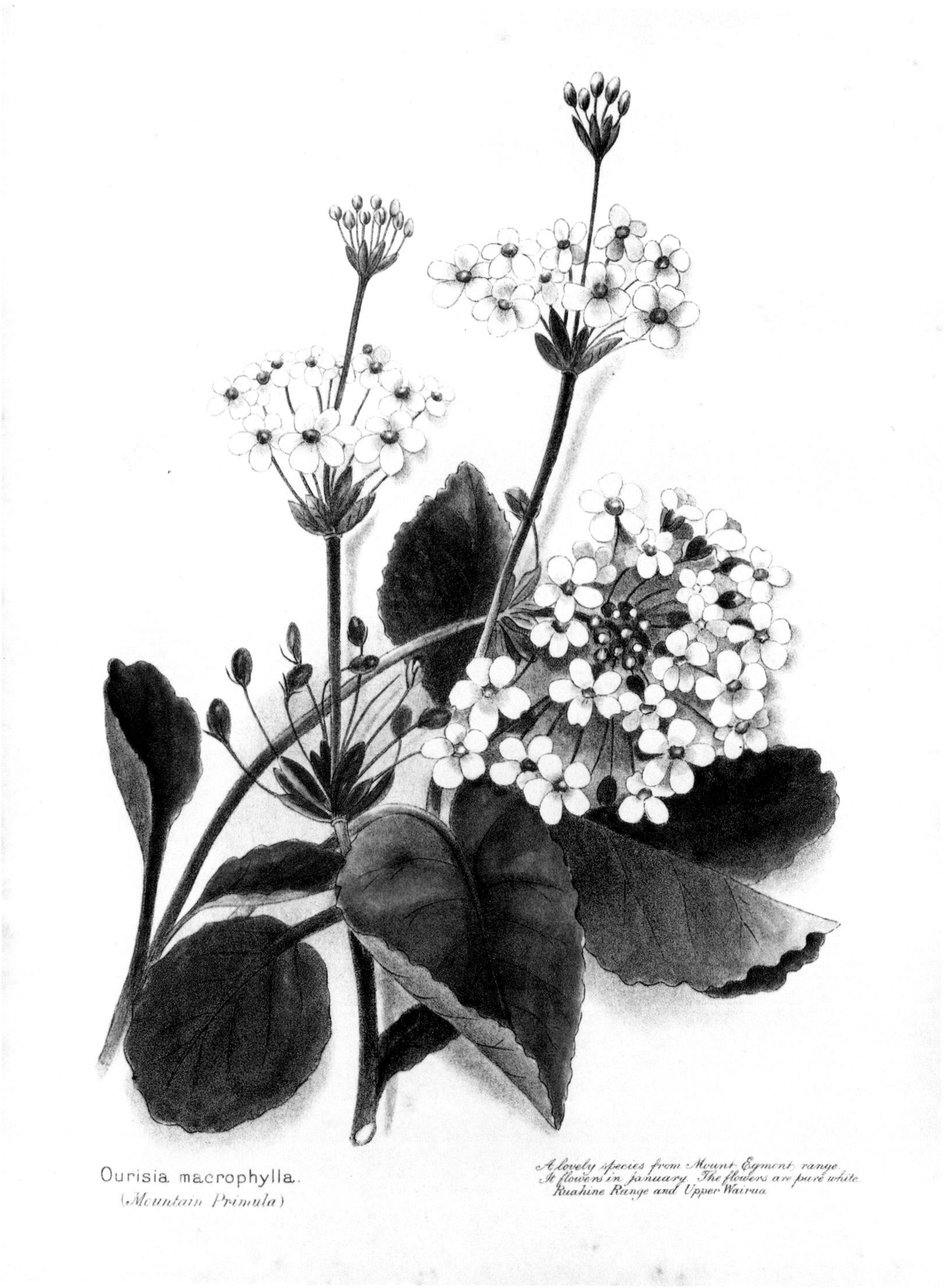

73 ▪ MOUNTAIN PRIMULA *Ourisia macrophylla*

"Ourisia macrophylla." Color-printed lithograph. In *New Zealand Flowers* by Emily C. Harris (1894). ▪ "A lovely species from Mount Egmont range. It flowers in January," Harris noted. Together with her *New Zealand Ferns* and *New Zealand Berries*, published in the same year, the author-artist provides us with a sketch of plant life of New Zealand, reminiscent in its informal style and pioneering spirit of the work of Maria Sibylla Merian.

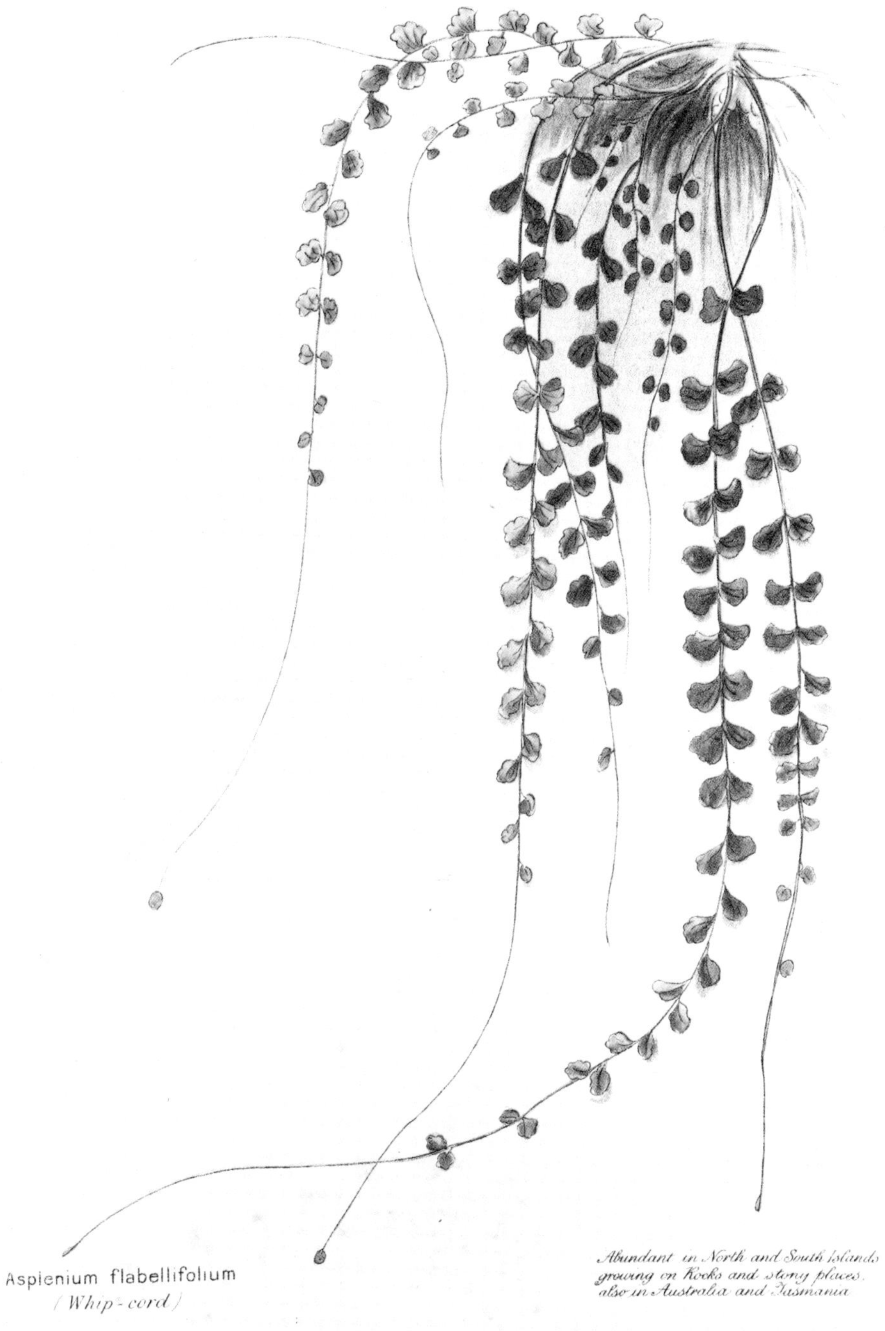

74 ▪ WHIP-CORD FERN *Asplenium flabellifolium*

"Asplenium flabellifolium." Color-printed lithograph. In *New Zealand Ferns* by Emily C. Harris (1894). ▪ Although visited by Captain Cook on one of his voyages in 1769, it was another seventy years before New Zealand was colonized, in 1840. This early work on its ferns is a small picture book of a somewhat amateur bent, with notes about the location of growth providing the only textual accompaniment to the illustrations.

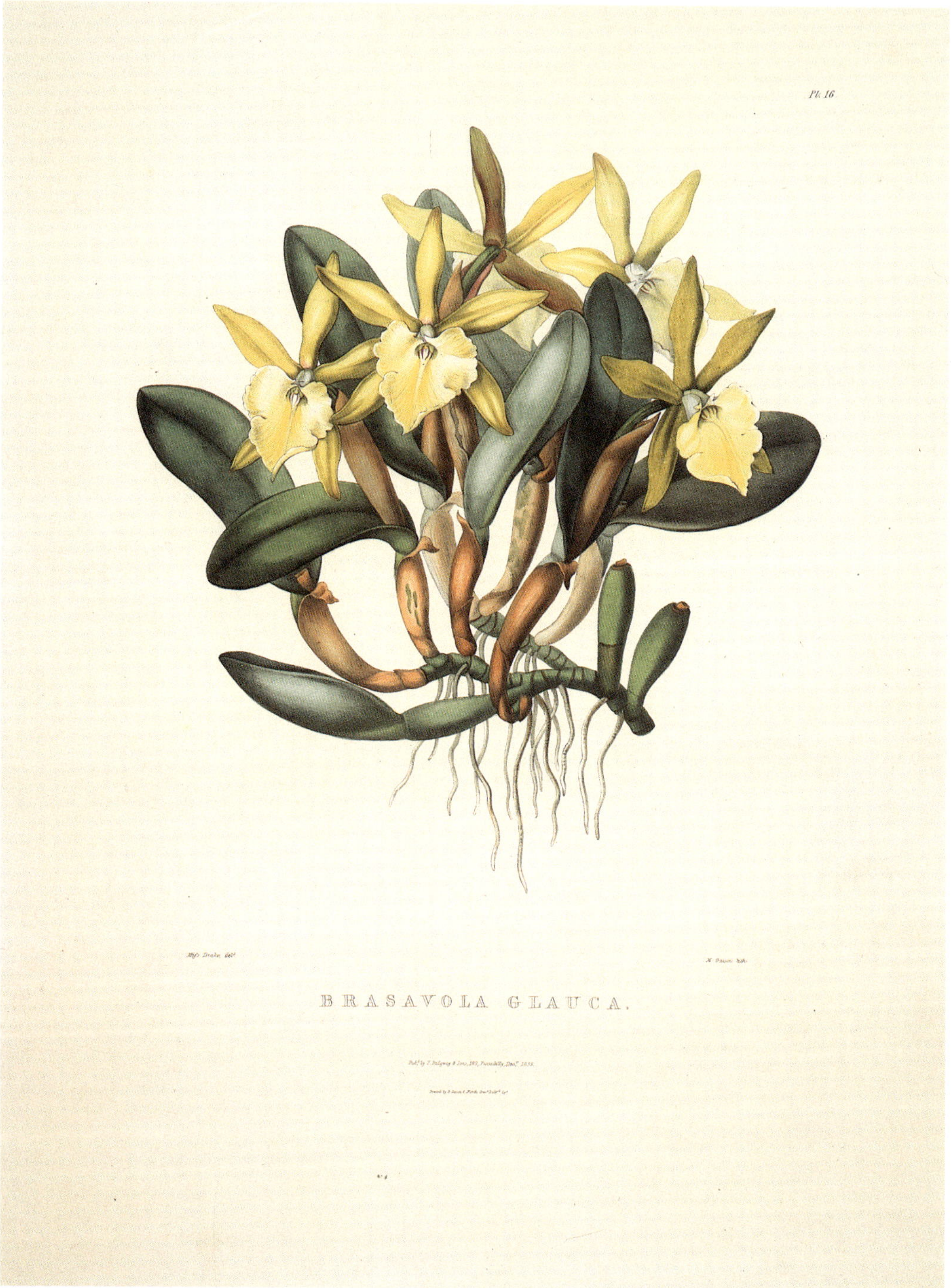

75 ▪ ORCHID *Brassavola glauca*

"Brasavola glauca." Color-printed lithograph, by Maxime Gauci from the drawing by Miss Drake. In *The Orchidaceae of Mexico and Guatemala* by James Bateman (1837–43). ▪ Bateman's was probably the largest book on orchids issued, an elephant folio having forty sizeable hand-colored lithographs by Maxime and Paul Gauci. Bateman, it should be noted, did not collect the specimens for his book.

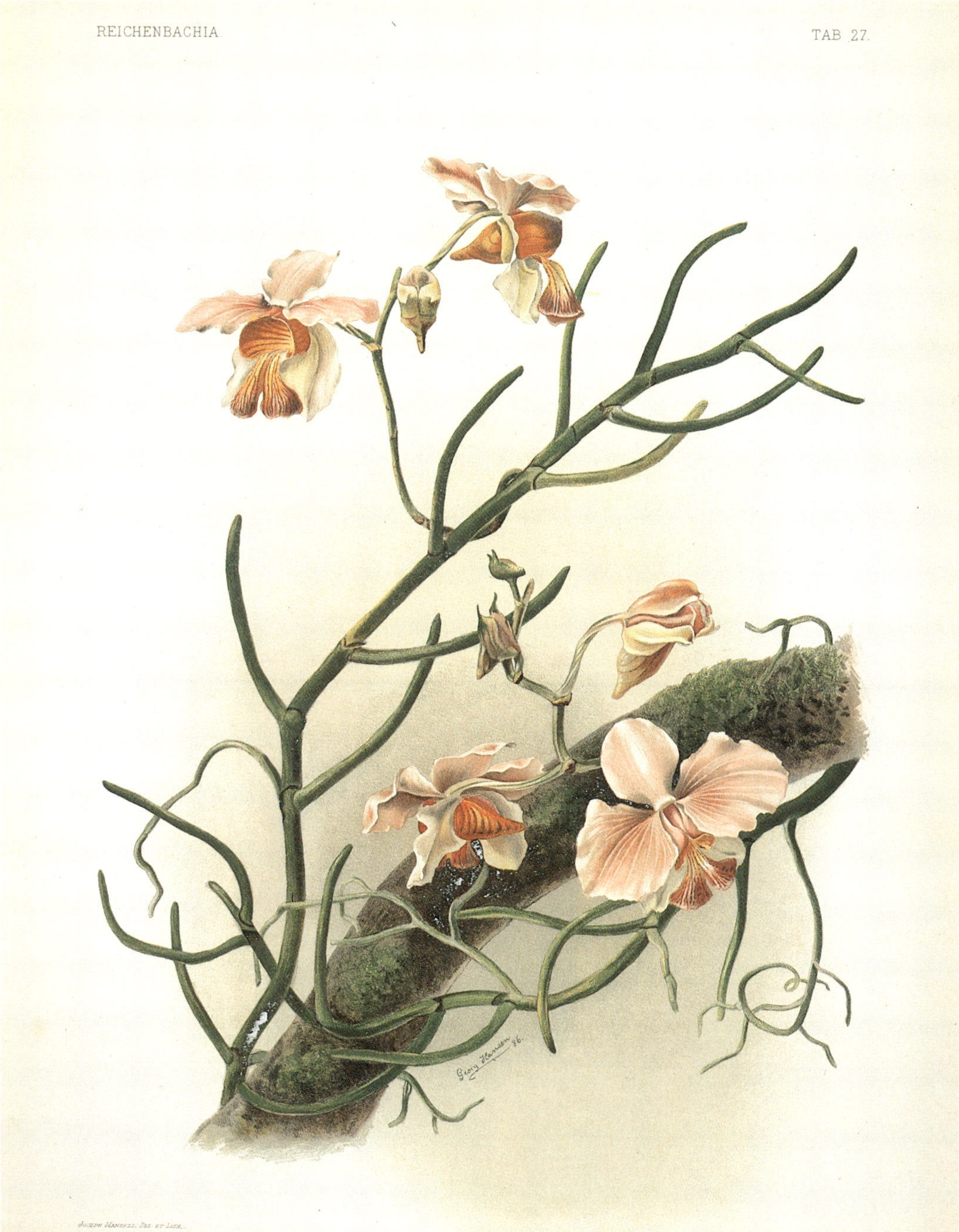

76 ▪ VANDA ORCHID *Vanda teres*

"Vanda Teres." Color-printed lithograph, by Joseph Mansell from his own drawing. In *Reichenbachia, Orchids Illustrated and Described* by Henry F. C. Sander (1886–95). ▪ The author, an important commercial nurseryman, was a grower and seller of orchids. Of this exquisitely portrayed pink orchid, Sander relates that it was introduced into England from Burma in the 1920s.

TREES AND SHRUBS

The history of plant science may be seen, on one level, as humankind's struggle to come to terms with the natural world. On another level, it is the history of a way of looking at the world, literally in the case of the illustrations that have accompanied botanical texts. These two aspects combine exploration and discovery, particularly as documented by the method and substance of the illustration of trees over the last four hundred years. "The Drunken Date Tree" in John Gerard's *Herball* (1597) is a simple woodcut, an outline of a tree. But it is also an evocation of far-off lands, for Gerard gives the tree's name in Arabic and Latin. His interest is not in offering his readers information about the means of growing or cultivating this tree to which the English climate was unsuitable. Rather he is concerned, like most of the herbalists of the sixteenth and seventeenth centuries, with its medicinal properties and uses. ▪ This medicinal concern is less pronounced in the botanical literature of the eighteenth century, but the sense of discovery of unfamiliar plants from distant lands is no less evident. Maria Sibylla Merian had traveled to the South American Dutch colony of Surinam because of her interests in the tropical insects of that region, examples of which she had seen in Amsterdam. The result of her journey was one of the most magnificently illustrated books of the early eighteenth century: *Metamorphosis insectarum Surinamensium* (1705), revised twenty years later and published under the title *Dissertation sur la Génération et les Transformations des Insectes de Surinam* (1726). ▪ Similar to Merian only in his combination of natural history and botanical subject matter in the same image was Mark Catesby, who produced one of the monumental studies of North American natural life in his *The Natural History of Carolina, Florida and the Bahama Islands* (1730–47). Catesby evoked for his English readers a distinctive American region, one which reverberates in the mythology of our own time. ▪ Where Merian was trained as an engraver by her father, lack of funds drove Catesby to make his own drawings and engravings. Altogether different was the case of the French botanist André Michaux and his son, François-André. When it came time to publish their researches on the trees of North America, they turned to Pierre-Joseph Redouté. The greatest of flower painters, Redouté shows a simpler, less baroque side to his talent in André Michaux's *Histoire des Chênes de L'Amérique* (1801) and in François-André Michaux's *Histoire des Arbres Forestiers de L'Amérique Septentrionale* (1810–13). ▪ Joseph Dalton Hooker trekked through the Himalayas in search of Rhododendrons. The published results of his journey, *The Rhododendrons of Sikkim-Himalaya* (1849–51) is a work which, with its glossy lithographic plates, epitomizes mid-Victorian botanical illustration. In his text he reports on the grandeur of the region as well as on the shrubs which were the main object of his concern. He manages to share with the reader that sense of delight and awe that is at the heart of the experience of discovery, qualities which imbue the greatest works of botanical literature.

Van Geneuer. Cap. lxxviiij.

¶ Tgheslacht.

GEneueren sijn tweederleye als Dioscorides scrijft. Daer es een gheslacht dat groot ende hooghe wordt/ende een dat cleyn ende neer blijft/dat hier te lande bekent es.

¶ Tfatloen.

Iuniperus minor. Cleyn Geneuer.

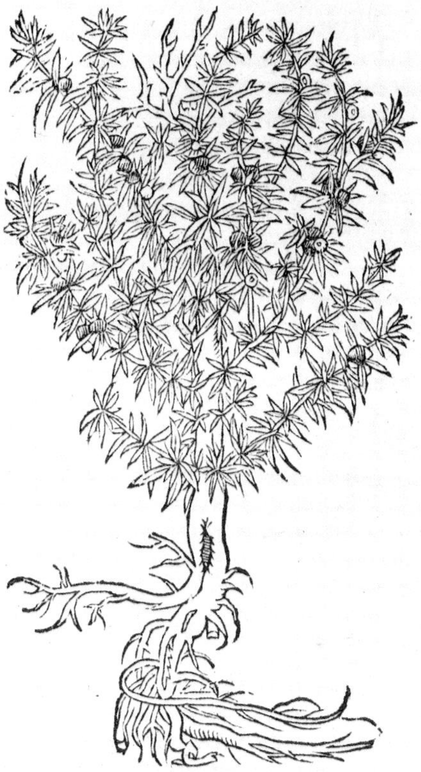

Die cleyne oft ghemeyne Geneuer wast somtijts om hooghe ende wordt grootachtich ghelijck ghemeyne boomkens/maer meest zoo blijft hy neer ende groeyet in maniere van den haghen. Die tacken van desen Geneuer sijn met dunne scorssen bedeckt die lichtelijcken splijten/ende daer wt vloeyet somtijts sonderlinghe in heete lãden tzoomers een gumme oft vettichept ghelijck wieroock oft spiegelherst. Die bladeren sijn cleyn smal hert scerp ende stekẽde/ende wassen rõtsomme die steelkens ende rijskẽs/ sy blyuen altijt gruen ende en vergaẽ tswinters niet. Die vruchten sijn cleyne ronde besiekens/die ierst gruen sijn ende naermaels swert/ende dan zoo sijnse oock goet van rueccke/ende van smaecke suet met een bitterachtich naersmaecxken.

iii iiij Die

77 ▪ SMALL JUNIPER *Juniperus communis*

"Juniperus minor." Woodcut. In *Cruydeboeck* by Rembert Dodoens (1552–54) ▪ Dodoens, a Flemish physician, was interested in investigatory classification systems other than those of the Ancients.

Areca, ſiue Faufel.
The drunken Date tree.

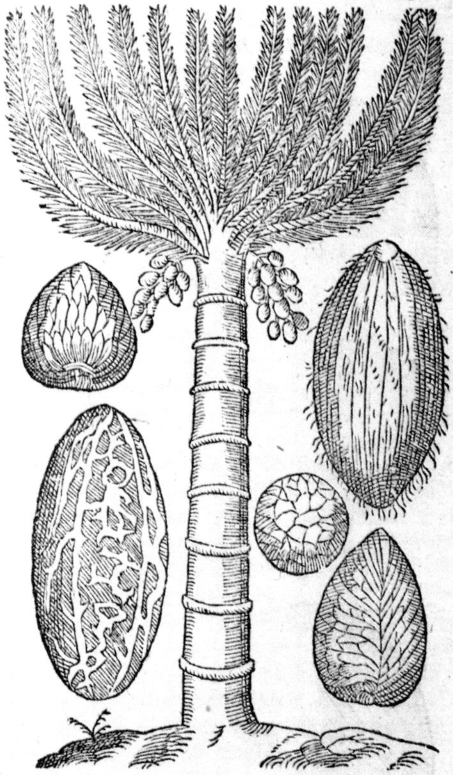

The place, time and names.

This Date tree which the Arabians call *Faufel*, that is by interpretation *Auellana Indica*, the Indian Nut or Filberd: *Auicen* and *Serapio* call it *Filfel* and *Fufel*. It groweth in the Eaſt Indies in diuers and ſundrie places, as in Malauar, where vulgarly it is called *Pac*, and of the nobles and gentlemen *Areca*, which name is vſed amongſt the Portingales which dwell in thoſe Indies; in Guzarate and Decan it is called *Cupare*, in Zeilan *Poaz*: in Malaca *Pinan*: in Cochin *Chacani*. In Engliſh the drunken Date tree, which name we haue coyned from his qualitie, bicauſe the fruite doth make thoſe drunke that eate thereof.

The temperature.

It is cold and drie in the ſecond degree.

The vertues.

A The fruit of *Areca* before it be ripe, is reckoned amongſt the ſtupefactiue or aſtoniſhing medicines; for whoſoeuer eateth thereof waxeth drunke, bicauſe it doth exceedingly amaze and aſtoniſh the ſenſes.

B When the Indians are vexed with ſome intolerable ache or paine, or muſt of neceſſitie endure ſome great torment or torture, then do they take of this fruite, whereby the rigor of that paine (which otherwiſe they ſhould feele) is very much mitigated.

C The iuice of the fruit of *Areca* doth ſtrengthen the gums, faſten the teeth, comfort the ſtomacke, ſtay vomiting, and looſeneſſe of the belly; it doth alſo purge the bodie from congealed or clotted blood gathered within the ſame.

78 ▪ BETEL NUT PALM *Areca catechu*

"The drunken Date tree." Woodcut. In *The Herball* by John Gerard (1597). ▪ Leaning heavily on the work of Dodoens, Gerard, an apothecary and botanist, brings a vibrant Elizabethan style to his descriptions, noting of this tree, for example, that its "fruit is reckoned among the stupefactive or astonishing medicines" and thus mitigates pain. He maintained his own garden in Holborn in London, and was in charge of the London gardens of William Cecil, Lord Burghley. Part of the value in Gerard's book was his references to specific locations where plants could be found, especially in England.

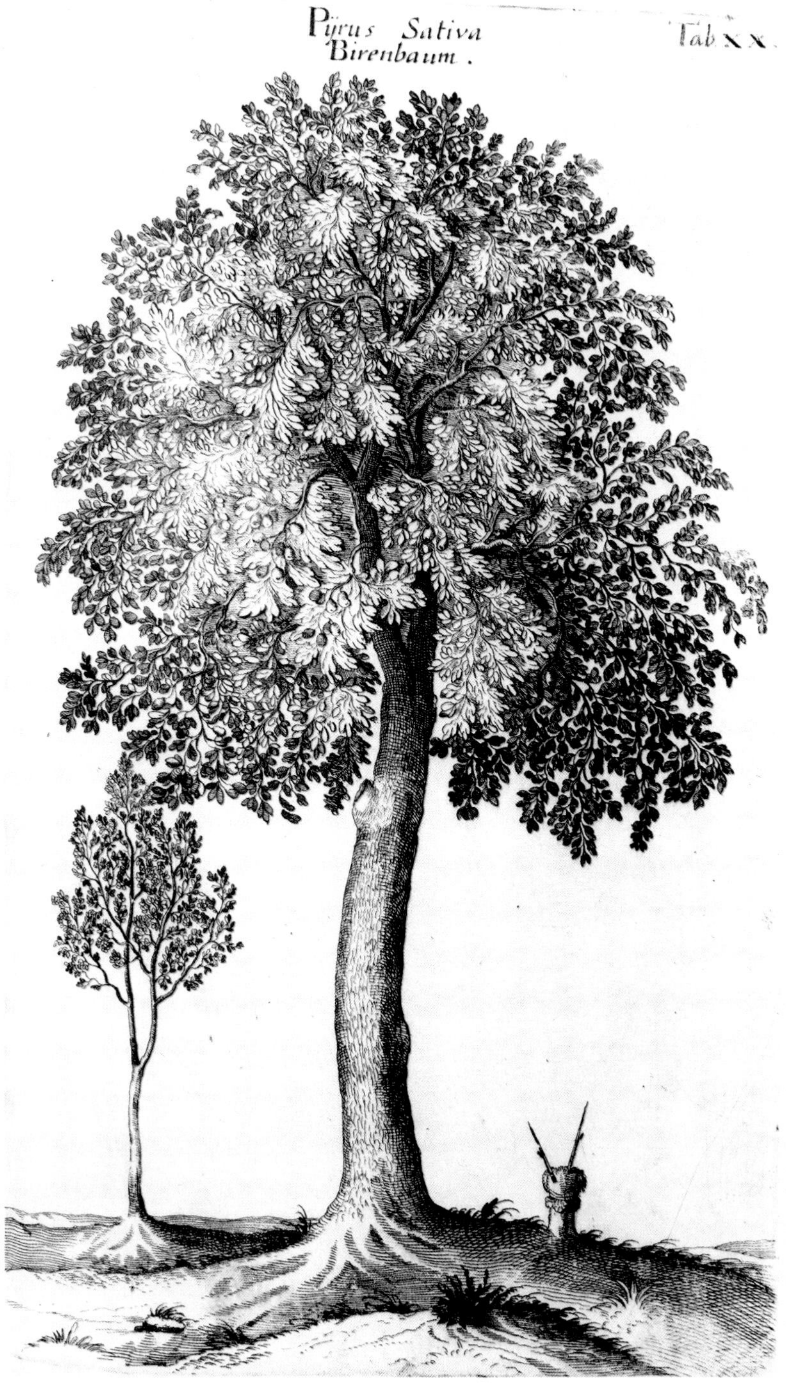

79 ▪ PEAR TREE *Pyrus communis*

"Pÿrus Sativa." Engraving. In *Dendographias* by John Jonston (1662). ▪ This work on trees and their fruit and nuts owes much to the research of the sixteenth- and seventeenth-century herbalists and botanists. Like many botanical works of the period, however, it also leans heavily on the authors of classical antiquity, with references to Dioscorides, Pliny, and Hippocrates throughout the text.

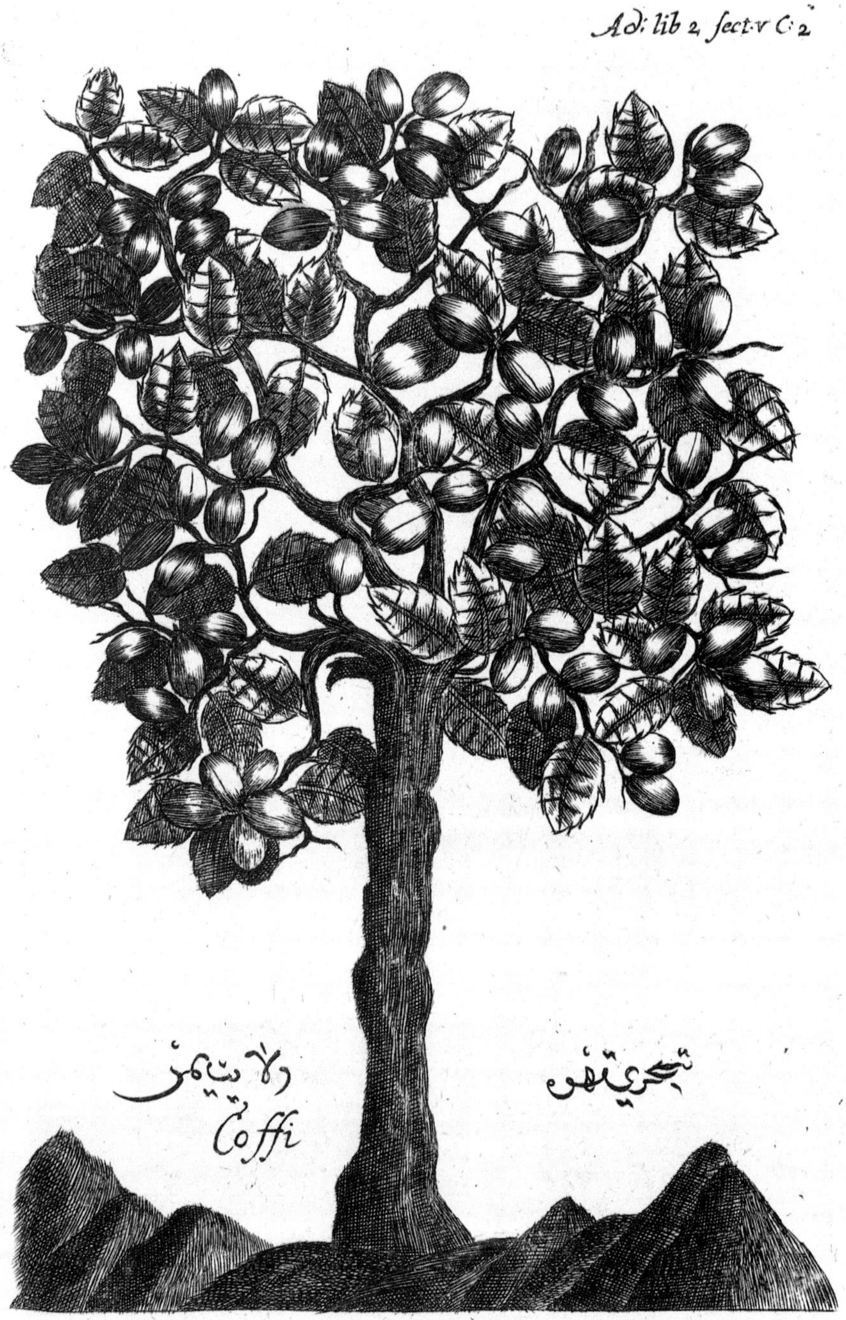

80 ▪ COFFEE *Coffea arabica*

Engraving. In *Historia Simplicium Reformata* by Michael Bernard Valentini (1716). ▪ When the Turks waged battle unsuccessfully in Vienna in 1683, coffee was a part of the captured booty. Tradition holds that this "spoil of war" introduced all Europe to the pleasures of drinking coffee. Valentini, in addition to describing the plant, relates the method for preparing the drink by grinding the beans into a powder and adding boiling water.

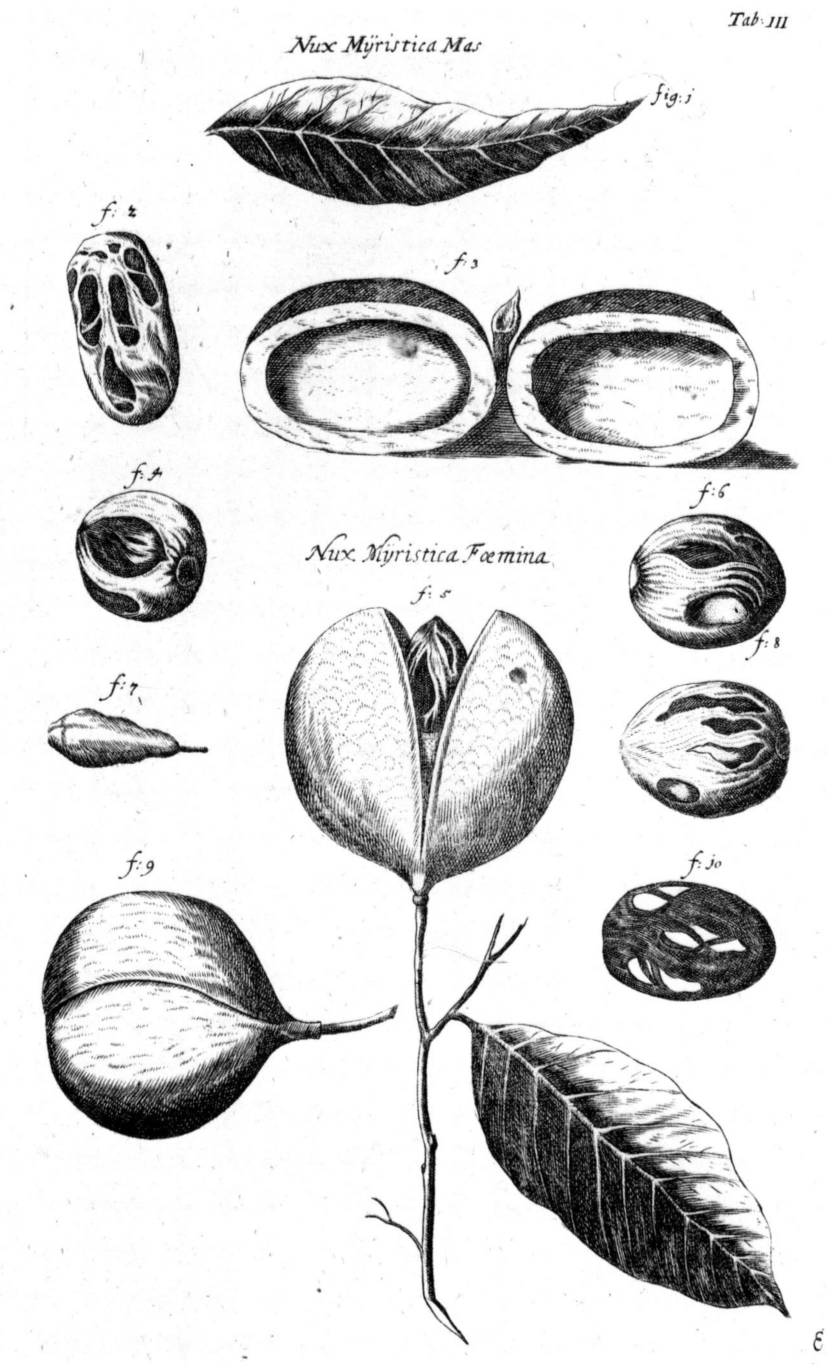

81 ▪ NUTMEG AND MACE *Myristica fragrans*

"Nux Mÿristica Mas; Nux Mÿristica Fœmina." Engraving. In *Historia Simplicium Reformata* by Michael Bernard Valentini (1716). ▪ The interest in trading spices between Europe and the Near and Far East was behind a good deal of the motivation for early voyages by European explorers. This fascination with different worlds is reflected in this work where Valentini provides the Indian and Javan nomenclature for spices as well as the European names. The coating over the nutmeg is known as mace.

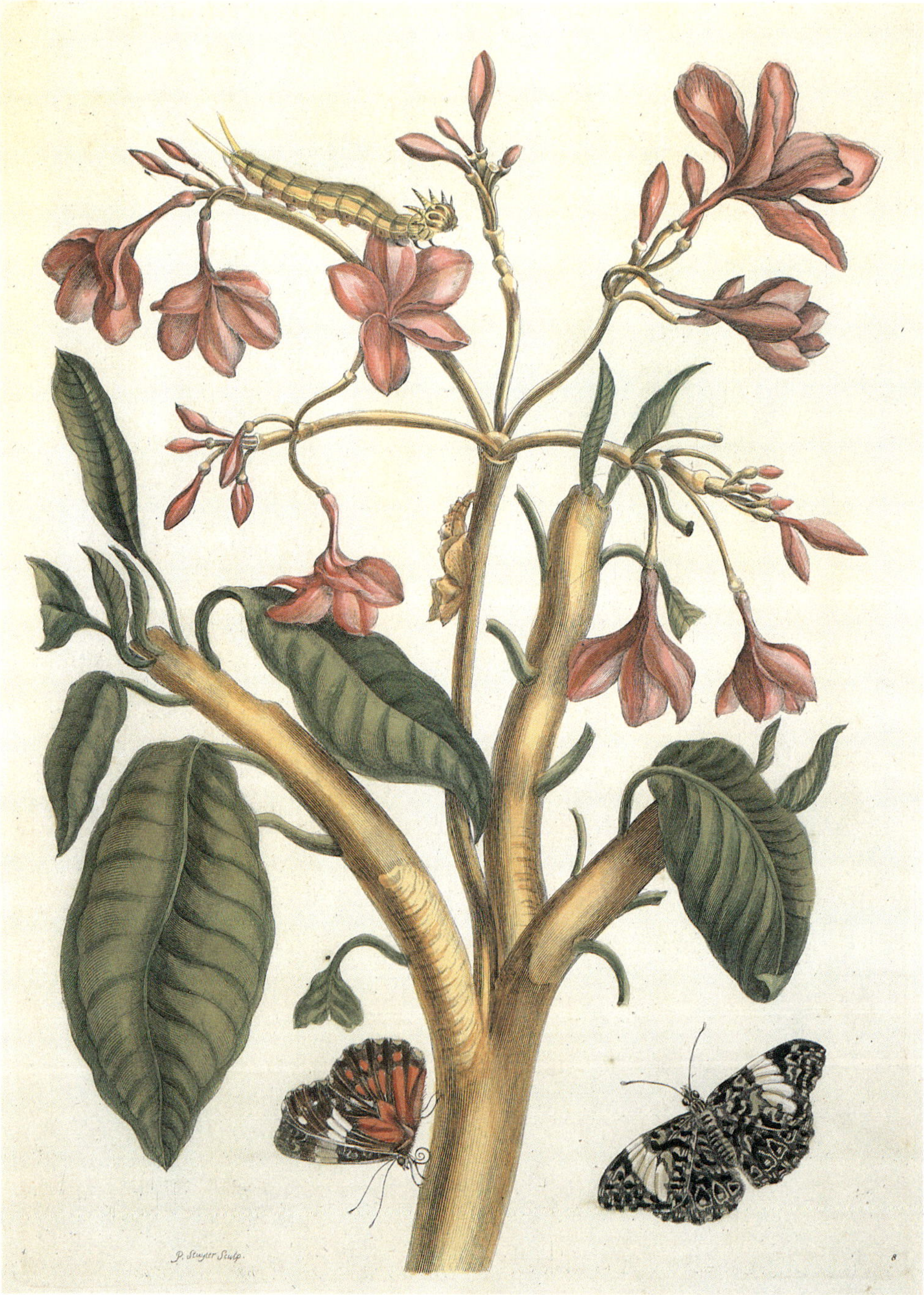

82 ▪ RED JASMINE *Plumeria rubra*

Hand-colored engraving, by P. Sluyter from the drawing by Maria Sibylla Merian. In *Dissertation Sur La Génération et Les Transformations des Insectes de Surinam* by Maria Sibylla Merian (1726). ▪ In her preface to this work Merian notes that she made her drawings for the pleasure of others. Nonetheless, her interest in the insects of Surinam was a serious one, for as oppressive as was the climate, she assiduously studied while there, taking pains to paint the insects against their host plants.

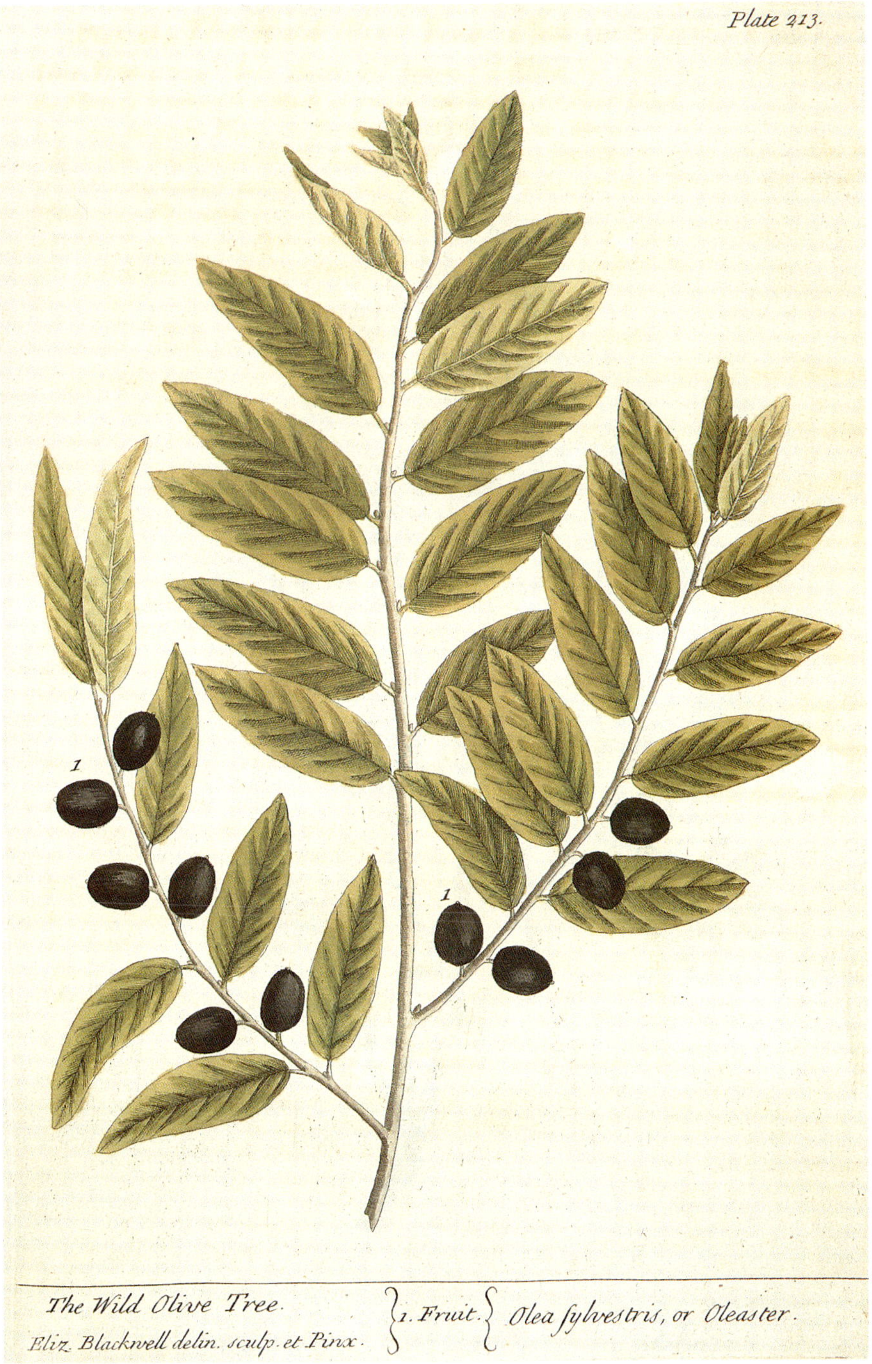

83 ▪ WILD OLIVE TREE *Olea europaea*

"The Wild Olive Tree." Hand-colored engraving, by Elizabeth Blackwell from her own drawing. In *A Curious Herbal Containing 500 Cuts, of the Most Useful Plants Which Are Now Used in the Practice of Physick* by Elizabeth Blackwell (1737–39). ▪ Women were frequently active in the production of drawings and engravings for botanical works in the eighteenth century. Mrs. Blackwell was one of the few to receive full credit for both text and image. She found the subjects for her drawings in London in the Chelsea Physic Garden.

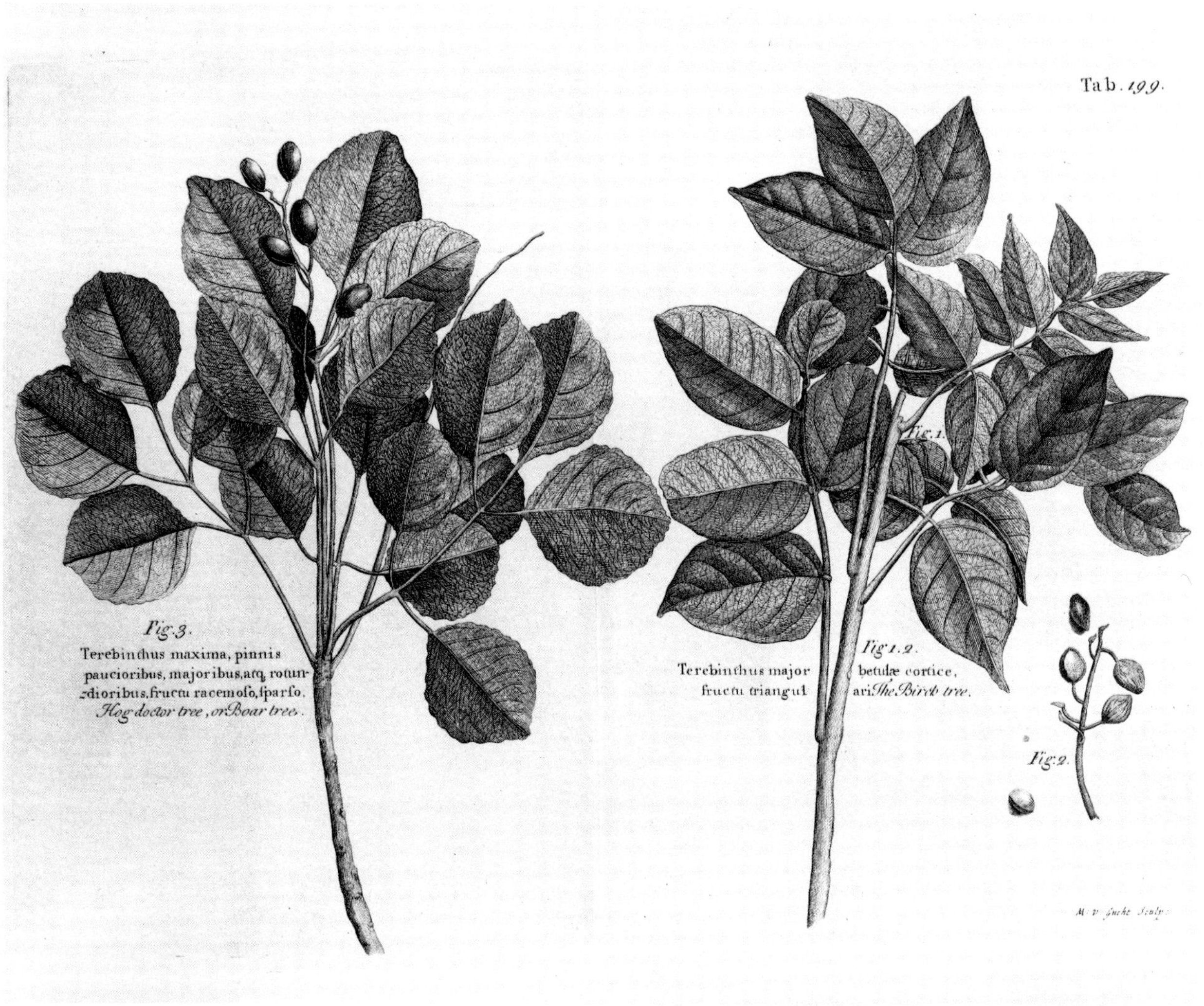

84 ▪ HOG DOCTOR TREE *Rhus metopium* ▪ BIRCH TREE *Bursera gummifera*

"Hog doctor tree, or Boar tree; The Birch Tree." Engraving, by M. van der Gucht from the drawing by E. Kickius. In *A Voyage to the Islands. . . .* by Sir Hans Sloane (1707–25). ▪ The Hog Doctor tree, Sir Hans reports, takes its name from the local belief "that wild Hogs when wounded, by natural instinct come to this tree, where, by rubbing its balsam on their wounds, they are cured." The Birch tree seems to be less useful to suffering swine, although Sir Hans does note that its trunk may sometimes be as thick as a hogshead.

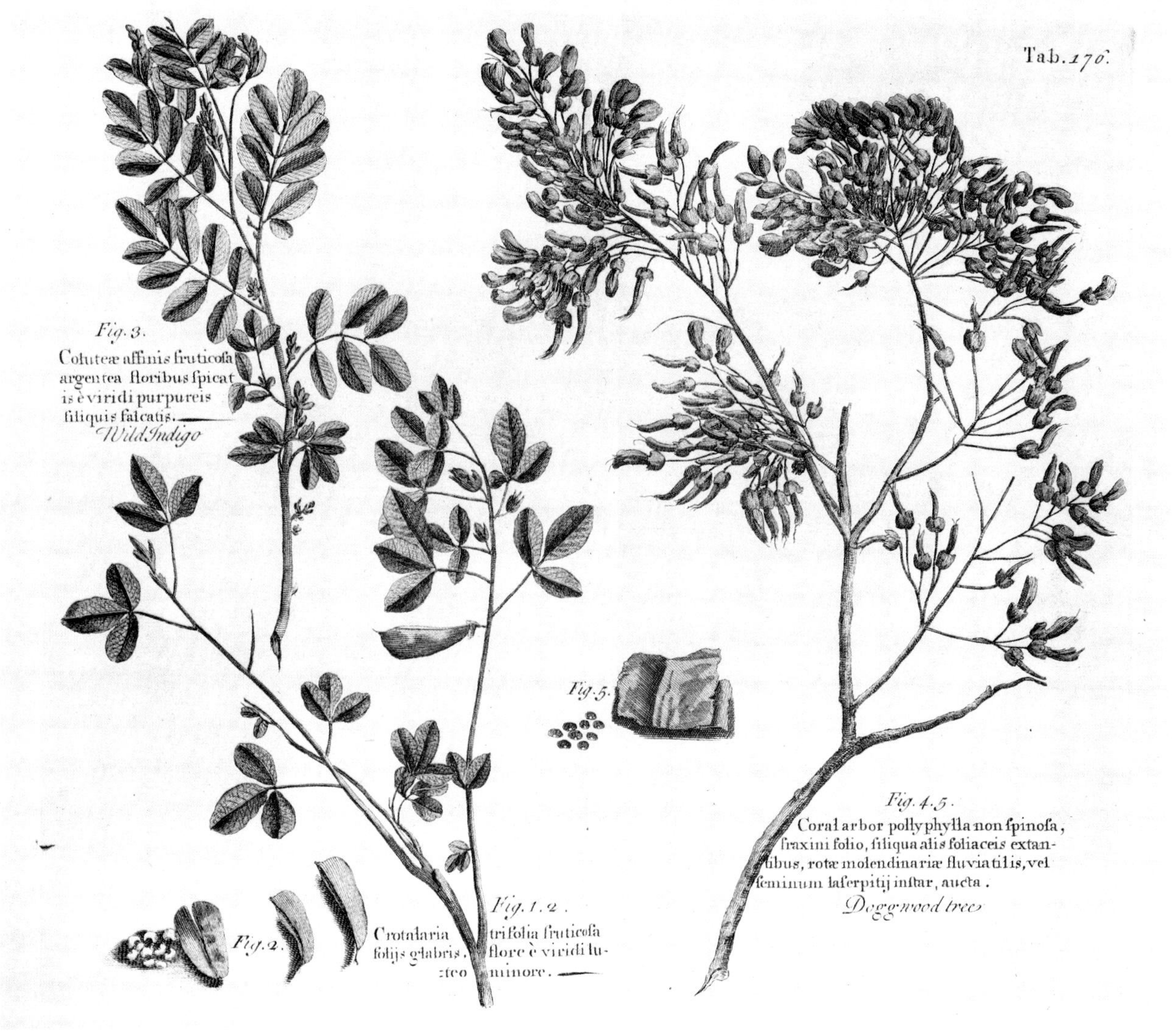

85 ▪ INDIGO *Indigofera tinctoria* ▪ DOGWOOD *Piscidia piscipula*

"Wild Indigo; Doggwood tree." Engraving, by M. van der Gucht from the drawing by E. Kickius. In *A Voyage to the Islands. . . .* by Sir Hans Sloane (1707–25). ▪ The bark of the Dogwood is helpful in fishing according to the author; if a piece of it is flattened out and tossed into still water it "intoxicates" the fish therein "for some time, they turning their bellies up, and coming above water." Sloane's *Voyage* was the earliest published representation of Jamaican flora and fauna; Sir Hans himself collected the specimens upon which the illustrations were based.

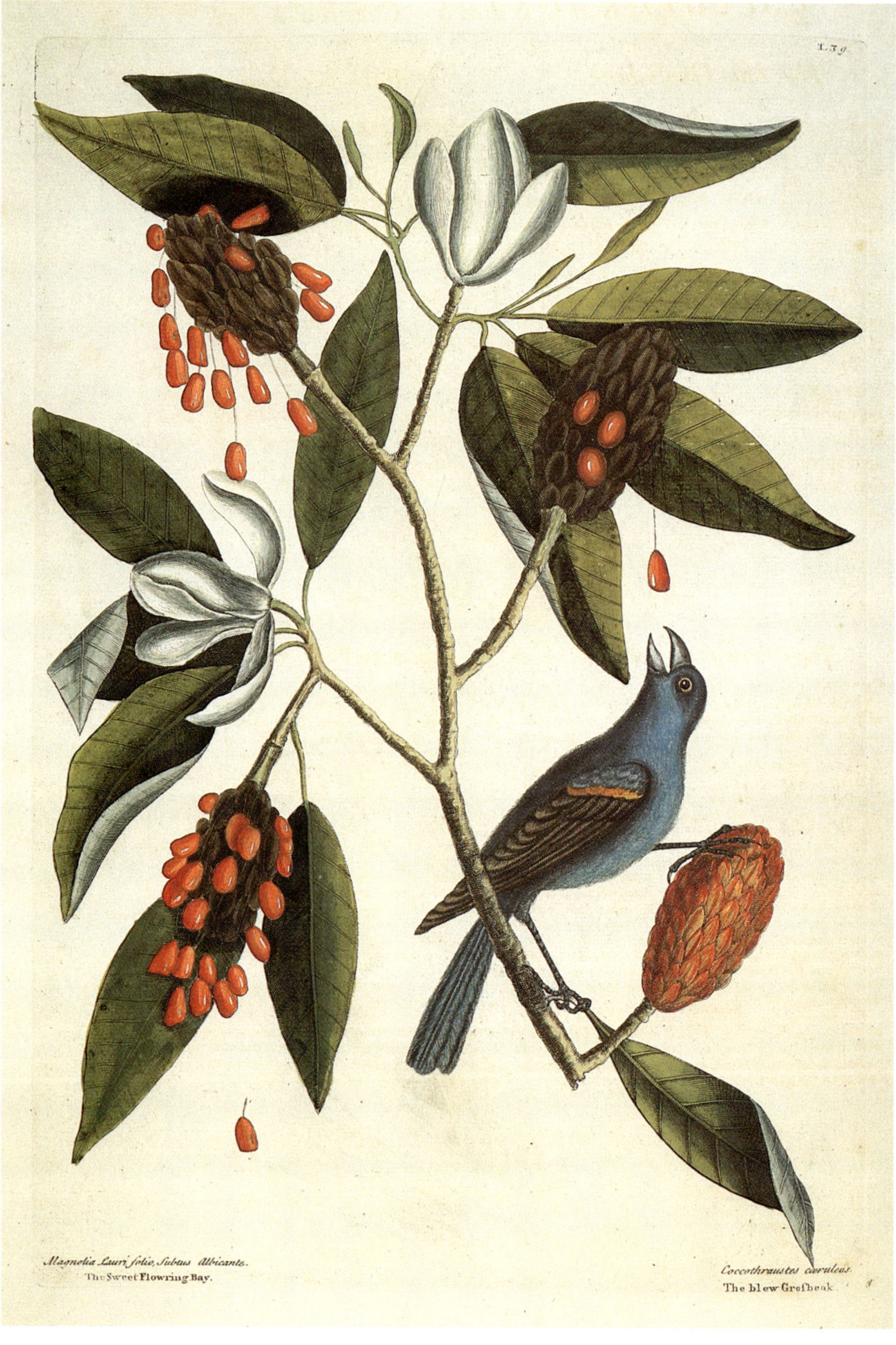

86 ▪ SWEET FLOWERING BAY TREE *Magnolia virginiana*

"The Sweet Flowring Bay." Hand-colored engraving, by Mark Catesby from his own drawing. In *The Natural History of Carolina, Florida and the Bahama Islands. . . .* by Mark Catesby (2d ed., 1754). ▪ The author-artist was rather apologetic about his style of illustration, noting that "things done in a flat, though exact manner, may serve the purpose of natural history better . . . than in a more bold and painter-like way." Catesby's modesty was genuine: lacking the necessary funds to pay an engraver, he studied etching and so prepared all but three plates himself.

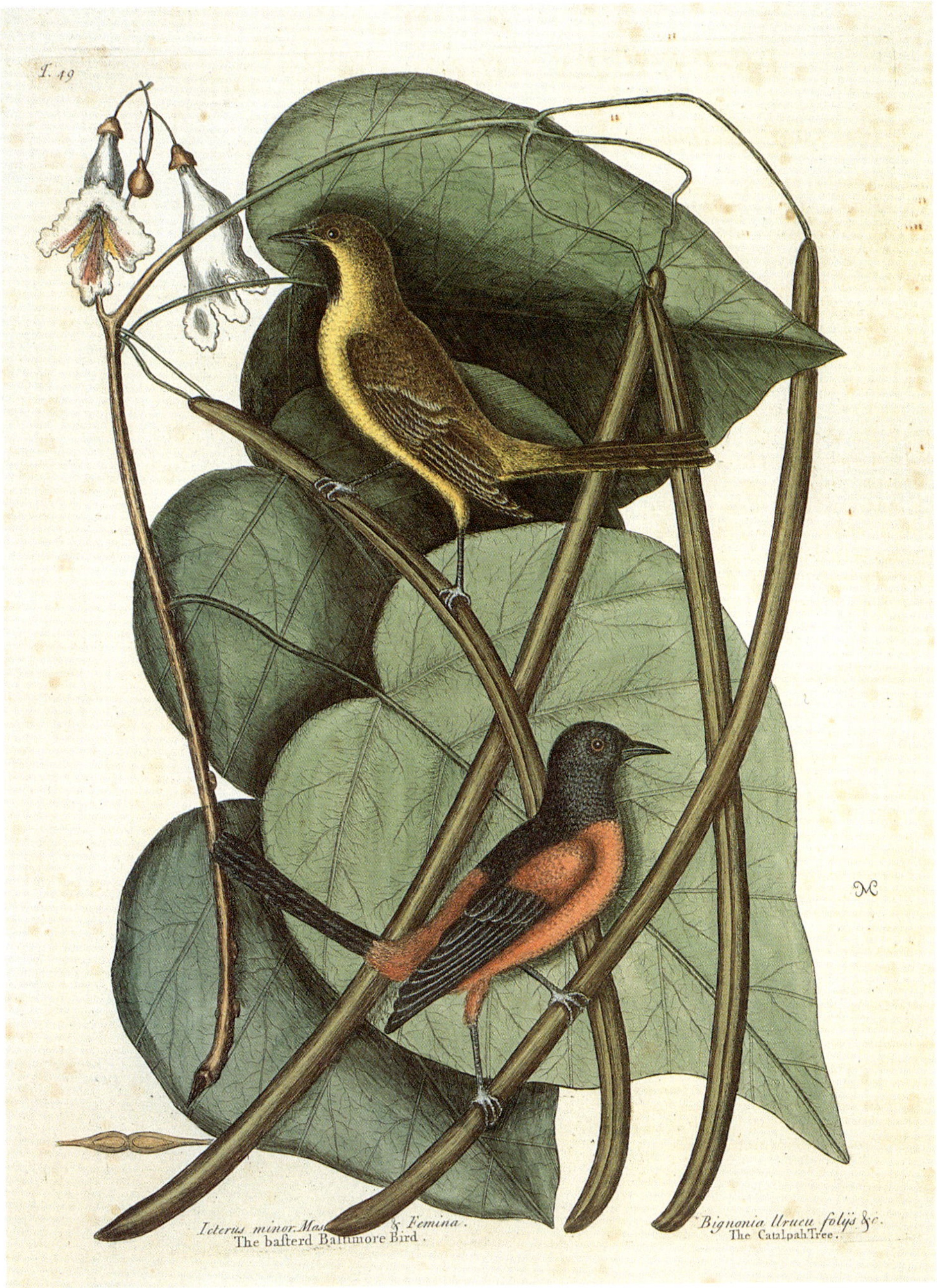

87 ▪ CATALPA TREE *Catalpa bignonioides*

"The Catalpah Tree." Hand-colored engraving, by Mark Catesby from his own drawing. In *The Natural History of Carolina, Florida and the Bahama Islands. . . .* by Mark Catesby (2d ed., 1754). ▪ Catesby's work on American plant and animal life was based on two visits he made to the southern English colonies in 1712 to 1719 and 1722 to 1726. His use of posing birds against a background was botanically correct, anticipating Audubon's technique by almost a century. But it was also due to limitations of space that Catesby merged bird and plant.

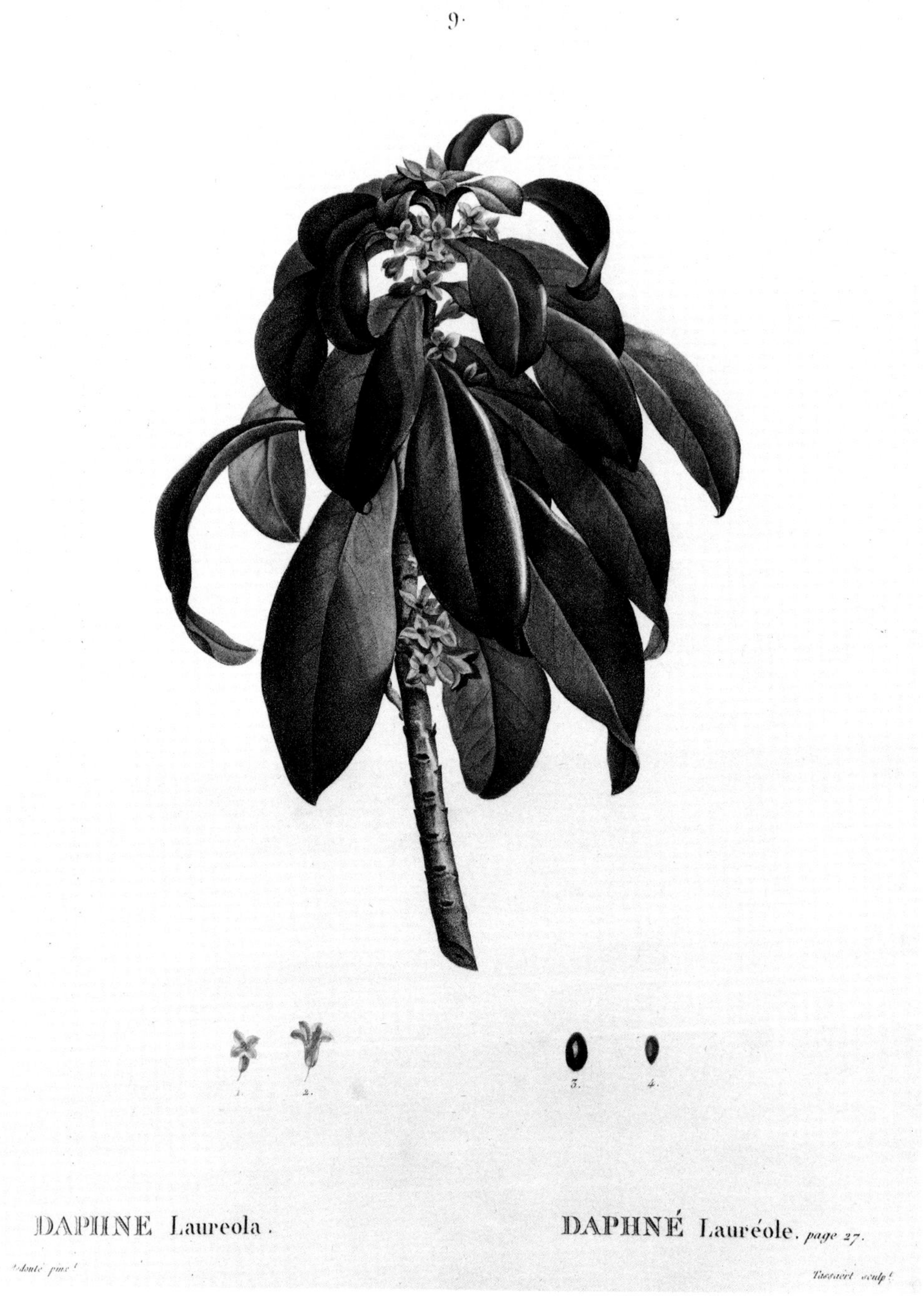

88 ▪ DAPHNE *Daphne laureola*

"Daphne Laureola." Color-printed and hand-finished engraving, by Tassaert from the drawing by Pierre-Joseph Redouté. In *Traité Des Arbres et Arbustes Que L'On Cultive en France en Pleine Terre* by Henri Louis Duhamel du Monceau (1800–19). ▪ This is one of the most beautiful as well as one of the most scientifically important books published on trees and shrubs in the nineteenth century. The comprehensiveness of its text is suggested by the fact that some twenty-three varieties of Daphne alone are described. Tassaert was also the principal engraver for Redouté's *Les Liliacées.*

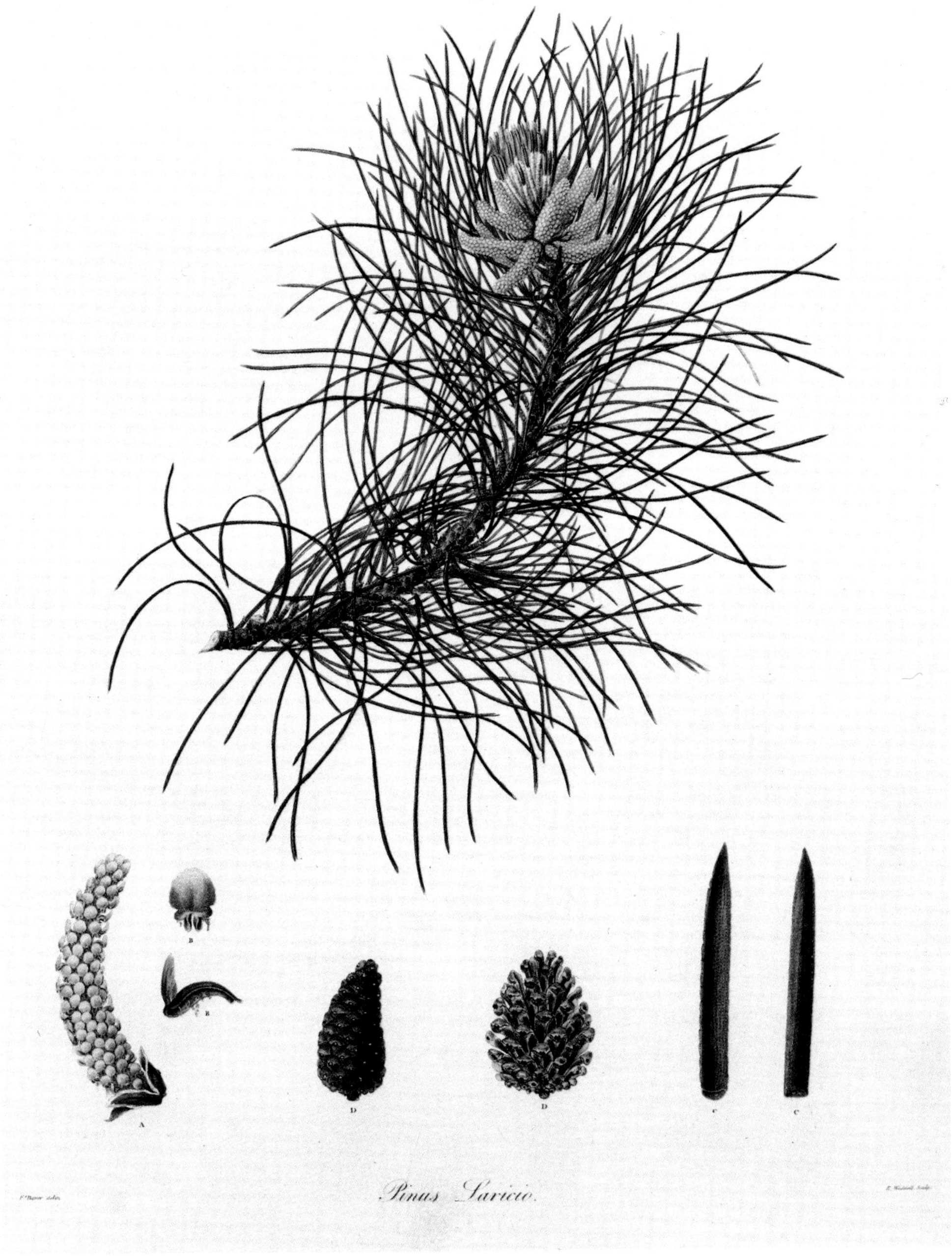

89 ▪ CORSICAN PINE *Pinus nigra*

"Pinus Laricio." Color-printed engraving, by E. Weddell from the drawing by Ferdinand Bauer. In *A Description of the Genus Pinus* by Aylmer Bourke Lambert (1828–37). ▪ First published in 1803–24, the illustrations in this work were admired by Goethe who wrote of them that "Nature is visible, Art concealed." The importance of travel outside Europe to the expansion of botanical knowledge is emphasized in the preface to this work where it is noted that travel has "tended infinitely to enlarge our views in every branch of Natural History, not only by the vast increase of new species, but by the accession of a rich fund of interesting facts and observations."

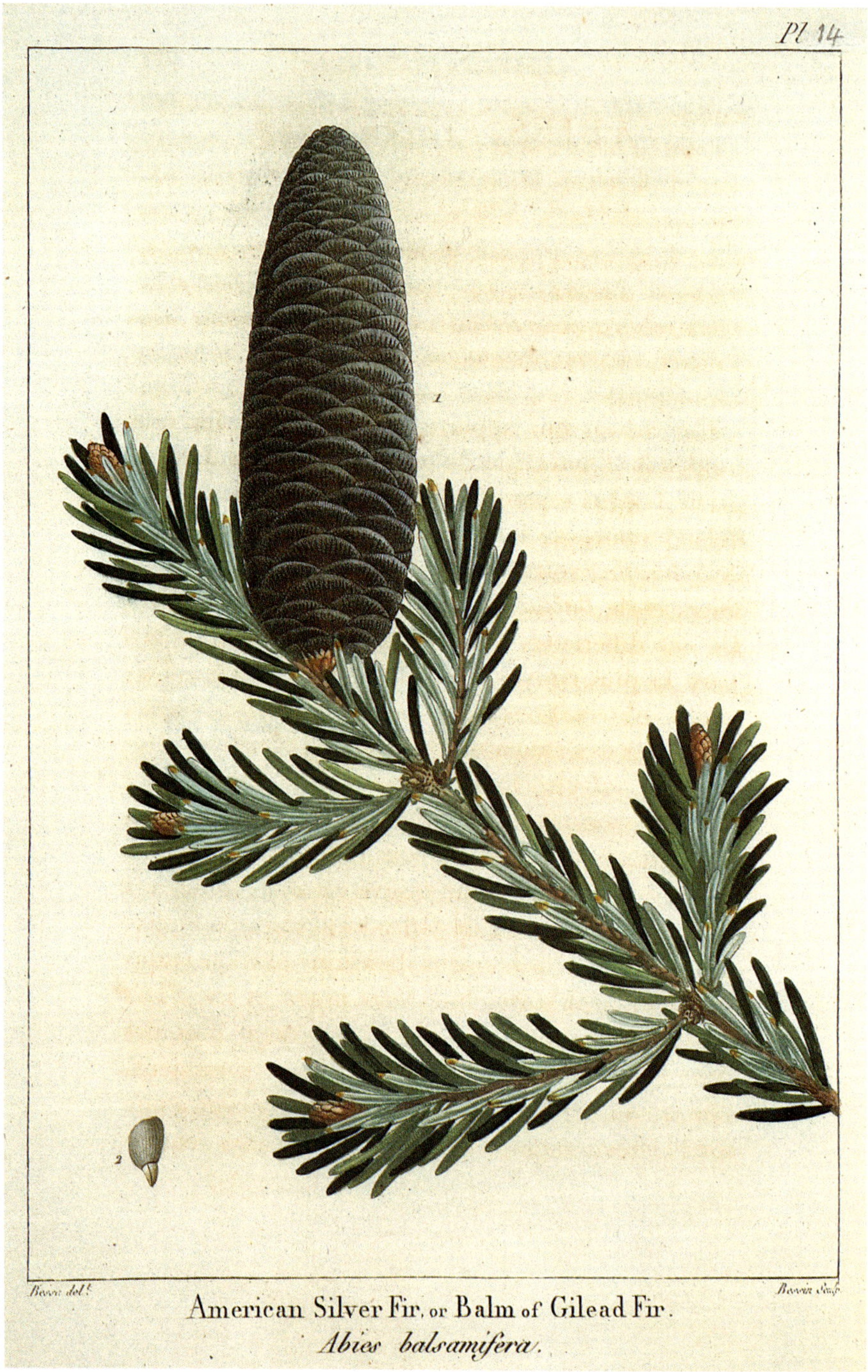

90 ▪ THE AMERICAN SILVER FIR *Abies balsamea*

"American Silver Fir, or Balm of Gilead Fir." Color-printed and hand-finished stipple engraving, by Bessin from the drawing by Bessa. In *Histoire des Arbres Forestiers de L'Amérique Septentrionale* by François-André Michaux (1810–13). ▪ This tree, Michaux tells us, is particularly suitable for the embellishment of parks and gardens. His interests, however, were not limited to the aesthetic appeal of trees; he was concerned with their economic uses and in forest conservation.

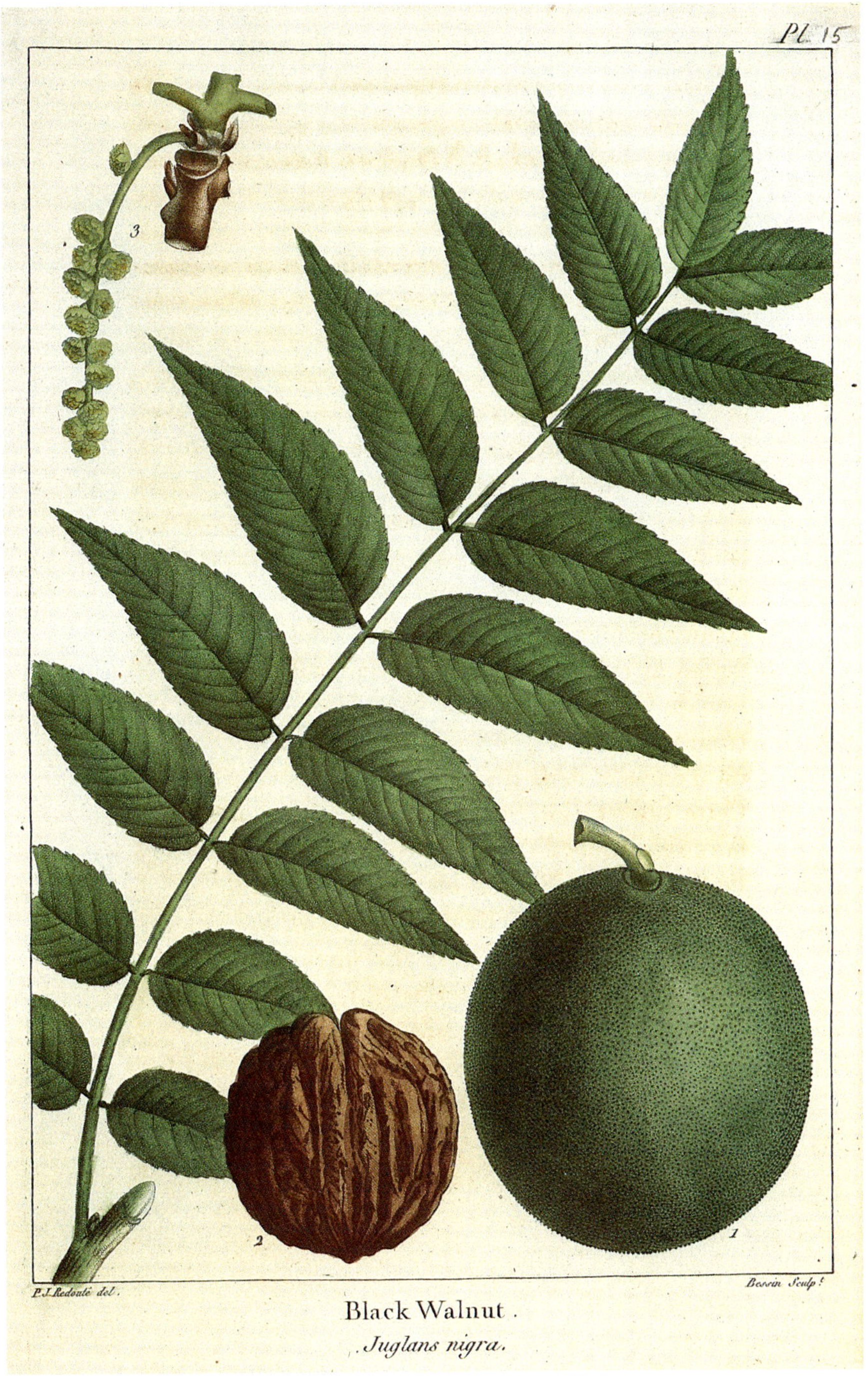

91 ▪ BLACK WALNUT *Juglans nigra*

"Black Walnut." Color-printed and hand-finished stipple engraving, by Bessin from the drawing by Pierre-Joseph Redouté. ▪ In *Histoire des Arbres Forestiers de L'Amérique Septentrionale* by François-André Michaux (1810–13). F.-A. Michaux first went to the United States with his father, André, in 1785 to 1790. He subsequently made two additional trips—1801 to 1803 and 1806 to 1807—the result of which was this book, the first sylva of North America.

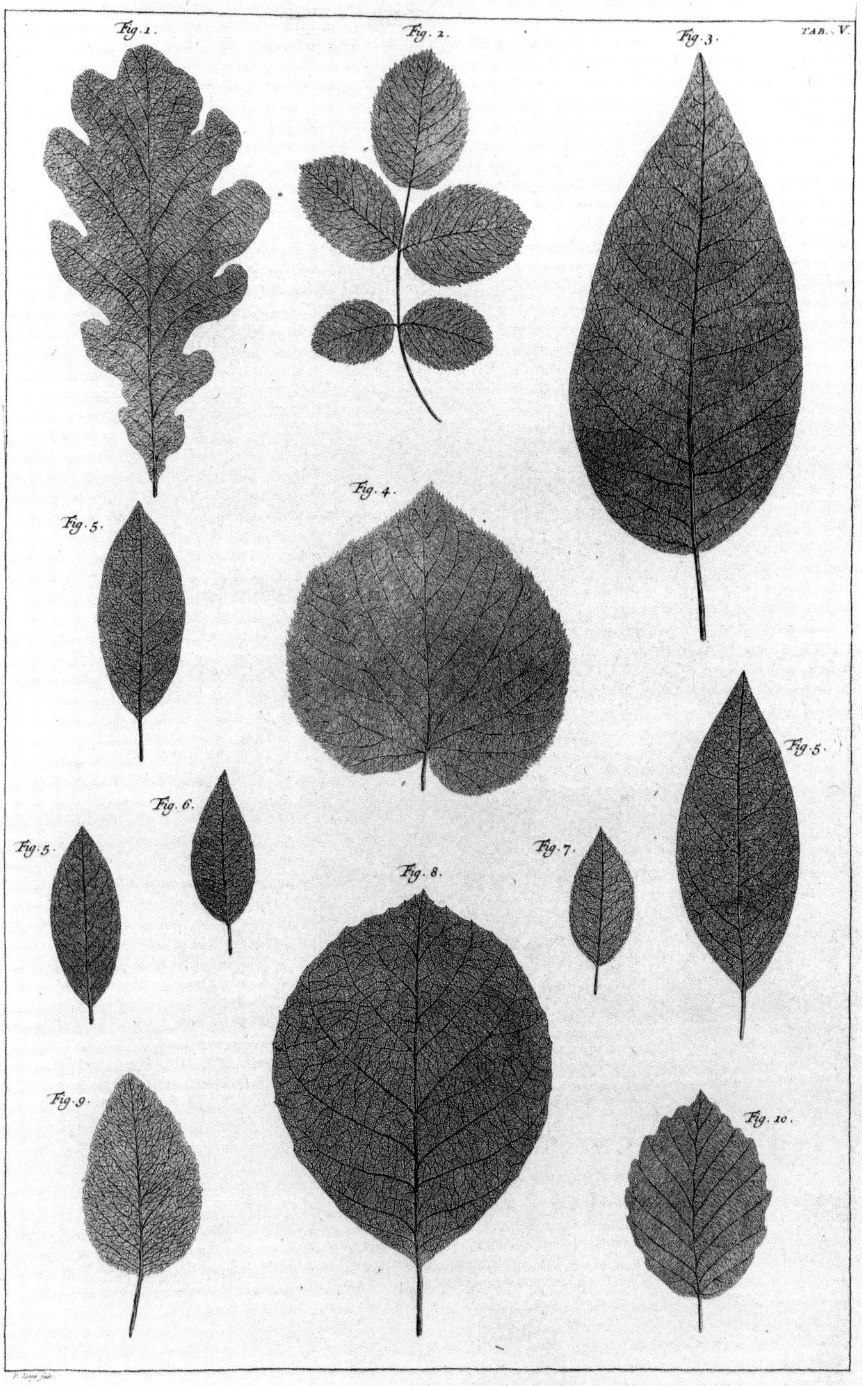

92 ▪ LEAVES

Etching, from the drawing by P. Taugé. In *Locupletissimi rerum naturalium thesauri. . . .* by Albert Seba (1734–65). ▪ An Amsterdam apothecary, the author assembled collections of natural objects, some rare and others common, like these leaves from trees and flowers. His goal was to produce an encyclopedia of the natural world—animal, mineral, and vegetable.

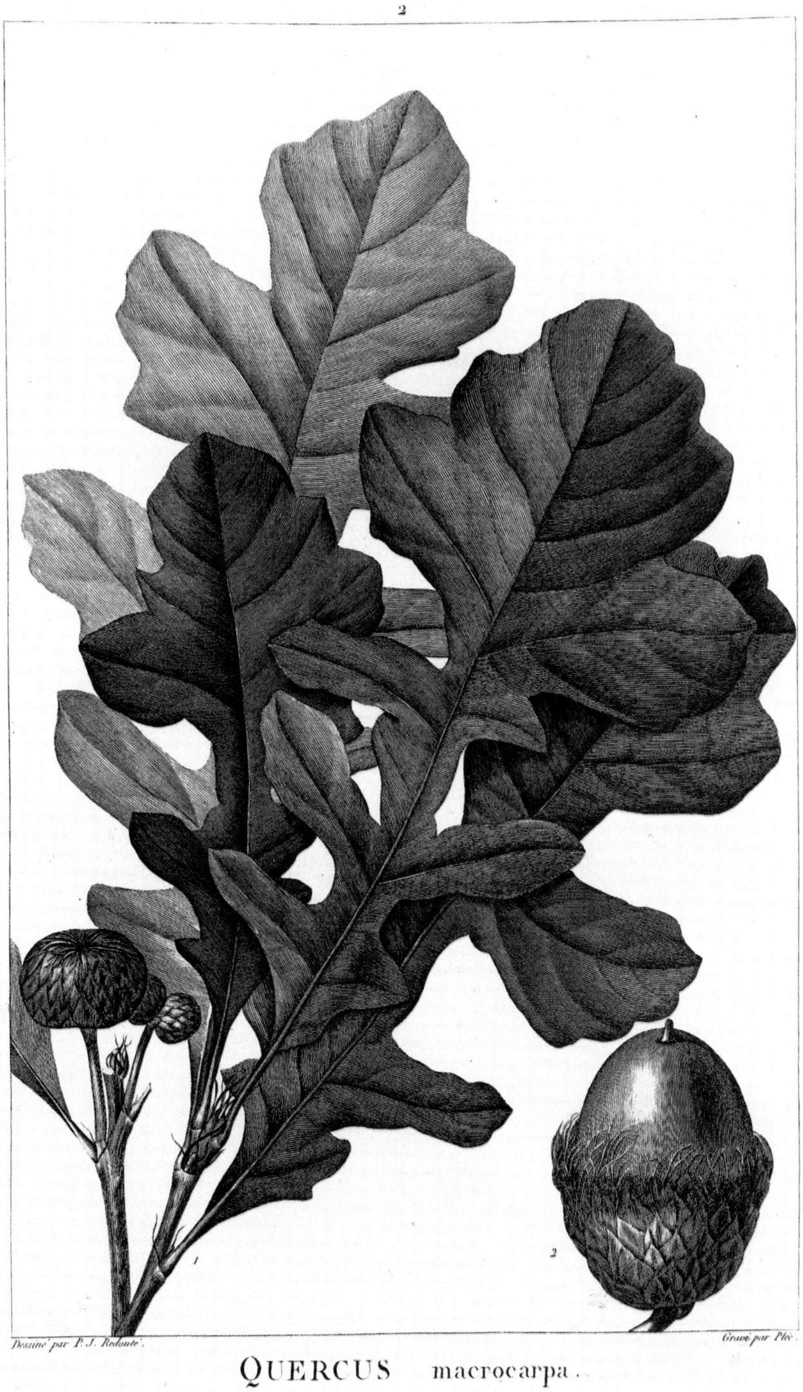

93 ▪ WHITE OAK *Quercus macrocarpa*

"Quercus macrocarpa." Engraving, by Auguste Plée from the drawing by Pierre-Joseph Redouté. In *Histoire des Chênes de L'Amérique* by André Michaux (1801). ▪ Together with his son and fellow botanist, François-André, Michaux made an enormous contribution to the systematic knowledge of the plant life of North America, particularly its trees.

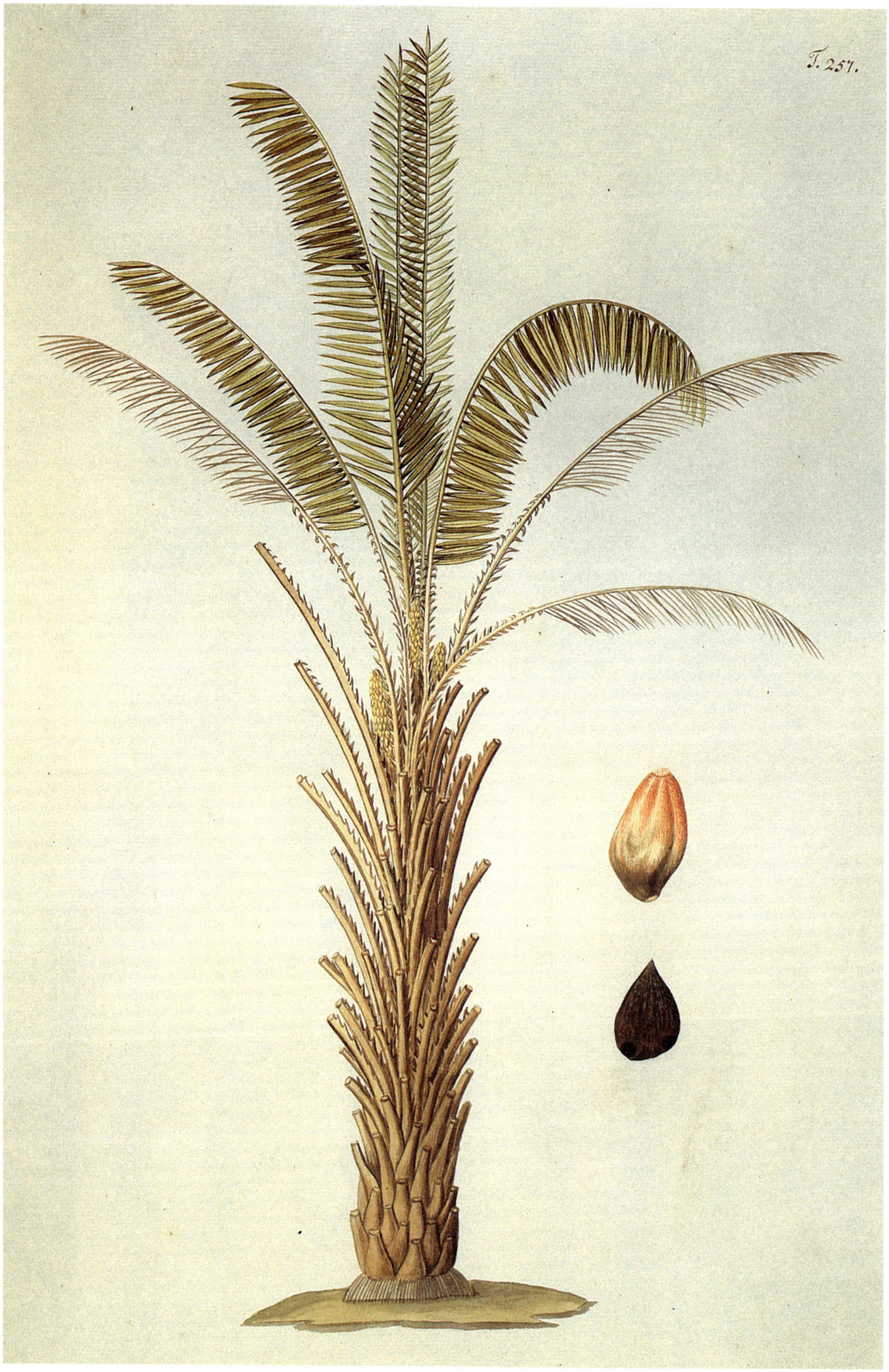

94 ▪ AFRICAN OIL PALM *Elaeis guineensis*

Hand-colored engraving, from the drawing by Nikolaus Joseph Jacquin. In *Selectarum Stirpium Americanarum Historia* by Nikolaus Joseph Jacquin (1780–81). ▪ The fruit of this tree yields an oil sometimes used in the manufacture of soap and candles.

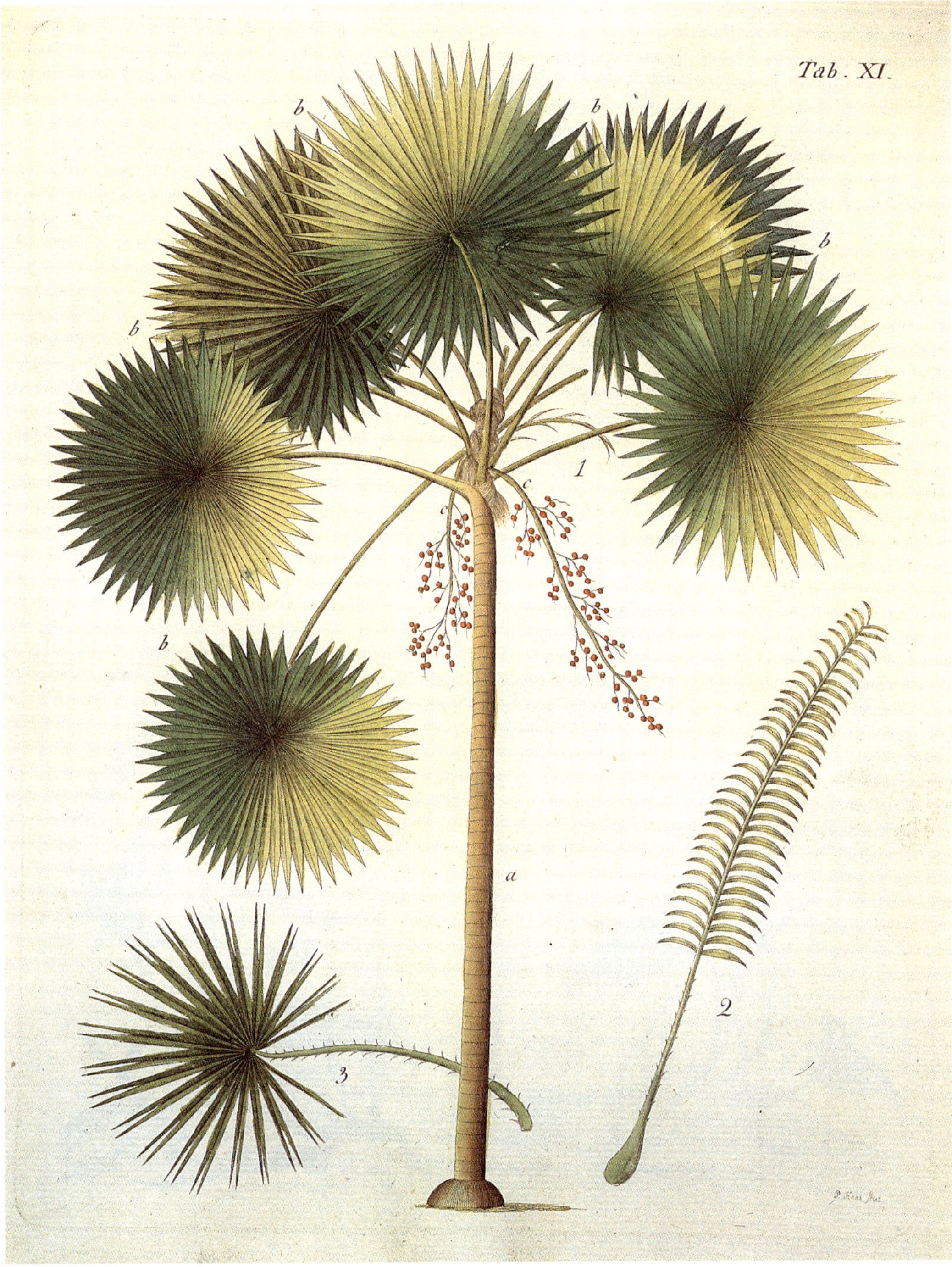

95 ▪ FAN PALM *Livistona rotundifolia*

Hand-colored engraving, by P. Haas. In *Termini Botanici. . . .* by Friedrich Gottlieb Hayne (1799–1812). ▪ With its bilingual text in Latin and German, this work sought to provide general definitions of botanical terms. Issued in paper-bound parts over a period of thirteen years, Hayne's work suggests the popularity of botanical subjects among amateurs and professionals which developed in the early nineteenth century.

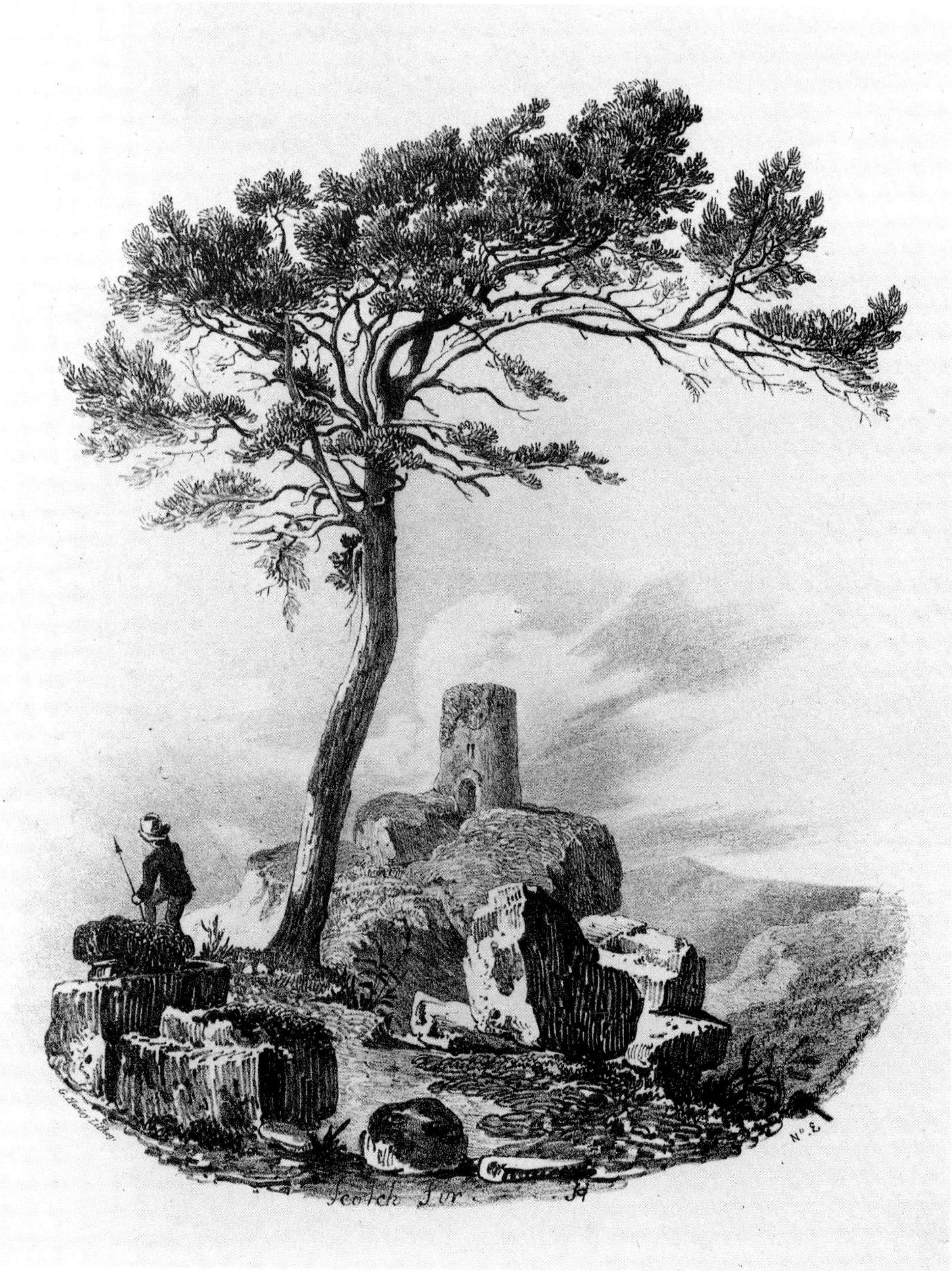

96 ▪ SCOTCH FIR *Pinus sylvestris*

"Scotch Fur." Lithograph, by George Harley. In *Portraits of Trees, Sketched From Nature And On Stone* by George Harley (1821). ▪ The fascination with Nature that was a hallmark of the Romantic schools of poetry and painting likewise infected the popular imagination. As a result there were published drawing books such as this to inspire and instruct the weekend artist.

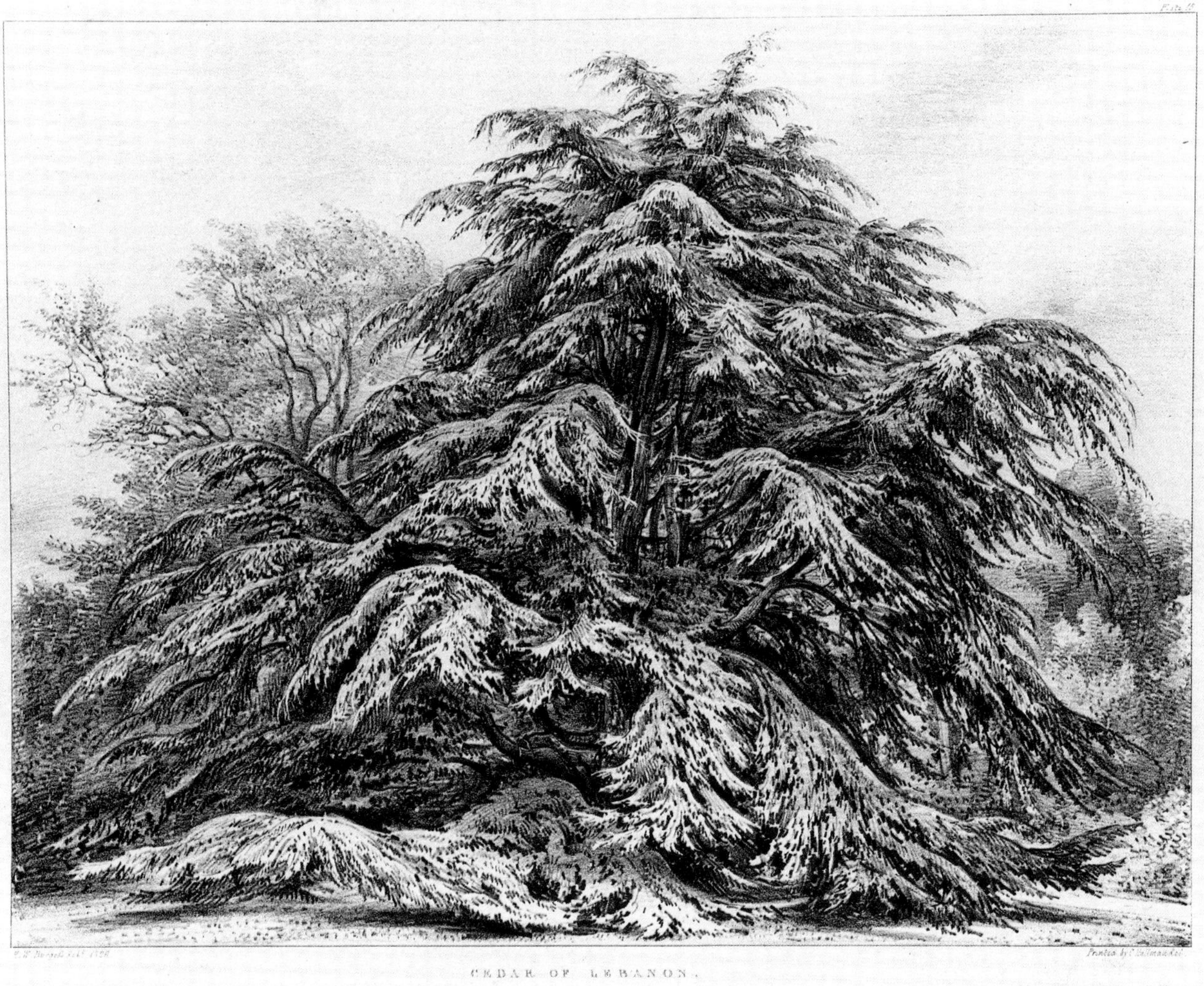

97 ▪ CEDAR OF LEBANON *Cedrus libani*

"Cedar of Lebanon." Lithograph, by H. W. Burgess. In *Eidodendron* by H. W. Burgess (1827). ▪ Imbued with the Romantic notion of trees as an essential element of the picturesque, this work mingles chauvinism with aestheticism as when the author notes that "there are no forests like our own." The Romantics, under the influence of J. J. Rousseau and others, had contributed to the notion of Nature as sacred and inspiring. Trees, flowers, mountains and valleys were not merely pretty things whose visual splendors were to be noted, but they broadened the spirit.

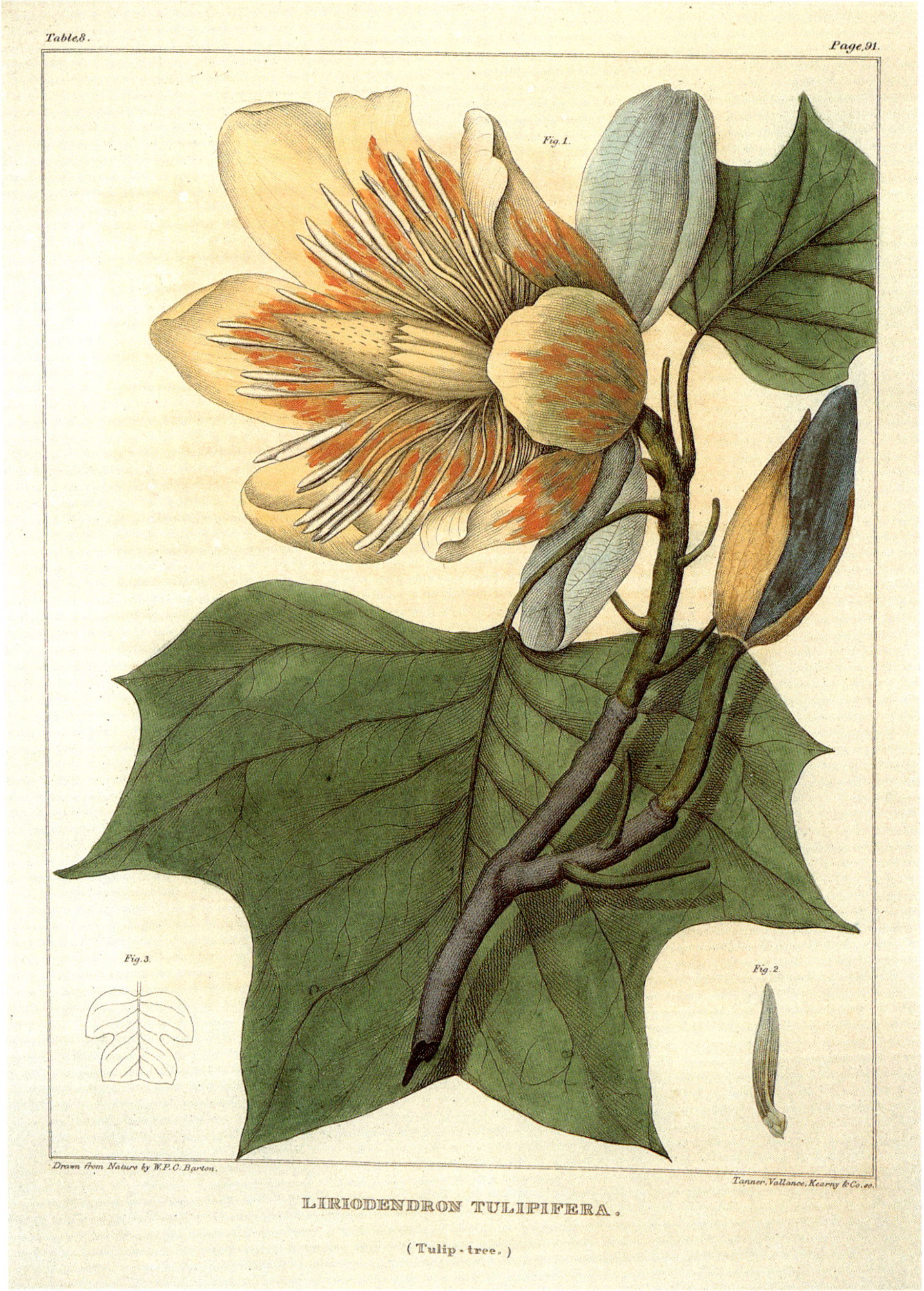

98 ▪ TULIP TREE *Liriodendron tulipfera*

"Liriodendron Tulipifera." Hand-colored engraving, by Tanner, Vallance, Kearny & Co. from the drawing by William P. C. Barton. In *Vegetable Materia Medica of The United States; or, Medical Botany* by William Barton (1817–18). ▪ Among the illnesses which the bark of this tree may cure, Barton reports, are gout, rheumatism, and hysteria.

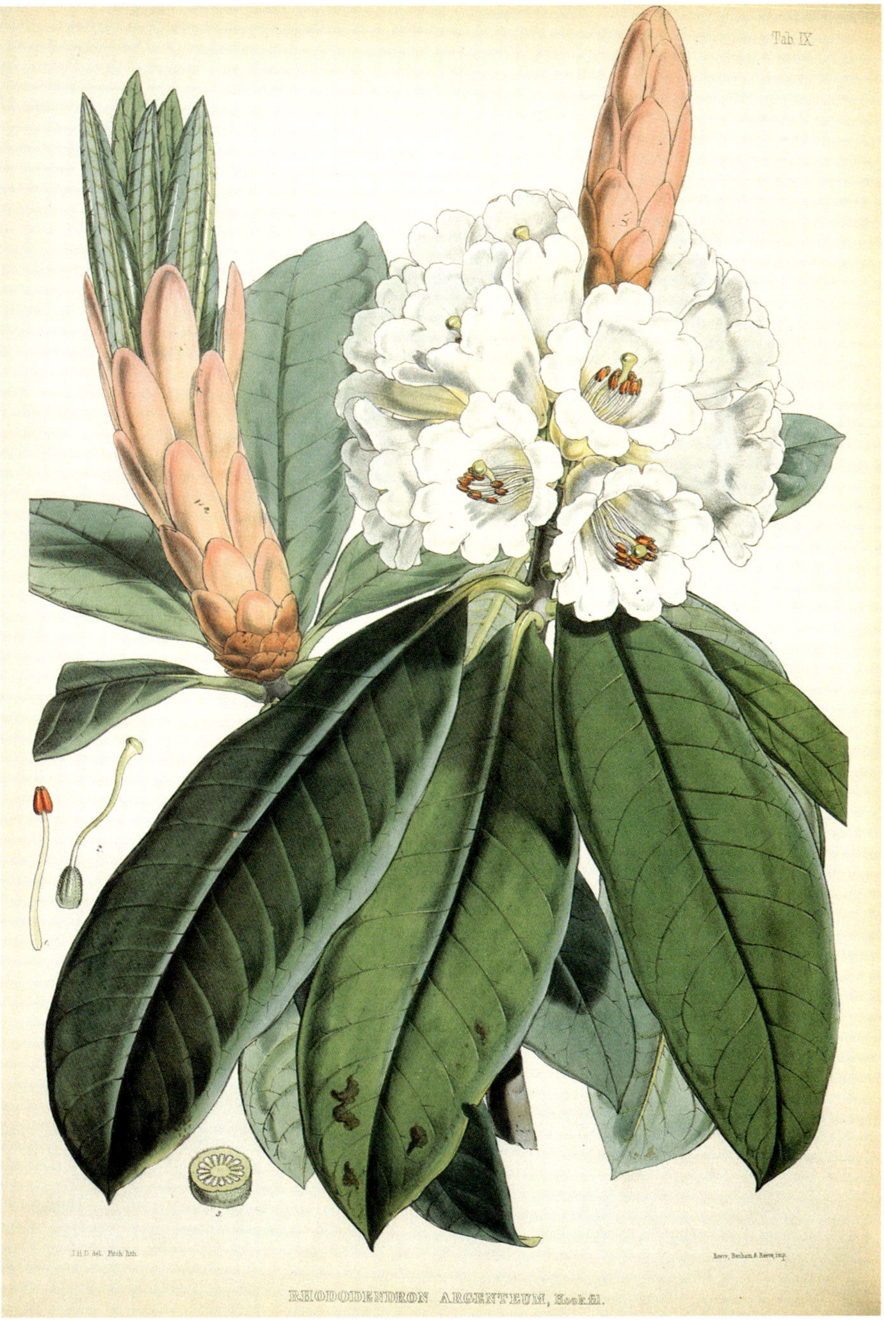

99 ▪ SILVERY RHODODENDRON *Rhododendron grande*

"Rhododendron argenteum." Hand-colored lithograph, by Walter Hood Fitch from the drawing by Joseph Dalton Hooker. In *The Rhododendrons of Sikkim-Himalaya* by Joseph Dalton Hooker (1849–51). ▪ As in the case of the European exploration and conquest of the Americas, the British were active in documenting the plant life of their Indian empire. Hooker, in addition to trekking through the Himalayas, traveled to Antarctica. Director of the Royal Botanic Gardens, Kew, from 1865 to 1885, Hooker was a man of intellectual distinction as well as physical energy; Charles Darwin consulted him when preparing his epochal *On the Origin of Species.*

BIBLIOGRAPHY OF WORKS ILLUSTRATED

References Cited:

ARBER, AGNES. *Herbals.* 3rd ed. Cambridge: Cambridge University Press, 1986.

HENREY, BLANCHE. *British botanical and horticultural literature before 1800.* 3 vols. London: Oxford University Press, 1975.

NISSEN, CLAUS. *Die botanische buchillustration.* 2 vols. Stuttgart: Hiersemann, 1951–66.

STAFLEU, FRANS A. and RICHARD S. COWAN. *Taxonomic Literature.* 2d ed. 7 vols. Utrecht: Bohn, 1976–88.

ALÉCHAMPS, JACQUES D'. *De l'histoire générale des plantes.* 2 vols. Lyon: Rouille, 1615. *Ref: Nissen, 447.*

BARTON, WILLIAM P. C. *Vegetable Materia Medica of the United States; or, Medical Botany:* Philadelphia: Mathew Carey and Son, 1817–18. *Ref: Stafleu, 324.*

BATEMAN, JAMES. *The Orchidaceae of Mexico and Guatemala.* London: Ridgway & Sons, 1837–43. *Ref: Stafleu, 342.*

Beautiful collection of drawings of flowers. Album of 131 watercolors on vellum. [German? c. 1700?]

BESLER, BASIL. *Hortus Eystettensis.* Altdorf: K. Bauer, 1613. *Ref: Nissen, 158.*

BIGELOW, JACOB. *American Medical Botany:* Boston: Cummings & Hilliard, 1817–20. *Ref: Stafleu, 514.*

BLACKWELL, ELIZABETH. *A Curious herbal, containing 500 cuts, of the most useful plants which are now used in the practice of physick.* 2 vols. London: Printed for John Nourse, 1737–39. *Ref: Nissen, 168.*

BONAFOUS, MATHIEU. *Histoire naturelle, agricole et économique du mais.* Paris: Huzard, 1836. *Ref: Nissen, 198.*

BONELLI, GIORGIO ET AL. *Hortus Romanus.* 5 vols. Rome: Bouchard & Gravier, 1772–93. *Ref: Stafleu, 634.*

BROOKSHAW, GEORGE. *Pomona Britannica.* London: the author, 1804–12. *Ref: Nissen, 244.*

———. *Pomona Britannica.* London: Longman et al, 1816–17. *Ref: Nissen, 244.*

BROWNE, PATRICK. *The civil and natural history of Jamaica.* London: B. White, 1789. *Ref: Nissen, 255.*

BRUNSCHWIG, HIERONYMUS. *Kleines Distillierbuch.* Frankfurt: Erben, c. 1565. *Ref: Nissen, 270.*

BURGESS, HENRY W. *Eidodendron.* London: J. Dickins, 1827. *Ref: Stafleu, 924.*

BURY, PRISCILLA SUSAN. *A selection of Hexandrian plants.* London: R. Havell, 1831–34. *Ref: Stafleu, 937.*

CAMERARIUS, JOACHIM. *Hortus medicus et philosophicus.* Frankfurt: Feyerabend, 1588. *Ref: Arber, 281.*

CATESBY, MARK. *The Natural History of Carolina, Florida and the Bahama Islands: containing the figures of Birds, Beasts, Fishes, Serpents, Insects, and Plants . . . Together with their descriptions in English and French. . . .* 2d ed. 2 vols. London: Marsh, 1754. *Ref: Stafleu, 1057.*

CORNUT, JACQUES. *Canadensium plantarum . . . historia.* Paris: Le Moyne, 1635. *Ref: Stafleu, 1233.*

CURTIS, SAMUEL. *A Monograph on the genus Camellia.* London: Arch, 1819. *Ref: Stafleu, 1283.*

DODOENS, REMBERT. *Cruydeboeck.* Antwerp: Jan van der Loe, 1552–54. *Ref: Arber, 277.*

DUHAMEL DU MONCEAU, HENRI LOUIS. *Traité des arbres et arbustes que l'on cultive en France en pleine terre.* 7 vols. Paris: Didot ainé, 1800–19. *Ref: Stafleu, 1547.*

DURANTE, CASTORE. *Herbario novo.* Venice: Sessa, 1602. *Ref: Arber, 102–03.*

FUCHS, LEONHART. *Historia de las yeruas, y plantas, sacada de Dioscoride . . .* Antwerp: Byreman, 1557. *Ref: Nissen, 666.*

GALLESIO, GIORGIO. *Pomona Italiana.* 2 vols. Pisa, 1817–39. *Ref: Nissen, 683.*

GERARD, JOHN. *The Herball.* London: John Norton, 1597. *Ref: Arber, 282.*

GRANDVILLE, JEAN IGNACE ISIDORE GÉRARD. *Les Fleurs animées.* 2 vols. Paris: de Gonet, 1847.

HARLEY, GEORGE. *Portraits of trees, sketched from nature and on stone.* London: Rowney and Forster, 1821.

HARRIS, EMILY C. *New Zealand Ferns, New Zealand Flowers.* 2 vols. Nelson, N. Z.: H. D. Jackson, 1894. *Ref: Nissen, 795, 796.*

HAYNE, FRIEDRICH G. *Termini Botanici Iconibus illustrati.* Berlin: Oehmigke, 1799–1812. *Ref: Stafleu, 2507.*

HOOKER, JOSEPH DALTON. *The Rhododendrons of Sikkim-Himalaya.* London: Reeve and Benham, 1849–51. *Ref: Stafleu, 2629.*

HOOKER, SIR W. J. *Victoria Regia; or illustrations of the Royal Water-Lily.* London: Reeve and Benham, 1851. *Ref: Nissen, 919.*

JACQUIN, NIKOLAUS JOSEPH. *Selectarum stirpium Americanarum Historia.* Vienna, 1780–81. *Ref: Stafleu, 3249.*

JONSTON, JOHN. *Dendographias.* Frankfurt: Merian, 1662. *Ref: Nissen, 1007.*

LAMBERT, AYLMER BOURKE. *A description of the Genus Pinus.* London: George White, 1828–37. *Ref: Stafleu, 4145.*

LAWRANCE, MARY. *A Collection of roses from nature.* London: the author, 1799. *Ref: Henrey, 948.*

L'HÉRITIER DE BRUTELLE, CHARLES LOUIS. *Stirpes novae aut minus cognitae. . . .* Paris: Pierres, 1784–91. *Ref: Stafleu, 4484.*

MATTHIOLI, PIER ANDREA. *Commentarii in sex libros Dioscoridis.* Venice: Valgrisi, 1565. *Ref: Arber, 276.*

MERIAN, MARIA SIBYLLA. *Dissertation sur la génération et les transformations des insectes de Surinam.* The Hague: Gosse, 1726.

MICHAUX, ANDRÉ. *Histoire des chênes de L'Amérique.* Paris: Crapelet, 1801. *Ref: Stafleu, 5957.*

MICHAUX, FRANÇOIS-ANDRÉ. *Histoire des arbres forestiers de L'Amérique septentrionale.* Paris: Haussmann, 1810–13. *Ref: Stafleu, 5961.*

MOORE, THOMAS. *The Ferns of Great Britain and Ireland.* 2d ed. London: Bradbury and Evans, 1857. *Ref: Stafleu, 6275.*

MORANDI, GIAMBATTISTA B. *Historia botanica-practica.* Milan: Malatesta, 1744. *Ref: Stafleu, 6290.*

PARKINSON, JOHN. *Paradisi in Sole.* London: Cotes, 1635. *Ref: Henrey, 284.*

PASSE, CRISPIJN VAN DE. *Hortus floridus.* Arnhem: Janson, 1614–16. *Ref: Nissen, 1494.*

PENA, PIERRE, and MATTHIAS DE L'OBEL. *Stirpium Adversaria Nova.* London: Purfoot, 1571. *Ref: Arber, 278.*

QUÉLUS, D. DE. *Histoire naturelle du cacao, et du sucre.* Paris: D'Houry, 1719.

REDOUTÉ, PIERRE-JOSEPH. *Les Liliacées.* 8 vols. Paris: Didot Jeune, 1802–16. *Ref: Nissen, 1597.*

REDOUTÉ, PIERRE-JOSEPH, and CLAUDE ANTOINE THORY. *Les Roses.* 3 vols. Paris: Didot, 1817–24. *Ref: Nissen, 1599.*

REGNAULT, NICOLAS FRANÇOIS. *La Botanique. . . .* 3 vols. Paris: the author, 1774–80. *Ref: Stafleu, 8810.*

RENEAULME, PAUL DE. *Specimen historiae plantarum.* Paris: Beys, 1611. *Ref: Nissen, 1621.*

RISSO, JOSEPH ANTOINE, and PIERRE ANTOINE POITEAU. *Histoire naturelle des orangers.* Paris: Hérissant Le Doux, 1818–22. *Ref: Stafleu, 9248.*

ROBERT, NICOLAS. *Diverses fleurs dessinées et gravées d'après le naturel.* Paris: Poilly, 1660. *Ref: Nissen, 1645.*

SANDER, HENRY F. C. *Reichenbachia, orchids illustrated and described.* 4 vols. London: Sotheran, 1886–95. *Ref: Nissen, 1722.*

SEBA, ALBERT. *Locupletissimi rerum naturalium thesauri. . . .* 4 vols. Amsterdam: Janssonius, 1734–65. *Ref: Nissen, 1825.*

SLOANE, SIR HANS. *A voyage to the islands. . . .* London, 1707–25. *Ref: Stafleu, 12.104.*

THORNTON, ROBERT JOHN. *New illustration of the sexual system of Carolus von Linnaeus . . . the temple of Flora, or Garden of Nature.* London: the author, 1798–1807. *Ref: Stafleu, 14.283.*

TOURNEFORT, JOSEPH PITTON DE. *Institutiones rei herbariae.* 3 vols. Paris: Typographia regia, 1719. *Ref: Nissen, 1977.*

TREW, CHRISTOPH JACOB. *Hortus Nitidissimus. . . .* Nuremberg: Fleischmann, 1750–86. *Ref: Stafleu, 15.130.*

———. *Uitgezochte Planten.* Amsterdam: Sepp, 1770–73. *Ref: Nissen, 1998.*

TURNER, WILLIAM. *A new herball.* London: Mierdman, 1551. *Ref: Arber, 276.*

VALENTINI, MICHAEL BERNARD. *Historia simplicium reformata.* Frankfurt: Ex Officina Zunneriana, 1716. *Ref: Nissen, 2036.*

WEINMANN, JOHANN WILHELM. *Phytanthoza iconographia. . . .* Regensburg: Lenz, 1737–45. *Ref: Nissen, 2126.*

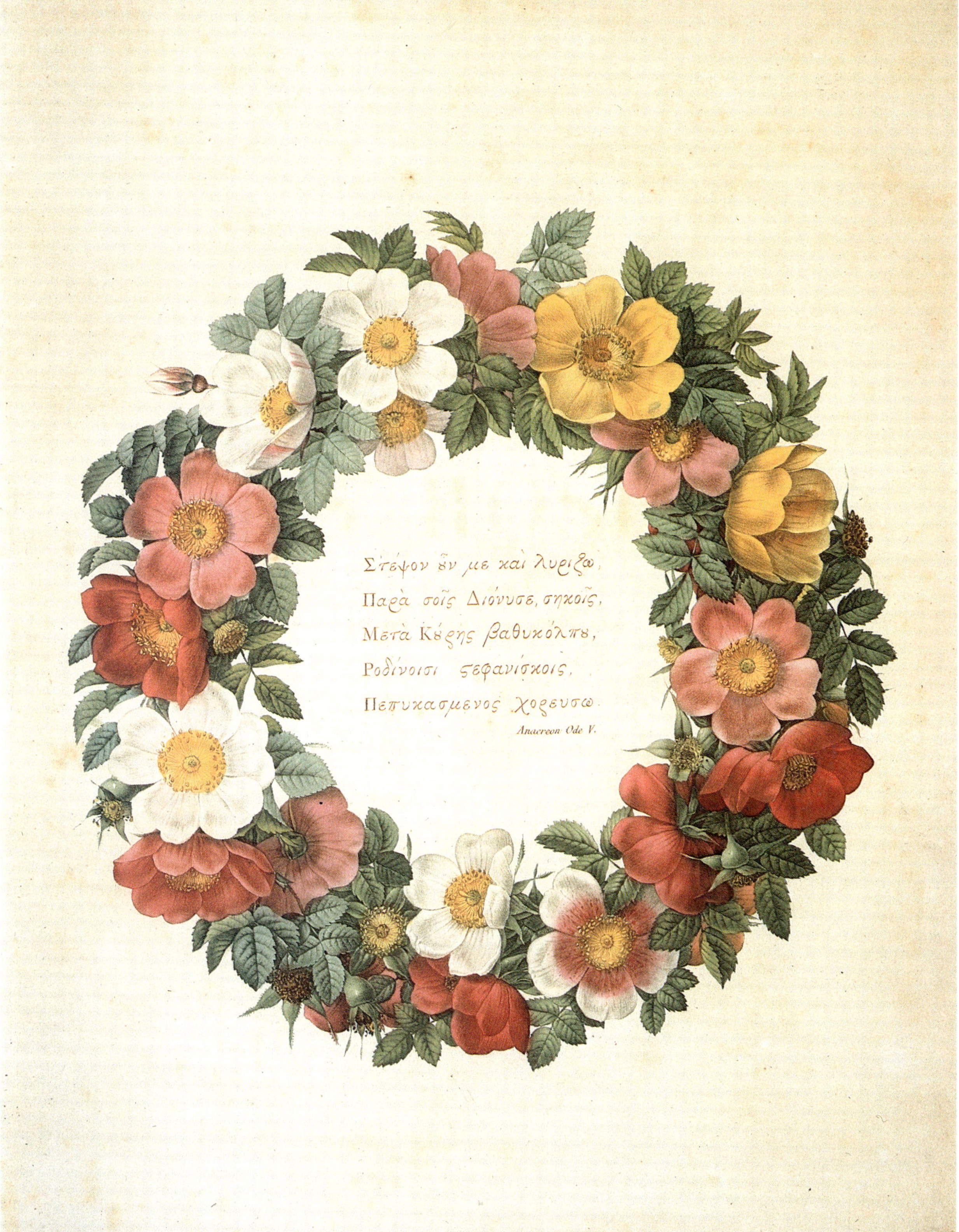
Στέψον ȣ̃ν με καὶ λυρίζω,
Παρὰ σοῖς Διόνυσε, σηκοῖς,
Μετὰ Κȣ́ρης βαθυκόλπȣ,
Ροδίνοισι ςεφανίσκοις,
Πεπυκασμενος χορευσω.
Anacreon Ode V.
P. J. Redouté pinx.
Imprimerie de Rémond
Charlin sculp.

INDEX

ACKNOWLEDGEMENTS

This book owes its genesis to many people. First among them are James Lenox and John Jacob Astor whose original endowments helped form The Library's core collection of illustrated botanical works. A collection without the expertise to perceive its merits is a useless thing, and I owe many thanks to Miriam Gross, Librarian in The Library's General Research Division, for her efforts in helping me plumb the depths of these rich collections. ▪ Richard Newman, Manager of Publications at The Library, was enthusiastic in his support of this project and his assistant, Lawrence Parke Murphy, provided helpful assistance in arranging for the photography of the illustrations contained in this book. ▪ My long-suffering colleagues in The Rare Books and Manuscripts Division made the work involved in producing a manuscript in a short time less burdensome than it might otherwise have been. Wilhelmina Clayton assisted me with her usual efficiency in typing the manuscript. Lisa Browar, Isaac Gewirtz, John Rathe, Daniel Tierney, and Anastacio Teodoro gave me moral and logistical support. In other units of The Library, Robert Rainwater, Roberta Waddell, Theresa Salgado, and, especially, Margaret Glover were extremely considerate and helpful in this undertaking. ▪ Outside The Library, Bernadette Callery, Research Librarian at the New York Botanical Garden, was an invaluable source of advice and information. Such errors of fact that this book may contain will have occurred because of my own ineptitude and in spite of Ms. Callery's best efforts. ▪ At Harry N. Abrams, Inc., Ruth Peltason, my editor, and Elissa Ichiyasu, the book's designer, brought their thoroughgoing professionalism to bear on this project. ▪ To all of the above I am most grateful and delighted at having had their cooperation and expertise to enable me to complete this book. ▪ *Bernard McTigue*

Oriens

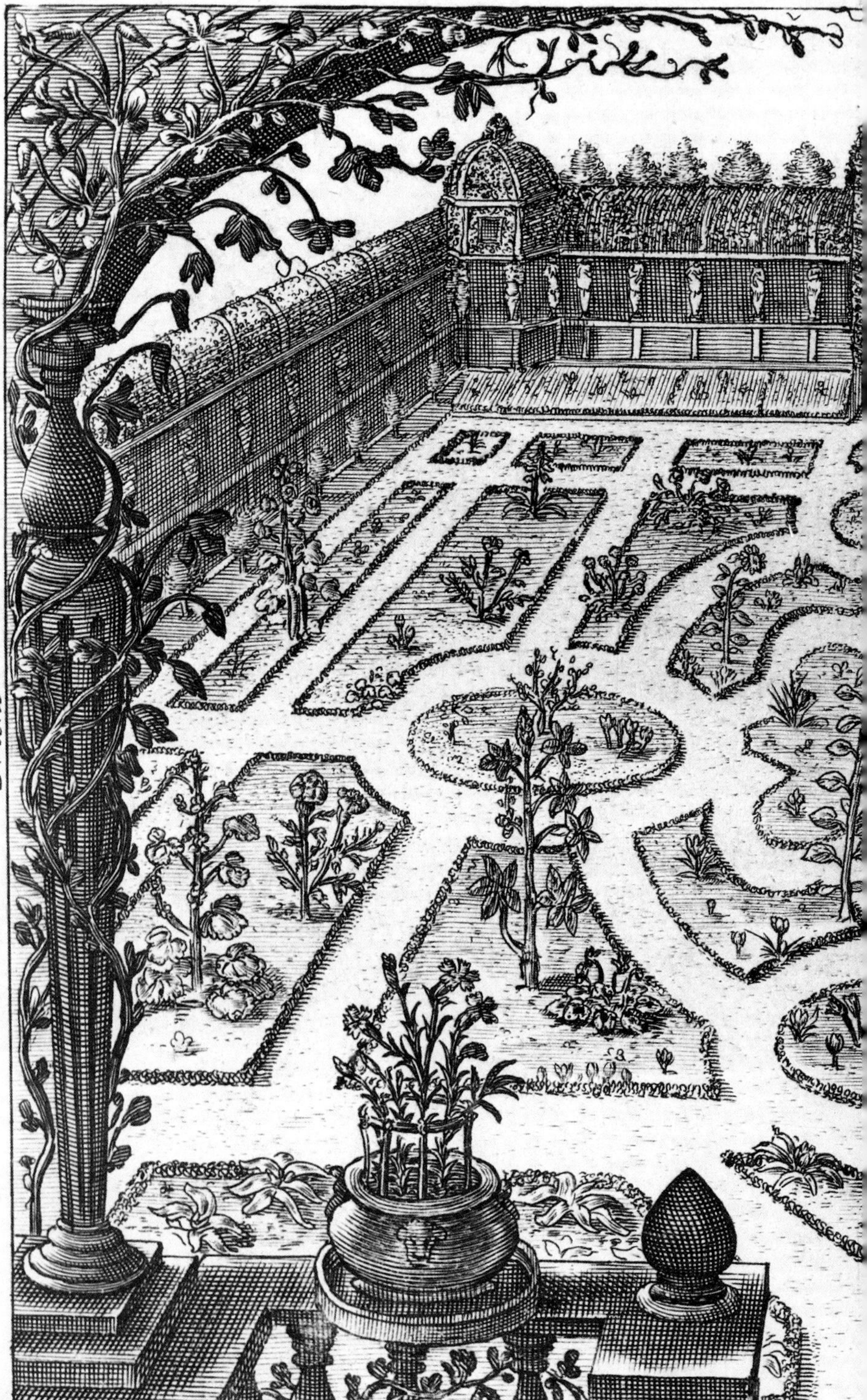